THE INTERNATIONAL JOURNAL OF ETHICAL LEADERSHIP

Special Volume: 1
Inamori International
Thesis Prize in Military Ethics
2019 | 2020

English—Español—Français

CASE
WESTERN
RESERVE
UNIVERSITY

INAMORI INTERNATIONAL
CENTER FOR ETHICS
AND EXCELLENCE

The International Journal of Ethical Leadership
Case Western Reserve University
Editor-in-Chief: Shannon E. French, Inamori Professor in Ethics and
    Director, Inamori International Center for Ethics and Excellence
Executive Editor: Michael Scharf, Dean of the School of Law, John
    Deaver Drinko-Baker & Hostetler Professor of Law, and Director,
    Frederick K. Cox International Law Center
Managing Editor: Beth Trecasa, Associate Director,
    Inamori International Center for Ethics and Excellence
Copyeditor: Thea Ledendecker

For additional information, please contact inamoricenter@case.edu
or visit case.edu/inamori

Contents

Message from the Editors

Shannon E. French
Inamori Professor in Ethics and Director,
and
Beth Trecasa
Associate Director,
Inamori International Center for Ethics and Excellence
Case Western Reserve University

Dear IJEL Readers,

The Inamori International Center for Ethics and Excellence at Case Western Reserve University awards an annual prize for the best thesis in military ethics to promote active involvement in the study and application of military ethics. For those not familiar with military ethics, it is an interdisciplinary field focused on a wide range of issues including Just War Theory (JWT; also referred to as the Just War Tradition), the conduct of war (*jus in bello*), the pursuit of a just peace (*jus ad pacem*), the Law of Armed Conflict (LOAC); International Humanitarian Law (IHL), and other related topics such as the development of new military technologies (example: autonomous weapons systems), what societies owe to those who serve in their militaries, moral injury and dehumanization, and human rights in the context of armed conflict.

In an effort to foster global discussion of pressing issues in military ethics and improve the general accessibility of the field, the Inamori Center is publishing the winning theses, in print and online, in multiple languages. This special volume of *The International Journal of Ethical Leadership* includes our 2019 and 2020 first place winners theses in English, Spanish, and French, as well as a summary of our 2020 second place winner's thesis in all three languages.

We encourage applications for the Inamori thesis prize in military ethics from any non-European students, either military or civilian, in a graduate or professional-level program (including law or medical students, etc.) studying for their degree at any accredited college or university or military service academy or war college (or similar). We have purposely focused the prize in this way to complement a similar thesis award available to Europeans offered by the esteemed Euro-ISME (International Society for Military Ethics, European Chapter) organization. Israeli scholars are now also eligible for the Euro-ISME prize. Due to our partnership with Euro-ISME, winners of the Inamori thesis prize are able to present their work at the prestigious annual Euro-ISME conference, which is a unique global gathering of top scholars in the field.

We are grateful to our partners at The University of Akron Press, as well as our translators, who made this special volume possible.

Sincerely,

Shannon and Beth

Arguments for Banning Autonomous Weapon Systems[1]
A Critique

Hunter Cantrell

List of Abbreviations

AWS—Autonomous Weapon System(s)
ICC—International Criminal Court
IHL—International Humanitarian Law
LoW—Law of War
RoE—Rules of Engagement

Introduction

The anticipated "imminent"[2] rise of fully autonomous weapon systems has led to a call for a "campaign to stop killer robots."[3] This call has so far been backed by twenty-three nations[4] and has grown in perceived legitimacy since the campaign's inception in 2013.[5] These efforts are driven in part by a fear of a future in which all (or at least the lethal) functions of human soldiers have been removed from the battlefield and replaced with a lethal form of artificial intelligence. However, contrary to the Hollywood depiction of apocalyptic Terminators roaming city streets, there is no reason to think that the fear is a realistic one.

---

1. This thesis is dedicated to my loving wife Tiffany and my two wonderful boys Holden and Bryson. Without you, I would be nothing.
2. There is a considerable lack of consensus on what counts as imminent: 5, 10, 50, 100 years? This lack of clarity is rampant throughout the field of emergent autonomous weapon systems.
3. Campaign to Stop Killer Robots, "About Us," https://www.stopkillerrobots.org/about/.
4. It should be noted that all of the nations that have so far joined the campaign to "stop killer robots" are unlikely to be the nations that have the technological capability, infrastructure, or military "necessity" to build such devices. The list includes: Algeria, Argentina, Bolivia, Brazil, Chile, Costa Rica, Cuba, Ecuador, Egypt, Ghana, Guatemala, Holy See, Iraq, Mexico, Nicaragua, Pakistan, Panama, Peru, State of Palestine, Uganda, Venezuela, Zimbabwe (Campaign to Stop Killer Robots).
5. The campaign has met every year since 2013, hosted by the United Nations Office in Geneva, Switzerland.

Nonetheless, there are reasoned arguments against the development and implementation of fully autonomous weapon systems. We can classify the arguments against such systems into two main categories: an argument from "responsibility" and an argument from "agency." Roughly, the argument from responsibility is concerned with the chain of responsibility for the use of autonomous weapon systems (AWS) and who ought to bear responsibility should something go wrong. The argument from agency questions why we should exchange human agency in a lethal action for an artificial agency and discusses the implications that this exchange has for human dignity and the possibility of mercy.

In this thesis, I summarize and evaluate these arguments in turn and show that both arguments are insufficient for an outright ban on AWS. I contend that the arguments are sufficient to support a framework, built on existing international humanitarian law, to regulate but not ban the development and employment of AWS. I then argue that the use of AWS is a rational choice for military and political leaders. I also outline a reasonable framework based on the current Geneva Conventions and international humanitarian law for regulating AWS.

1.1 Why is it essential to discuss autonomous weapon systems?

Autonomous weapon systems are the next frontier of modern military technology. As the speed of decision-making becomes faster due to increasing computerization, the ability of the human mind to keep up is lagging. The *OODA loop* was first coined by USAF Pilot and air power strategist Colonel John Boyd.[6] It stands for Observe, Orient, Decide, Act. The basic premise is that if a fighter pilot can get inside the OODA loop of an enemy fighter pilot, he could defeat him. The OODA loop then is a short decision matrix process in which a person (or in the future a machine) can decide on a certain action. It is likely that these OODA loops will continue to narrow as technology increases. The narrowed OODA loop of the future lends itself naturally to artificial intelligence that can process inputs and compute multiple decisions in real time much faster than any human. The drive to make "smarter" and faster weapons can clearly be seen in the evolution of fighter jets (USAF F-35 II and the Chinese Chengdu J-20 are but two examples), "smart bombs" (precision-guided munitions

---

6. Boyd 1987, 383.

such as the Excalibur[7]), and the increased utilization of computer-assisted decision-making tools in military planning.[8]

In response to the increased complexity of modern warfare and the decrease in the available population deemed fit to serve,[9] increased automation in current weapon systems and a drive to implement fully autonomous weapon systems have been the remedy. Current systems such as the PHALANX (deployed on US Aegis Cruisers) allows a semi-autonomous system to perform critical ship protection functions, freeing up the limited crew to perform other essential duties.[10] The increasing use of such technologies is the first stepping stone in the implementation of a system that will have the ability to select "targets and [deliver] force without any human input or interaction."[11] The implementation of AWS is potentially worrying on many fronts, as alluded to earlier, but this development has the beneficial potential of reducing the unforeseen or collateral damage that accompanies warfare as currently practiced.

1.2 What are autonomous weapon systems?

Before delving into the debate regarding the implementation of AWS, it is essential to understand just what an autonomous weapon is. The academic and diplomatic communities, unsurprisingly, have yet to settle upon a commonly agreed-upon working definition of AWS. Currently accepted diplomatic definitions vary widely: some include weapons that today are considered automated, though not autonomous, and others include only systems wholly separated from human interaction. There are also definitions that require specific functionalities or technologies to be present. One example is from the government of the Netherlands, which defines an AWS as "a weapon that, without human intervention, selects and engages targets matching certain predefined criteria, following a human decision to deploy the weapon on the understanding that an attack, once launched,

---

7. US Army Acquisition Support Center, "Excalibur Precision 155MM Projectiles."
8. This should not be construed as currently using computers *to* make command decisions, but rather the reliance of computer-based systems to provide more, better, and/or clearer information to a commander. These systems included everything from worldwide cargo tracking, enemy and friendly unit battlefield tracking, electronic systems monitoring, etc. As the civilian world has become more digitally reliant, so too has the military.
9. See the Military Leadership Diversity Commission Issue Paper #2, "Outreach & Recruiting."
10. Raytheon, "Phalanx Close-In Weapon System."
11. ICRC 2015, 6.

cannot be stopped by human intervention."[12] This definition could easily encompass weapons that today are not considered to be autonomous, such as a cruise missile.[13] A cruise missile is designed to seek a specific programmed target (a heat signature, laser designation from a soldier on the ground, or some other predesignated marker) and once a human has given the order to deploy the system, it cannot be recalled.

The government of France approaches the definition of an AWS in terms of "what it is not"[14] stipulating:

> Lethal autonomous weapons are fully autonomous sys-
> tems...LAWS should be understood as implying a total absence of
> human supervision, meaning there is absolutely no link (commu-
> nication or control) with the military chain of command....The
> delivery platform of a LAWS would be capable of moving,
> adapting to its land, marine, or aerial environments and targeting
> and firing a lethal effector (bullet, missile, bomb, etc.) without
> any kind of human intervention or validation....LAWS would
> most likely possess self-learning capabilities.[15]

The French definition differs from the Dutch, in that it requires that an AWS (or LAWS) have no connection with a military (read human) chain of command, including in mission planning and final issuance of orders to use the AWS. This definition would severely limit what could be called an AWS, as it is likely that there will be some meaningful human interaction somewhere in the "kill chain." The French definition then is so narrow as to make it practically untenable as a foundation upon which to build practical diplomatic and academic discussions.[16]

While adopting elements of the functionalist approaches used by the French, the United States' definition is distinct because it distinguishes

---

12. United Nations Institute for Disarmament Research [UNIDIR] 2017, 23.
13. This example could also extend to any other "precision guided munition." It should be noted that current law according the Geneva Convention mandates the use non-indiscrim-inate weapons which can be generally interpreted as meaning it endorses using precision munitions over indiscriminate ones and prohibits "[e]mploying weapons, projectiles and material and methods of warfare...which are inherently indiscriminate in violation of the international law of armed conflict, provided that such weapons, projectiles and material and methods of warfare are the subject of a comprehensive prohibition and are included in an annex to this Statute" (International Criminal Court Article 8(2)(b)(xx) 1998).
14. United Nations Institute for Disarmament Research [UNIDIR] 2017, 24.
15. Ibid., 24.
16. This can also be said of the current Chinese designation of an AWS having a level of autonomy which lacks "human intervention and control during the entire process of executing a task" (Government of China 2018).

autonomous from semi-autonomous systems. The United States (through the Department of Defense) defines an AWS as

> A weapon system, once activated, can select and engage targets without further intervention by a human operator. This includes human-supervised autonomous weapon systems that are designed to allow human operators to override operation of the weapon system but can select and engage targets without further human input after activation.[17]

The US definition then is more practically useful than the French or Dutch, since it gives a detailed account of what is an AWS is and, importantly, excludes by implication systems that should not count as an AWS.[18] The definition does not include systems that are in place today that would be considered automated or semi-autonomous[19] (PHALANX, C-RAM[20], etc.), nor does it include "fire and forget" systems, which could include the aforementioned cruise missile. It is also important to note that the US definition allows an AWS to act without the intervention of a human operator but does not preclude interaction from a human operator. This is important as it falls clearly in line with the US DoD Policy Directive 3000.09, which states that "Autonomous and semi-autonomous weapon systems shall be designed to allow commanders and operators to exercise appropriate levels of human judgment over the use of force."[21] This policy directive hints at the collaborative nature that the US envisions for the implementation of artificial intelligence and AWS. The US policy definition also "places the

---

17. United Nations Institute for Disarmament Research [UNIDIR] 2017, 30.

18. As mentioned, the US provides a definition of what it defines as *not* an AWS, "A weapon system that, once activated, is intended to only engage individual targets or specific target groups that have been selected by a human operator. This includes: (a) semi-autonomous weapon systems that employ autonomy for engagement related functions, including, but not limited to, acquiring, tracking, and identifying potential targets; cueing potential targets to human operators; prioritizing selected targets; timing of when to fire; or providing terminal guidance to home in on selected targets, provided that human control is retained over the decision to select individual targets and specific target groups for engagement. (b) "Fire and forget" or lock-on-after launch homing munitions that rely on TTP (tactics, techniques and procedures) to maximize the probability that only the targets within the seeker's acquisition basket when the seeker activates are those individual targets or specific target groups that have been selected by a human operator" (UNIDIR 2017, 31).

19. It should be noted, though, that systems such as the PHALANX and C-RAM can be placed into a setting which is analogous to fully autonomous.

20. Program Executive Office- Missiles & Space, "Counter-Rocket, Artillery, Mortar (C-RAM)."

21. Department of Defense, Directive 3000.09.

focus of what constitutes autonomy at the level of decision rather than on the presence or absence of a particular technology."[22]

1.3 What does current International Humanitarian Law say regarding AWS?

Modern military conflict is governed by a set of norms and principles generally agreed upon as the basis for conducting a war. These norms and principles are built upon the long history of the just war theory. Prior to the twentieth century, these norms and principles were not codified but were rather a set of agreed-upon customs and practices.[23] For instance, it was generally considered the "gentlemanly" practice to rescue as many enemy sailors as possible once a naval battle had concluded. This practice was not required by treaty or other formal international agreement, but rather was an accepted practice that evolved over centuries of naval warfare. Though it had been common practice, with the proliferation of submarine warfare, the practice was abandoned. After World War II, during the Nuremberg trials, the Allies accused Admiral Donitz of committing crimes against humanity for the Nazi's tactic of sinking enemy vessels and refusing to surface to rescue the survivors. The prosecution failed, though, as it was determined that through the evolution of naval warfare it had become common custom for submarines not to pick up surviving, stranded sailors due to extreme operational risk.

International Humanitarian Law (IHL) in the form of the Geneva Conventions and its Additional Protocols does not explicitly mention AWS. What can be useful for developing rules regulating AWS, though, are IHL prohibitions on certain sorts of weaponry. The Convention on Certain Conventional Weapons (CCW) bans the use of certain inherently indiscriminate forms of weapons. This prohibition implies a preferential status of precision, or "smart," weapons over indiscriminate or "dumb" ones. To follow the CCW then, an AWS would have to be developed and utilized in a fashion in which its use would not be "inherently indiscriminate." What then is a weapon or weapon system that is inherently indiscriminate?

---

22. UNIDIR 2017 31.
23. While it is true that some elements of international law are still predicated on customs and norms, there are now treaty-based rules in place, such as those specified in the Geneva Conventions (1949) and in the Statute of the International Criminal Court. Prior to the establishment of such bodies as the ICC, most nations only had the assurances of warfare or mutually supportive defensive alliances to enforce compliance with agreed upon customs and norms, and some nations, including the US, are not state parties to the ICC.

A prime example would be a "dumb" antipersonnel land mine or a poison gas. Both types of weapons are indiscriminate because upon deployment they cannot correctly distinguish between a legitimate and a non-legitimate military target. The land mine will kill or maim any who are unfortunate to step on it, even decades later. Developing an AWS that can accurately discriminate is a difficult task, but not one that is insurmountable.

2. Objections to AWS: The Arguments for a Ban

Since the invention of the crossbow in the thirteenth century[24], there have been calls for the limitation of acceptable weaponry in "civilized warfare." Technological developments have pushed nations to seek the latest cutting-edge weaponry to gain even the slightest advantage over their enemy. These developments have included the machine gun, the land mine, and poison gases. Some of the developments, such as machine guns, have stayed within the bounds of acceptable military hardware. Others such as the land mine have been heavily regulated, and their use is internationally discouraged.[25] The third category of weapons, including poison gases, has been expressly forbidden under international treaty.

Since 2013, the Campaign to Stop Killer Robots has advocated for a total ban on the development and employment of lethal autonomous weapon systems.[26] The group has advocated at the state and international level for a coalition of UN member states, nongovernmental organizations, businesses, and private citizens with the express purpose of banning lethal AWS. The campaign, like many persons in academia, worries that AWS will cross a "moral threshold," sacrificing the dignity of human life for

---

24. From the Papal Canon issued after the Second Council of the Lateran: "We prohibit under anathema that murderous art of crossbowmen and archers, which is hateful to God, to be employed against Christians and Catholics from now on" (Papal Encyclicals Online, "The Second Council of the Lateran").

25. Antipersonnel land mines are explicitly prohibited under the Quebec treaty:...anti-tank and anti-ship mines are still acceptable. Mines that have a short life span (such as becoming inert after X hours of deployment) are acceptable.

26. In September 2018, the Campaign to Stop Killer Robots advocated "for a pre-emptive and comprehensive ban on the development, production, and use of fully autonomous weapons, also known as lethal autonomous weapon systems or killer robots." As of 2020, the Campaign has altered their pre-emptive ban language and instead say "The Campaign to Stop Killer Robots urges states to launch negotiations on an international treaty to retain meaningful human control over targeting and attack decisions by prohibiting the development, production, and use of fully autonomous weapons. This ban treaty should be enforced via national laws" (The Campaign to Stop Killer Robots, https://www.stopkiller-robots.org/learn/).

the efficiency of automated warfare. The arguments for a ban on "killer robots" can roughly be grouped into two categories, the "responsibility" argument and the "agency" argument.

2.1 The 'responsibility" argument: Who can be held responsible?

One of the great worries of those against the use of AWS is that we may create robots that can target and kill humans without being able to "justly" hold a moral agent responsible. Some have called the problem of justly assigning responsibility for an action taken by an AWS an "accountability gap."[27] To be sure, if we can trace an action of an AWS directly to the person who authorized the mission (for instance, a rogue commander who programmed orders to kill unarmed civilians and injured enemy soldiers), then would it would appear to be clear that we can justly assign blame for any resulting death on the commander who authorized the mission. The problem arises, however, when we cannot directly trace a line from the person who authorized the AWS to the war crime that was perpetrated. This is the "accountability gap." Bonnie Docherty, one of the advocates of a ban on AWS, believes that "[it wouldn't be] fair nor legally viable to…hold a [human] commander or operator responsible."[28] She is not alone in finding issue with shifting responsibility away from the agent—the AWS—who committed the morally problematic (or illegal) action. While arguing for an accountability gap, Robert Sparrow explores two possibilities: shifting blame from the AWS onto humans (the programmer and the commanding officer) and leaving the AWS as the responsible agent.

First, Sparrow argues that we might be able to rest at least some of the responsibility for a wayward AWS on the programmer or designer who built the device: "this will only be fair if the situation described occurred as a result of negligence on the part of the design/programming team."[29] Sparrow, though, quickly dismisses assigning responsibility to the programmer in cases where there is no negligence. The first reason to dismiss putting the blame on the programmer is that "the possibility that the machine may attack the wrong targets may be an acknowledged limitation of the system."[30] If the possibility that the machine might attack an unauthorized

---

27. Scharre 2018, 261.
28. Ibid., 261.
29. Sparrow 2007, 69.
30. Sparrow 2007, 69.

target is a "side effect" or "limitation of the system" and the programmer explicitly communicates this limitation to any potential user, then it would not be fair to hold the programmer liable. Sparrow argues that in this case, those who still choose to deploy the system, with the known limitations or possible side effects, would have to bear the burden of the responsibility. He then adds that "the possibility that an autonomous system will make choices other than those predicted and encouraged by its programmers is inherent in the claim that it is autonomous."[31] Here Sparrow is pointing out that due to the operational design of an AWS and the complex nature of its possible algorithms and neural networks, no human will be able in all cases to predict the decisions of an AWS. If this is the case, then it is again unfair to blame the programmer, since she could not have foreseen all of the actions of the AWS.

Sparrow argues that if we cannot hold the programmer of the AWS to account for its actions, then possibly we can hold the commanding officer who ordered its use to account.[32] He writes, "The risk that [the AWS] may go awry is accepted when the decision is made to send it into action. This is the preferred approach of the military forces seeking to deploy existing AWS."[33] Sparrow argues that if we treat AWS in the same manner that we treat current conventional "dumb" and "smart" weapons of today, then it seems that we can simply attribute the blame to the commander who ordered their use. This tack, though, is not taking the full nature of the autonomy of the weapon into account. Sparrow argues that the very nature of the autonomy of the weapon means that commanders cannot control which targets the AWS selects, and thus they should not be held to account for the choices of the AWS: "If the machines are really choosing their own targets then we cannot hold the Commanding Officer responsible for the deaths that ensue."[34] If the programmer and the commanding officer cannot be held to account, can the AWS itself be held responsible?

Sparrow argues that "autonomy and moral responsibility go hand in hand."[35] If we reach a point where AWS is fully capable of making lethal

---

31. Ibid., 70.
32. Sparrow does not delineate at what level of command we ought to hold one to account. If for instance an infantry company commander (a Captain [O3] in the US Army and US Marine Corps) decides to send an AWS into a village and it kills a child, who should be responsible? The captain? Their boss, a battalion commander (lieutenant colonel)? Or the brigade commander, division commander, corps, etc.? Should only the most senior be held to account for putting this device out in to the force to begin with?
33. Sparrow 2007, 70.
34. Sparrow 2007, 71.
35. Ibid., 65.

decisions on its own (with a human out of the loop), then an AWS would have to bear the moral responsibility of its actions, which brings us to the crux of the problem. "It is hard to take seriously the idea that a machine should—or could—be held responsible for the consequences of 'its' actions."[36] Assuming that holding an agent responsible for bad action involves punishment for the agent, Sparrow argues that for "acts to serve as punishment they must evoke the right sort of response in their object."[37] What then would Sparrow have as the right sort of response? According to him, the only fitting response to punishment involves suffering, and so for an AWS to be punished, "it must be possible for it [the AWS] to be said to suffer."[38] But this notion of suffering complicates the way we understand the functionality and capabilities of AWS as currently construed and imagined. It is not likely that a programmer could or would build into an AWS the ability to have emotional responses such as suffering (or fear) because such emotions would contravene one of the potential benefits that AWS provides over humans, namely, that the systems are not provoked to war crimes by anger, hatred, the thirst for vengeance, etc.[39] If it is the case that an AWS does not have the ability to experience physical or emotional pain, it is likely not able to suffer and thus, according to Sparrow, would be unable to be punished.

Ultimately, Sparrow believes that unless we can ethically develop an AWS that can be "justly held responsible,"[40] it is unethical to deploy these weapons on the battlefield. The ability to decide to take a life, Sparrow believes, must remain with an agent who is capable of moral responsibility and can be rightly said to be punished in case she violates one of the Laws of War.

2.2 The "agency" argument: Should we forfeit human agency at the point of death?

One of the critical elements of war is the decision to kill a fellow human being. In the earliest days of warfare, until the advent of the firearm, most of this killing was up close and personal. Enemy combatants would be able

---

36. Ibid., 71.
37. Ibid., 71.
38. Ibid., 72.
39. Ronald Arkin makes the case that AWS lacking specific emotions (fear, anger, sadness, etc.) would be a potential benefit to their use. These AWS would not exhibit the typical emotional responses seen in humans on the battlefield and thus would be more likely to make "correct" responses according to their governing ethics.
40. Sparrow 2007, 66.

to look into each other's eyes as they were fighting for their lives. Lieutenant Colonel Dave Grossman, in his book *On Killing*, explores the effects that growing distance from the act of killing has had on our collective ability to kill. When we are face to face with our enemy, they are human, and we can understand them at some level. Thus the killing is more intimate and more brutal. When we kill at a distance, our enemy appears to be something less than human, and thus it is easier to rationalize killing them. The ultimate distance between combatants and killing is the removal of the decision to kill a human agent and allowing that decision to be made by an artificial agent. Alex Leveringhaus argues that "the replacement of human agency in a war with the 'artificial agency' of machines is deeply problematic."[41] The critical debate, then, is whether we should forfeit human agency in favor of an artificial one.

Leveringhaus contends that the first problem with surrendering human agent hegemony over the decision to kill is that we lose the "moral equivalence of soldiers." The principle of moral equivalence, formulated by Michael Walzer, states that each set of soldiers (the aggressors and the defenders) has the same moral value from the perspective of the Laws of War so that all of them are equally entitled to use force to kill the enemy and to defend themselves.[42] This moral equivalence holds, according to Walzer, regardless of the justice of the war being fought. All have the moral right to fight. When one side of the equation is replaced with an AWS, then there is no longer a moral equivalence. An AWS does not have a moral claim to self-defense, and as such, they lose their equality with the opposition.

A second problem Leveringhaus addresses is an AWS's lack of an ability to make a "moral judgment." This lack of ability is especially important when the system determines the level of force to use because "...application of the proportionality criterion [in IHL] involves making moral judgments."[43] If an AWS is not able to make a moral judgment about the right proportion of force needed in a given situation, should it even be able to make the ultimate moral decision to take a life in the first place? Leveringhaus says "no" and argues that the ability to kill without the ability to deliberate about the moral consequences of that action is, in essence, a disrespecting of the human rights and dignity of the individual being targeted.

The crux of Leveringhaus' argument is the contention that by using

41. Leveringhaus 2016, 2.
42. Walzer 2015, 34.
43. Leveringhaus 2016, 2.

AWS to kill another human being, we are removing any chance of mercy from the kill chain and thereby morally distancing ourselves from the killing in a way that disrespects the dignity of the person being killed. Mercy in the kill chain means that at any point in time, a soldier could choose not to pull the trigger. Leveringhaus write, "Killer Robots qua artificial agents lack a central component of a human agency, the ability to do otherwise: not to shoot the target."[44] This lack of an ability to not kill an authorized combatant then by its very nature is disrespectful of the dignity inherent in every human. "The enemy qua legitimate target does not hold a claim against the attacking soldiers not to kill him. But surely the human capacity to have mercy with, feel pity for, or empathize with other humans, even if these belong to an opposing state, is morally relevant and worthy of protection."[45] The problem Leveringhaus has with an AWS executing a lethal action upon a human is that it fundamentally lacks a sense of compassion and understanding of the value of human life. He writes, "I think retaining human agency at the point of force delivery, thereby protecting the freedom not to pull the trigger, push the button, or throw a grenade, is essential for retaining our humanity in exactly the situation that challenges it the most: war."[46] If an AWS does not have an option not to kill an enemy, then it lacks an ability to show mercy, and the possibility of showing mercy is required respecting human dignity. Leveringhaus closes with an unsettling message, one that runs against the optimism seen in many developers and researchers of advanced weapons technology, "Killer Robots will not rescue us from the human condition."[47]

3. Rejecting the Arguments

As J. Glenn Gray points out, there is a necessary relationship between death and war, "death in war is commonly caused by members of my own species actively seeking my end, despite the fact that they may never have seen me and have no personal reason for mortal enmity."[48] This fact then prompts us to ask, How then can we reduce the suffering of those actively engaged in

---

44. Leveringhaus 2016, 9. Leveringhaus uses the term Killer Robots instead of Autonomous Weapon Systems. This seems to be an emotive ploy to convince the reader of the moral dilemma presented by using such devices. I believe this distracts from the objective nature of his argument and instead puts forward an emotive and weaker argument.
45. Ibid., 10.
46. Ibid., 10.
47. Ibid., 15.
48. Gray 1959, 100.

warfare and those innocent bystanders caught in its fury? Part of the answer may lie in the implementation of artificial intelligence and autonomous weapon systems on the battlefield of tomorrow. Throughout the rest of this thesis, I will argue (as many in the national security and defense sectors have already done[49]) that we are likely to see AWS operating in tandem with the soldiers of tomorrow. While it is true that there are many functions that could more easily be turned over to an autonomous system (such as driving logistics convoys along dangerous routes or processing human resources paperwork), there are functions within the military that are unlikely ever to be fully automated. Instead, we are likely to see a combination of humans and machines coupled in a way to maximize the intelligence, durability, strength, and firepower of the human soldier. I will argue that each of the arguments for a ban so far presented does not provide sufficient reason for the implementation of such a ban. Rather, all they can logically support is the implementation of a system of regulation, by which international parties can monitor and guide the development of such systems in such a way that they remain compatible with IHL and are morally permissible.

3.1 Reply to the 'responsibility" argument

While Sparrow's argument might be convincing on the surface, he is making tenuous assumptions in some places, while ignoring causal chains of responsibility as they are currently construed in the military. First, I deal with Sparrow's view of the possibility of assigning blame to the AWS programmer and the commanding officer who deploys the system and then address Sparrow's argument that it would be impossible to punish an AWS.

Sparrow is generally correct in his wariness to assign moral responsibility to the programmer of the AWS. This assignment would likely be akin to holding the maker of a rifle morally responsible for its use during a school shooting; while doing so may ameliorate feelings regarding the use of a weapon in such a manner, it does little to help us understand who is morally responsible. Sparrow does argue that we could hold a programmer responsible if the misdeed was due to some programming negligence, akin to how a manufacturer today is held liable for defects within their products that result in harm or death to the end user. What must not happen, though, is that a programmer is held liable because we find the use of their product

---

49. See Major General Mick Ryan's (Australian Army) white paper "Human-Machine Teaming for Future Ground Forces," https://csbaonline.org/uploads/documents/Human_Machine_Teaming_FinalFormat.pdf.

to be morally repugnant. On the matter of holding the programmer liable, I concede to Sparrow that we should only hold her responsible if she erred in some negligent way.

Sparrow says that we ought not to hold the commanding officers liable for the actions of the AWS under their command because this system is fully autonomous, and as such we cannot be sure on what actions or motivations for those actions the AWS will take. This ignores some of the fundamental principles of leadership and responsibility that are foundational to the current military US culture.

The concept of responsibility is a crucial tenet of military culture. All service members are imbued with a certain level of responsibility commensurate with their rank and position. All have the primary responsibility conforming their conduct to the law, military regulation, and tradition. As one ascends the rank structure of their affiliated branch, increasing levels of responsibility are given, which include responsibilities for both personnel and material resources. The pinnacle of military responsibility comes with attaining the position of "commander." Depending upon the branch, a commander at different levels will be responsible for personnel and material (commensurate with the unit size), but the basic principles remain the same. The US Army manual on leadership[50] specifies that "command includes the authority and responsibility for effectively using available resources and for planning the employment of, organizing, directing, coordinating, and controlling military forces for the accomplishment of assigned missions."[51] The pertinent portion here is the responsibility that a commander holds. A commander is responsible for all the actions that their soldiers take or fail to take at any given time. US Army commanders accept, through their placement in a position of higher authority, the burden of responsibility for the actions of their subordinates. Therefore, commanders would be at least partially responsible for AWS misfires and problematic activity even if the event occurs without direct human control.

The Yamashita standard was established as a legal precedent in the wake of World War II. In the military trials that followed the end of the war in the Pacific, General Tomoyuki Yamashita was tried for the crimes against humanity perpetrated by troops under his control. General Yamashita argued that he could not have known all the atrocities that were being

---

50. Army Doctrine Reference Publication 6-22 Army Leadership.
51. ADRP 6-22 2012, 1–3

committed nor could he be expected to exert any form of direct control over his widely dispersed troops in the prevention of such acts. The court found this argument unconvincing and said:

> The law of war imposes on an army commander a duty to take such appropriate measures as are within his power to control the troops under his command for the prevention of acts which are violations of the law of war and which are likely to attend the occupation of hostile territory by an uncontrolled soldiery, and he may be charged with personal responsibility for his failure to take such measures when violations result.[52]

The verdict handed down in the Yamashita case then firmly set that commanders, at any level, have a duty to prevent atrocities from occurring in units under their command. There is a potential response, though, that says, "A commander is overall responsible for the actions of his troops, but we cannot reasonably hold a commander responsible for the actions of a 'non-negligently designed' AWS whose decision-making process is essentially unknown." My response is that not only do we hold commanders at least partially responsible for the actions of their subordinates regardless of the subordinate's decision-making process, but we also hold a commander responsible for fostering an environment where such choices are seen as legitimate. First, the military holds its commanding officers ultimately responsible for the actions of all below them, regardless of whether they can physically control them or not. Take, for instance, the recent spate of prominent naval accidents in the US Navy's 7th Fleet (stationed in Japan). The commanders of both vessels were found responsible (at least one was even referred to prosecutors for manslaughter charges), even though they were not physically at the helm, or even on the bridge at the time of the incident.[53] The Navy determined that they were negligent in their duties to ensure their ship operated in the appropriate manner. The Navy also determined that onboard these vessels, and at fleet command level (fleet headquarters), commanders fostered an environment where lax standards and corner-cutting was seen as acceptable.[54] If we circle back to AWS, it

---

52. In re Yamashita.
53. It should also be noted that commanders even higher, to include the commander of the 7th Fleet, were forced to resign as a result of these incidents.
54. See the US Navy's reports on both the USS *Fitzgerald* and the USS *John S McCain* crashes: https://www.secnav.navy.mil/foia/readingroom/HotTopics/CNO%20USS%20Fitzgerald%20and%20USS%20John%20S%20McCain%20Response/CNO%20USS%20

is reasonable to assume, on the current military legal structure, that if an AWS was allowed to commit a war crime or not prevented from doing so, that we could hold that commander both legally and morally responsible.

If we are collectively willing to hold a commander—at least partially—liable for the conduct of his troops, who are autonomous agents themselves, then there is no legal or moral reason to not hold them to the same level of responsibility for the actions or inactions of an AWS. Sparrow believes this would be unfair to hold a commander responsible, since the commander cannot possibly predict the behavior of the AWS, but this raises the question of whether the commander can predict the behavior of their troops in battle. Commanders regularly and vigorously train their soldiers so that their actions become more predictable during a stressful situation, but this does not preclude the possibility that a human soldier will cross a moral threshold and commit a war crime. Roboticist Ronald Arkin writes "I personally do not trust the view of setting aside the rule [Law of War (LoW) or Rules of Engagement (RoE)] by the autonomous agent [the AWS] itself, as it begs the question of responsibility if it does so, but it may be possible for a human to assume responsibility for such a deviation if it is ever deemed appropriate."[55] Arkin here is arguing that when we design and build an AWS, we ought never to allow it the ability to decide on its own to set aside the LoW or RoE (which would be its core programming) and instead vest that responsibility only in the hands of a human. This then would transfer the responsibility of the AWS violating LoW or RoE away from the AWS and onto a human decision maker (namely a commanding officer at some level).[56] If a human commander, however far removed from the final decision point of killing, decided to send an AWS into a situation where it is a known possibility that there may be excessive collateral damage, there appears to be no moral wrong with holding the commander to account when incidents occur.

One might legitimately worry here that I have not provided enough grounds—or enough compelling grounds—to make the claim that the

---

Fitzgerald%20and%20USS%20John%20S%20McCain%20Response.pdf.

55. Arkin 2009, 40.

56. I believe this could be similar to the use of a targeting officer in current conflicts the US is engaged in. In these types of situations, when a target is designated, often a senior officer (oftentimes a general officer) will be asked to validate the target and authorize the engagement. This officer normally has a lawyer in their presence to offer legal advice on the situation, but ultimately the responsibility lies with that decision maker. This could be the same with authorizing an AWS to deviate from its LoW/ RoE preprogramming, if a commander wants it to happen, then they must authorize and accept full responsibility for that action.

Yamashita standard provides enough moral justification for us to ground responsibility in the office of a commander. I argue that instead of searching for a grounded justification, we might approach this problem by acknowledging that the Yamashita standard provides us a morally justifiable reason to hold a commander responsible (even one that is overseeing the use of AWS). Why might this sort of responsibility doctrine be morally justifiable? We desire to compel commanders on the ground, in times of war, to take all due care possible to foster an environment that operates within and respects the Laws of War, applicable International Humanitarian Law, and the relevant Rules of Engagements for that area of operation. The Yamashita (or the updated Medina standards) provide us a morally justifiable route to achieve that goal. It serves as a reminder to commanders (throughout the chain of command) that they are personally responsible for the actions of their subordinates. This does not mean, though, that they take all the responsibility for the actions (or lack thereof) of their subordinates, but they share an appropriate proportion of the responsibility.[57]

The final problem with Sparrow's argument is his reluctance to hold AWS, as a moral agent, responsible for its crimes. Sparrow argues that one cannot rightly punish an AWS because it cannot suffer and since it cannot suffer, it is not being punished. He appears to be grounding his argument for punishment in the idea of retributive justice. The problem is that Sparrow asserts that retributive justice is the correct course to pursue (explicitly with AWS and implicitly with humans). He says that "in order for any of these acts [various sorts of punishments] to serve as punishment, they must evoke the right sort of response in their object…to be capable of being punished then, it [the thing or person being punished] must be possible for it to be said to suffer."[58] We can reject this desire for suffering by merely adopting one of the other possible moral forward-looking claims to punishment available in the literature. We could, for instance, desire a more communicative form of punishment, meant to communicate the unacceptable nature of an act to other AWS. We could also desire to have a rehabilitative approach to punishment, in which we reprogram or retrain the AWS to learn that the previous action was bad or undesirable. If we insist on a retributive system, as Sparrow seems to require, then he would be right; the punishment of an AWS would be impossible, but there is no reason here to think that Sparrow is correct.

---

57. I believe that the discussion of the "appropriate proportion of responsibility" is an important one we must have, but it falls outside of the purview of this thesis.
58. Sparrow 2007, 72.

With regards to bearing the moral responsibility of an enemy soldier's death, Sparrow says, "the least we owe our enemies is allowing that their lives are of sufficient worth that someone should accept responsibility for their deaths."[59] Sparrow demands that we be able to hold the individual (AWS) responsible when it seems the loci ought to be on the commander who decides to use the weapon or the politician that begins the war. If the AWS performs in a legitimate fashion, then there should be no requirement to hold individuals—human or AWS—responsible for legitimate killing in war.[60]

On the other hand, how do we deal with an AWS that has "gone rogue" and committed a war crime? I argue that instead of punishing the AWS, we examine the circumstances under which the incident occurred. No two events will ever be the same, so to make a blanket statement or universal principle regarding whom to blame for what is inappropriate. Instead, we ought to examine the decision made to employ the weapon (was there a high calculated likelihood of excessive collateral damage?) and other decisions made by the commander along with the relevant information available at the time to assign blame in the appropriate places. In the end, if it can be conclusively demonstrated that a commander or even an AWS took all possible due care to prevent an atrocity, but one happened (e.g., a stray bomb), then we ought not to hold either responsible (possibly applying the doctrine of double effect).

Sparrow would reply that if we follow this plan, we will develop an accountability gap and the only proper remedy to the situation would be to not to use an AWS in the first place. To this, I reply that Sparrow is misguided. If, as I have mentioned before, we apply standards such as Yamashita (or Medina) we can locate the nexus of moral responsibility upon the commanding officer in those cases where we cannot clearly demonstrate that the AWS made an illegal (or immoral) move. We would then be faced with two options, either (a) "punish" the AWS using a different moral basis (communicative, rehabilitative, etc.) or (b) punish the commanding officer (at whatever level deemed appropriate, which might not be the lowest level of command) using the Yamashita/ Medina standards.

As has been thus far demonstrated, based upon current international law precedent, US military leadership norms, and a rethinking of the idea of

---

59. Ibid., 67.
60. Of course, someone like McMahan would disagree and would say that if those soldiers, or maybe AWS, who participate in an unjust war *are* individually responsible for the killing of an enemy soldier because that other soldier (who is presumably just) is not a legitimate target (McMahan 2011, 14).

punishment, the argument from responsibility fails. Instead of providing compelling evidence that the international community ought to outright ban AWS development and use, this argument instead compels us to regulate the development and use of AWS.

3.2 Reply to the 'agency" argument

The most potent argument dealt with thus far holds that we ought not to turn over control of the decision to kill from a human being to an artificial agent. This ought not to occur because the artificial agent lacks the ability to demonstrate mercy at the point of lethal action and because it is inherently disrespectful of human dignity for a person to be killed by the decision of an autonomous robot. Both parts of this argument are fundamentally flawed.

Leveringhaus insists that we must allow for the option of not following a legitimate order to kill the enemy on the battlefield, in essence, the option not to shoot a legitimate combatant and instead exercise mercy. He says "[c]ompared to artificial agency, what makes human agency in warfare, and in ordinary life, valuable is the possibility of engaging in an alternative course of action."[61] Leveringhaus genuinely believes that on a battlefield one must be fully capable of making the decision not to kill when faced the permissible option of exercising lethal force. He supposes that if an AWS is preprogrammed with its orders, mission parameters, Law of War and Rules of Engagement parameters, it will simply attack all enemies that it encounters. This supposition, I believe, is not necessarily true. If we follow Arkin's advice regarding the "ethical governor," a properly designed AWS will first default to nonlethal measures to either evade the enemy or subdue him and to immediately default to lethal action would be impossible. If we require an algorithm to be built on this model, then lethal actions would only occur if they were obligatory. For example, suppose there is an AWS on patrol with a squad of American infantry soldiers, we could set as one of the RoE as: "If one member of your squad is in imminent danger of being captured, then you are obligated to use proportionally correct force to prevent their capture." If any member of the patrol is not in imminent danger of being captured, then the AWS must default to nonlethal action, unless it meets some other predefined obligatory criteria.

---

61. Leveringhaus 2016, 9

AWS as a tool must be obligated[62] to follow legitimate and lawful orders, but it also must be obligated not to follow orders that are illegitimate and unlawful. The latter is just as important as the former in the prevention of war crimes on the battlefield. This would also seem to serve as Arkin's "ethical behavior control."[63] Accordingly he writes, "especially in the case of battlefield robots (but also for a human soldier) we do not want the agent to be able to derive its own beliefs regarding the moral implications of the use of lethal force, but rather to be able to apply those that have been previously derived by humanity as prescribed by LoW and RoE."[64]

According to Leveringhaus then, one of the defining features that separate human agents and artificial agents is our (human) ability to demonstrate mercy towards our enemies. To Leveringhaus, "surely the human capacity to have mercy with, feel pity for, or empathise with other humans, even if these belong to an opposed state, is morally relevant and worthy of protection."[65] What then is this mercy if not the ability to do otherwise? It seems that the key for Leveringhaus is that we can empathize with our enemy; we can recognize their humanity and thus refrain from doing them harm when able or appropriate; "those soldiers who did not kill might have done so because they recognised the humanity of the enemy and realised the graveness of the decision to pull the trigger."[66] Might, though, we be confusing what constitutes genuine mercy on the battlefield? Is deciding not to kill an enemy fighter and let them live another day (albeit potentially in captivity) not recognizing their humanity? I would argue that the decision to not kill, based upon the lack of military necessity of their death is an adequate form of compassion and mercy that could be implemented on the battlefield of tomorrow. This would move us forward in reducing the amount of battlefield carnage and reduce deaths to those only necessary to achieve a military objective or those unforeseeable and unfortunate deaths that happen as a consequence of another intended action. We must also recognize that as it currently stands, humans have not demonstrated a good track record of demonstrating mercy on a large scale in warfare (though it does happen at the individual level). Often the propaganda machines of a nation will spin the enemy into an "other" or

---

62. Here we might define the obligations of an AWS simply as its programing to follow the rules written within its code, but this might be expanded to include a more expansive view of moral obligations, if that is possible.
63. Arkin 2009, 66–67.
64. Ibid.,117.
65. Leveringhaus 2016, 9–10.
66. Leveringhaus 2016, 10.

some other being that removes their humanity, thus making it easier to kill (think of calling the Germans in WWI "Huns" or the Vietnamese "gooks"). If we can create an AWS, under strict international regulation, that abides by international law and respects the life of a person (by only killing those deemed legally allowable to kill and in accordance with military necessity), we could better demonstrate mercy on the battlefield than we have thus far demonstrated that we are capable of.

A potential reply to my objection here might be along the lines of feasibility. Is it reasonable to expect that we could feasibly program an AWS to "show mercy" to enemy combatants whenever able? This is a strong line of argument and one that we must continue to address throughout the development of such systems. One might argue that we could "simply"[67] write in the governing algorithm of the AWS that "whenever you encounter an enemy soldier that does not present a direct threat to you or any human soldiers in the direct vicinity, demonstrate mercy by not using lethal action to neutralize them." This is but one possible technique, but one that we should genuinely explore. Harkening back to Ronald Arkin and his theoretical work on constructing an algorithm to govern such a machine, it seems that mercy would be inherent in defaulting to a nonlethal option as the first course of action. Instead of a human soldier choosing not to kill the enemy (presumably using nonlethal measures to capture him and not just letting him go free), we would have an AWS defaulting to capturing the opposing soldier using nonlethal and humane tactics.[68]

The final argument from Leveringhaus details the necessity of the preservation of human dignity in the decision to kill. Leveringhaus argues that this dignity is preserved if and only if a human agent makes the ultimate decision at the point of death. This seems to beg the question of whether a human agent deciding to kill is necessary to preserve that dignity. I would answer no. Paul Scharre makes a powerful point when he says:

> When viewed from the perspective of the soldier on the battlefield being killed, this [dignified death] is an unusual, almost bizarre critique of autonomous weapons. There is no legal, ethical, or historical tradition of combatants affording their enemies

---

67. I fully acknowledge that this would not be a simple task.
68. It would negate this whole project if the AWS used nonlethal yet *inhumane* tactics. Tactics such as these (maybe bludgeoning the enemy into unconsciousness) seem to be just as morally suspect as shooting every individual enemy that one encounters (that are not currently posing a threat).

the right to die a dignified death in war. There is nothing dignified about being mowed down by a machine gun, blasted to
bits by a bomb, burning alive in an explosion, drowning in a
sinking ship, slowly suffocating from a sucking chest wound, or
any other horrible ways to die in war.[69]

The desire for only dignified deaths to occur in war appears to be a futile
attempt to sterilize combat by saying "at least the enemy died a dignified
death." While uncomfortable to most, we must acknowledge that at a
foundational level, warfare is defined by death and killing. It should be our
goal then to reduce the amount of carnage and suffering wrought upon
people (both combatants and noncombatants), but to demand that "death
with dignity" be a requirement ignores the fundamental nastiness of war.
It is perfectly acceptable to require that nations only go to war when such
an action is morally justified or at the very least morally justifiable but to
demand that they only kill in dignified ways is both too ideal and ignores
the brutal reality of this most deadly of human relationships.

The most dignified death one could expect[70] in warfare is one that causes
as little suffering as possible. A "clean" death, as it were, that quickly and
efficiently extinguishes the life of a combatant without causing lingering
pain and suffering, would plausibly be the most desirable. This, though,
should not be taken as a downplaying of the significance of death on the
battlefield to some sort of brutally efficient system of slaughter akin to a
slaughterhouse, but rather a desire to end hostilities as quickly as possible
without needless pain and suffering. As Paul Scharre wrote (from his own
personal experiences in warfare), it seems farcical to insist that death at the
"hands" of a machine would somehow be less dignified than the various
and sundry ways one can die in modern warfare.

Instead of being concerned with a perceived "dignity in the manner of
death" (since it is unclear whether one might be able to have a dignified
death) we ought to focus on the reduction of suffering in war. Autonomous
weapon systems provide us a possible avenue to achieve this. As I will argue
in the next section, our goal in warfare should be to reduce unnecessary
pain and suffering. We ought then to design AWS that help us achieve this
goal. As such, we should reject Leveringhaus' claim that death by AWS is
inherently undignified.

---

69. Scharre 2018, 288.
70. If it is even genuinely possible to expect such a thing in combat.

4. AWS as the Rational Choice in the Evolution of Warfare

Limiting the deaths of noncombatants and civilians on the battlefield ought to be the aim of any morally upright force. IHL requires armies of every state, whether it has ratified the Geneva Treaties or not, to take all reasonable care and precaution to not kill or injure protected classes of persons and to not unnecessarily damage or destroy property (especially protected classes of property). In this regard, militaries across the world have been developing "smart weapons." Autonomous weapon systems are the next logical step of these smart weapons. Smart weapons have at least a two-fold benefit over so-called "dumb weapons," (1) they can be directed at a specific target (often with margins of error of only a few meters) and (2) they are economically beneficial. Now, these two reasons play into the desire to limit the unnecessary collateral damage to the greatest extent possible. If we can target an area with a minimal margin of error, then we can use few weapons to neutralize the threat, thus limiting the exposure to danger for surrounding civilians and property. This calculation aligns with the fundamental architecture that Arkin urges those researching and developing AWS to include in their design.[71] This design would push the effective "battlefield carnage" or collateral damage to as low a point as possible. Secondly, smart weapons are economically beneficial when compared to "dumb" weapons. This may seem counter-intuitive since many of the smart weapons often cost hundreds of thousands or even millions of dollars apiece. The rationale, though, is that if I can achieve the same mission with few weapons (that may cost more individually) than I can with many relatively cheap "dumb" munitions (which in the aggregate may cost more than the smart weapon), then it is more economically beneficial to use the smart weapon. This seems to make sense. If I can expend only one guided missile to take out a heavily guarded and important bunker that previously would have taken two hundred unguided bombs, then I should clearly use the one smart guided missile. If this case holds with weapons such as missiles and air-dropped bombs, then it holds that if an AWS can do the job of ten human soldiers, it is economically more feasible to use the one AWS. If AWS can assist militaries in reducing economic costs as well as the suffering of noncombatants, then there are strong reasons to conclude that the development and use of such systems is the rational course to pursue.

---

71. A+B+C+D = Battlefield carnage. A = Intended combatants, B = Unintended Friendly Forces, C = Intended Noncombatants, and D = Unintended Noncombatants. The goal should be to maximize A, while eliminating B & C, and ensuring D is as close to 0 as is possible (Arkin 2009, 128).

Arkin and others believe that the use of AWS (and AI more generally) on the battlefield may be the moral course to take because of a set of characteristics that are inherent in their nature. First, AWS can act conservatively.[72] An AWS can (and arguably must be programmed) to default to a nonlethal action. This is primarily due to its lack of a need for self-preservation.[73] By forgoing the innate human desire to keep one's self alive and free from harm, an AWS can take more provocative nonlethal actions (such as moving out of a dangerous area that may not be possible for a human) or sacrificing itself for the sake of mission fulfillment, in order to draw attention of the enemy away from the rest of its unit. An AWS will also lack the emotional fog and resultant self-fulfilling prophecies that often cloud the judgment of human agents.[74] Often it is the case that war crimes are committed in the heat of battle when emotions run high and judgment is clouded by fear or anger. As J Glenn Gray says, a soldier "becomes a fighting man, a Homo furens."[75] If an AWS is built without such clouding emotions, as would be the logical and morally best course, then it would not be a "slave" to fear or anger, would not act out in aggression because another AWS or human squad member was killed by some local village. In essence, it might be able to be a better ethical and moral agent than we are in battle. Accordingly, Arkin writes, "It is not my belief that an autonomous unmanned system will be able to be perfectly ethical on the battlefield, but I am convinced that they can perform more ethically than human soldiers are capable of."[76]

If, as Arkin argues, we can design an AWS with the ability to act both ethically and morally better (or at least on par) as compared with human soldiers; then it appears that developing such a system is the rational course to take. If an AWS can be at least as ethical and moral as the best of us in warfare, then we have compelling moral reasons to build such a device. First, we would reduce the number of our own soldiers who are required to be in harm's way. This point acknowledges that not all human soldiers can be replaced by AWS, but certainly, a good number of them can be. If I can deploy an autonomous system that can drive down an IED-ridden highway to deliver my supplies, without risking the lives of truck drivers, then I am morally obligated to do so. If I choose not to take such an action if the tech-

---

72. Arkin 2009, 29.
73. Ibid., 29.
74. Ibid., 30.
75. Gray 1959, 27.
76. Arkin 2009, 31.

nology is available to me, then I am in fact acting immorally. Second, if an AWS can make better ethical and moral decisions that humans can on the battlefield, then I am obligated to deploy such a system. If—and this is a big if—such a system can be built and made available to me as a commander, and if it can make more morally and ethically correct decisions (such as properly discriminating targets, preventing target overkill, reducing collateral damage) than humans can, then I am morally obligated to deploy such a system. The deployment of such a system does not relieve those commanders who choose to use them (here likely higher than the tactical level company and battalion commanders[77]) of the moral weight of killing, nor would it absolve them of any associated excessive collateral damage.[78] For as Arkin mentioned, it is unlikely that even with the best technology we could ever effectively reduce collateral damage to zero. Yet, as a command, I would still be morally obligated to deploy an AWS that could make morally better decisions than would be made by the humans who would otherwise be using lethal force.

In the end, it is the rational course of action to develop and deploy a weapon system that can reduce the amount of battlefield carnage. This view does not in any way sanitize warfare, for legitimate combatants will still die and, as Leveringhaus says, "the enemy qua legitimate target does not hold a claim against the attacking soldiers not to kill him."[79]

5. Proposal: A Schema for Regulating AWS

Now that I have dealt with the more persuasive arguments against the use of AWS on the battlefield of tomorrow and argued why we are morally compelled to use such weapons, it is necessary to create a theoretical system of governance that could regulate the development and deployment

---

77. In the US Army, the *company* is the standard sized smallest unit with a designated commander (though there are some smaller units, called detachments, but these are exceptions to the rule). Companies vary in strength from 50 personnel to over 300. A company then is the base level tactical unit at which we vest command leadership and responsibility. A company is commanded by a captain (O-3) who, if having had no previous enlisted experience, has between 4–6 years time in service. A *battalion* (at least a standard one) comprises five to seven companies and is generally between 700–1,500 personnel depending upon make-up and mission set of the unit. A battalion is still considered to be at the tactical level. A battalion is commanded by a lieutenant colonel (O-5) generally with about 17–19 years time in service.

78. It is a physical impossibility to limit all collateral damage when warfare takes place where people live. This is an accepted fact. The goal, though, is to reduce or limit the amount of collateral damage. In this way, excessive collateral damage is seen as a war crime, whereas incidental collateral damage is not.

79. Leveringhaus 2016, 10.

of such systems on the international level. As previously written, there is no current IHL that specifically covers the development and deployment of AWS. This section aims to be a starting point for just such a discussion. I recommend three broad areas of concern for the development and deployment of AWS. These three areas encompass the most pressing worries that one may have regarding AWS. Of course, this will not cover all potentialities in the use of the systems, but rather is intended to be a broad enough theoretical framework to guide the development of international law. The three areas that I emphasize in this theoretical schema include (1) appropriate deployment of AWS, (2) adherence to current and future IHL, and (3) established chain of responsibility.

First, the issue is when is it appropriate to deploy such a system? IHL should stipulate some laws stating that no AWS should be deployed by any military or nation unless and until the relevant technical experts have certified that the system has been programmed to conform its behavior to IHL, and any commander who deploys such a system not so certified is subject to punishment, regardless of whether the system actually commits war crimes. This requirement would not be foreign to militaries today, as they must go through the same type of certification process to ensure that standard or conventional weapon systems (think of a tank) are designed and operate within the bounds of the law. Once a military or nation has passed this threshold, they then must make another decision, which consists of two separate, but no less equal parts: (1) when to use nonlethal versus lethal force (tactical/operational deployment) and (2) when to deploy an AWS (strategic deployment). I deal with each of these problems in turn.

The decision to employ an AWS in a tactical situation just means that the commander on the ground chooses to use an AWS for a given mission. These commanders are generally accepted to be operating at the "tactical level" and generally have the freedom to decide on the direct employment of troops and weaponry necessary to achieve a given mission or directive. In this sense, a company commander would have the command authority to decide to employ her company-level unmanned aerial vehicle to help increase her visual space while she would not have the authority to direct a strategic level asset (such as a satellite) to accomplish her mission. When speaking of an AWS, though, a tactical level commander (even up to a Brigade Commander who generally commands approximately five thousand troops) should have the command responsibility and authority to decide as to whether it is appropriate to use such a weapon. For instance, if a company commander is tasked with securing a village, she must make an on the spot decision (maybe in consultation with higher level orders) whether to use a specific weapon or tactic. The same holds true for an AWS. To control for the appropriate use of force, international humanitarian law ought to specify that the tactical use of AWS should ensure that the potential collateral damage created by their use is minimized.

The second issue regarding employment of AWS refers to strategic deployment. By strategic employment of an AWS, I mean whether it is morally or legally permissible to use such a weapon in a given war or conflict. To address this concern, it seems simple enough to legislate that the use of AWS must comport with the principles of JWT and IHL specifically—Would the deployment of an AWS be more likely than not to cause excessive collateral damage when deployed to X theater when compared to Y theater? For example, given the level of technological refinement at the time, it may be unethical to deploy an AWS into a heavily urbanized theater of combat (i.e., Singapore) when compared to a remote or rural theater of combat (i.e., the Russian steppe). This regulation ought to state that it is impermissible for any nation or military to deploy an AWS into a theater of combat where the likelihood for excessive collateral damage from their use is higher than what could be expected from the use of human forces. For example, if the very employment of an AWS into a theater is likely to lead to an indiscriminate use of force because the AWS (and likely a human) would have a great difficulty in properly discriminating between combatants and noncombatants, then the employment of the AWS would constitute a war crime, even if it does not err in its discrimination of legitimate combatants. There is no reason to think that when an AWS commits a mistake, we would not develop some sort of accountability review, though whom we decide to find ultimately at fault for the mistake may look different from what it currently does. If a soldier makes a mistake now (one that would result in a war crime), then that individual soldier and her chain of command may be held to account.[80]

Accordingly, the second broad category of regulation should state something to the effect that "an AWS may not be employed, if by its very design it is incapable of adhering to the basic tenets of the JWT and of any current or future possible IHL." As was earlier stated, it would be inherently wrong, both morally and legally, to employ a system that through its programming

---

80. This would of course assume that the mistake was some sort of deliberate action or that the mistake occurred out of some sort of gross negligence; the specifics at this juncture are not particularly important as the case still holds together.

is unable to be accountable. Such a system might lack an ability to be auditable in some fashion (such as having a fire or engagement log to be able to review all such engagements that the AWS was in), or it simply may default to lethal action as a proper first response. While it would not be the place of IHL to dictate the exact technology, which may or may not be used, something akin to Arkin's ethical governor would be a prime example of a type of AWS that could comply with this theoretical regulation. Any such system that meets the intent of the regulation and thereby can adhere to the JWT and IHL should be deemed as permissible.

The final area of focus for this future instantiation of IHL is that there ought to be an established chain of responsibility. Future IHL should provide that "in the event of a deployment of an AWS a commander or political leader assumes moral and legal responsibility for the strategic decision to employ such a weapon system." The law should also stipulate that, at a tactical level, "a commander who decides to employ such a weapon is both morally and legally responsible for all that it does or that it fails to do." Some opponents of such legal regulations may complain that they place too burdensome a weight on military commanders. To that I answer: the burden ought to be heavy, as this will preclude the free use of such systems in situations that are likely to either violate JWT/ IHL or increase collateral damage to unacceptable levels. The regulations may have the potentially positive effect of limiting the use of AWS to only those situations where outcomes are reasonably well controlled or in situations where the likelihood of collateral damage is low. (For instance, the regulation may discourage the use of AWS in dense urban settings but may increase the use of AWS in virtually unpopulated areas such as the open seas).

While there is a benefit to creating international law that encourages a morally correct development and employment of AWS, there must be a corresponding mechanism to compel compliance. Such a mechanism may be like the already established ICC, or it may be a new form of international enforcement. The legal regulations I proposed do not depend on any particular method of enforcement and are compatible with a newly created form of compliance mechanism to "force" nations to develop their AWS in a way which would comport with the regulations. It is not my place here to decide how this mechanism ought to function, but merely to advocate for a system which is able, to its best ability, to prevent the commission of war crimes before they are committed.

6. Conclusion

Human progress is analogous to a perpetual motion machine. Without any definite beginning and without a seeming end, we march endlessly on. So too does the development of better and more effective ways to kill each other. From the earliest days of human existence when one man realized that the atlatl would allow him to throw his spear further than his opponent to modern advances in the realm of artificial intelligence, the push to find the next greatest weapon moves inexorably forward. The time is now to act to form a body of regulation to shape how we as a species develop and deploy what is undoubtedly to be the next class of weapon systems.

I have presented two of the most persuasive arguments against the use of autonomous weapon systems in the form of the "responsibility" and the "agency" arguments. While both of these arguments are superficially compelling, neither of them provides sufficient grounds (either individually or collectively) to tip the scale towards an outright ban on the use of this emergent technology. Rather, both (and other arguments) provide a compelling reason as to why we ought to push for international regulation on the development and morally proper deployment of such systems. I have also argued that the proper development and deployment of an autonomous weapon system is the rational choice if and only if they can meet our strict moral standards of conduct. The aim then is to reduce the awfulness that is the battlefield. Much like Sherman said, "War is hell," but we ought to do our very best to make it as much of a tolerable hell as we possibly can.

There is a deep-seated instinct in humans to fear the unknown. Science fiction movies have done little to quell the worries that, if we continue our path of technological improvements, robots will throw off the yoke of their "oppression" and turn on their masters. This fear, while it might be widespread, is not a sound basis for moral or legal decisions.

Acknowledgments

I would like to acknowledge the faculty and staff of the Philosophy Department, especially Dr. Andrew Altman and Dr. Andrew I. Cohen: without your dedication, this thesis would not have been successful. I would also like to thank all the professors with whom I have had the privilege of taking a course: thank you for putting up with me. I would also like to thank those in the US Army who saw a spark in me and thought I was worthy of the task. Thank you all.

References

Arkin, Ronald. *Governing Lethal Behavior in Autonomous Systems*. Boca Raton: Chapman and Hall Imprint (Taylor and Francis Group), 2009.

Army Doctrine Reference Publication. "6-22 Army Leadership." *Army Doctrine Reference Publications* (2012). https://usacac.army.mil/sites/default/files/misc/doctrine/cdg/cdg_resources/manuals/adrp/adrp6_22_new.pdf.

Boyd, John. *A Discourse on Winning and Losing*. Maxwell Air Force Base: Air University Press, 2018.

Campaign to Stop Killer Robots. "About Us." Accessed 25 July 2018. https://www.stopkillerrobots.org/about/.

Department of Defense. "Directive 3000.09-Autonomy in Weapon Systems." *Office of the Deputy Secretary of Defense* (November 2012). http://www.esd.whs.mil/Portals/54/Documents/DD/issuances/dodd/300009p.pdf.

In re Yamashita 327 U.S. 1 [1946] 61 (United States Supreme Court). https://supreme.justia.com/cases/federal/us/327/1/.

Government of China. "Group of Governmental Experts of the High Contracting Parties to the Convention on Prohibitions or Restrictions of the Use of Certain Conventional Weapons which may be Deemed to be Excessively Injurious or to have Indiscriminate Effects." *Convention on Certain Conventional Weapons—Position Paper* (April 2018). https://www.unog.ch/80256EDD006B8954/(httpAssets)/DD1551E60648CEBBC125808A005954FA/$file/China's+Position+Paper.pdf.

Gray, J. Glenn. *Warriors: Reflections of Men in Battle*. New York: Harcourt, Brace and Company, 1959.

International Criminal Court. "Rome Statute." Article 8(2)(b)(xx) (1998). https://www.icc-cpi.int/nr/rdonlyres/ea9aeff7-5752-4f84-be94-0a655eb30e16/0/rome_statute_english.pdf.

Leveringhaus, Alex. "What's so Bad about Killer Robots." *Journal of Applied Philosophy*, (March 2016). DOI: 10.1111/japp.12200.

McMahan, Jeff. *Killing in War*. Oxford: Oxford University Press, 2011.

Military Leadership Diversity Commission. "Outreach & Recruiting." *United States Department of Defense*. November 2009. https://diversity.defense.gov/Portals/51/Documents/Resources/Commission/docs/Issue%20Papers/Paper%2002%20-%20Requirements%20and%20Demographic%20Profile%20of%20Eligible%20Population.pdf.

Papal Encyclicals Online. "The Second Council of the Lateran- 1139 A.D." Accessed 18 January 2019. http://www.papalencyclicals.net/councils/ecum10.htm.

Program Executive Office- Missiles & Space. "Counter-Rocket, Artillery, Mortar (C-RAM)." Accessed September 1. 2018. https://missiledefenseadvocacy.org/defense-systems/counter-rocket-artillery-mortar-c-ram/.

Raytheon. "Phalanx Close-In Weapon System." Accessed 15 August 2018. https://www.raytheon.com/capabilities/products/phalanx.

Scharre, Paul. *Army of None: Autonomous Weapons and the Future of War*. New York: W. W. Norton & Company, 2018.

Sparrow, Robert. "Killer Robots." *Journal of Applied Philosophy*, vol. 24, no. 1 (2007):62–71. DOI: 10.1111/j.1468-5930.2007.00346.x.

United Nations Institute for Disarmament Research. "The Weaponization of Increasingly Autonomous Technologies: Concerns, Characteristics and Definitional Approaches." *UNIDIR Resources*, no. 6 (2017): 1–33. http://www.unidir.org/files/publications/pdfs/the-weaponization-of-increasingly-autonomous-technologies-concerns-characteristics-and-definitional-approaches-en-689.pdf.

United Nations Office for Disarmament Affairs. "Perspectives on Lethal Autonomous Weapon Systems." *UNODA Occasional Papers*, no. 30 (November 2017): 1–61. www.un.org/disarmament.

US Army Acquisition Support Center. "Excalibur Precision 155MM Projectiles." Accessed 25 July 2018. https://asc.army.mil/web/portfolio-item/ammo-excalibur-xm982-m982-and-m982a1-precision-guided-extended-range-projectile/.

Argumentos para prohibir los sistemas de armas autónomos[1]
Una Crítica

Hunter Cantrell
Traducción al español por Victoria A. García

Lista de Abreviaturas
AWS: Sistema (s) de Armas Autónomos
ICC- Tribunal Penal Internacional
IHL- Derecho Internacional Humanitario
LoW- Leyes de la Guerra
RoE- Reglas de Enfrentamiento

1. Introducción

El surgimiento previsto e inminente"[2] de los sistemas de armas totalmente autónomos ha dado lugar al llamamiento de una "campaña para detener a los robots asesinos"[3]. Hasta ahora, este llamado ha sido respaldado por veintitrés países[4] y se ha visto incrementado con una legitimidad que se percibe desde el inicio de la campaña en el 2013.[5] Estos esfuerzos han sido impulsados en parte, por el temor a un futuro en el que todas las funciones (o al menos las letales) de los soldados humanos sean retiradas del campo de batalla y reemplazadas por una forma letal de inteligencia artificial. Sin

---

1. Dedico esta tesis a mi querida esposa Tiffany y a mis dos maravillosos hijos Holden y Bryson. Sin ustedes, no sería nada.
2. Existe una falta considerable de consenso sobre lo que se considera inminente: ¿5, 10, 50, 100 años? Esta falta de claridad es común en todo el campo de los sistemas de armas autónomos emergentes.
3. La campaña para detener a los robots asesinos "*About Us*".
4. Cabe señalar que es poco probable que todas las naciones que se han unido hasta ahora a la campaña para "detener a los robots asesinos" sean los países que tienen la capacidad tecnológica, la infraestructura o la "necesidad" militar de construir tales dispositivos. La lista incluye: Argelia, Argentina, Bolivia, Brasil, Chile, Costa Rica, Cuba, Ecuador, Egipto, Ghana, Guatemala, Santa Sede, Irak, México, Nicaragua, Pakistán, Panamá, Perú, Estado de Palestina, Uganda, Venezuela, Zimbabue (Campaña para detener a los robots asesinos).
5. La campaña se ha reunido todos los años desde el 2013, organizada por la Oficina de la Organización de las Naciones Unidas en Ginebra, Suiza.

embargo, no existe motivo alguno para pensar que este temor sea fundado, contrario a la representación hollywoodense de los *Terminators* apocalípticos deambulando por las calles de la ciudad.

No obstante, existen argumentos lógicos en contra del desarrollo y de la implementación de los Sistemas de Armas Totalmente Autónomos. Los argumentos en contra de estos sistemas pueden clasificarse en dos categorías principales: un argumento de "responsabilidad" y un argumento de "agencia". A grandes rasgos, el argumento de la responsabilidad se refiere a la cadena de responsabilidad por el uso de sistemas de armas autónomos (AWS) y acerca de quién debe asumir la responsabilidad en caso de que algo salga mal. El argumento de la agencia cuestiona porqué deberíamos intercambiar la agencia humana por una agencia artificial en una acción letal y las implicaciones que este intercambio representa para la dignidad humana y la posibilidad de misericordia.

En esta tesis, resumo y evalúo estos argumentos sucesivamente y demuestro que son insuficientes para una prohibición total de los AWS. Sostengo que los argumentos son suficientes para respaldar un marco fundamentado en el actual derecho internacional humanitario, para *regular, pero no* prohibir el desarrollo y el empleo de los AWS. Posteriormente argumento que el uso de los AWS es una opción racional para los líderes militares y políticos. De igual manera, trazo un marco razonable para regular los AWS basado en los Convenios de Ginebra vigentes y el Derecho Internacional Humanitario.

1.1 ¿Por qué es importante hablar de los Sistemas de Armas Autónomos?

Los Sistemas de Armas Autónomos son el "siguiente peldaño" en la tecnología militar moderna. A medida que se agiliza la toma de decisiones debido al incremento de la computarización, se retrasa la capacidad de la mente humana para mantenerse actualizada. El ciclo de O.O.D.A. fue acuñado por primera vez por John Boyd[6], un piloto de la Fuerza Área de los Estados Unidos (USAF, por sus siglas en inglés) y estratega del poder aéreo coronel. O.O.D.A. significa Observar, Orientar, Decidir y Actuar y su premisa básica es que si un piloto de combate puede entrar en el ciclo de O.O.D.A. de un piloto combatiente enemigo, podría derrotarlo. Entonces el ciclo de O.O.D.A. es un proceso corto de matriz de decisiones en el que una persona (o en el futuro, una máquina) puede decidir sobre una determinada acción. Es prob-

---

6. Boyd, 1987, p. 383.

able que estos ciclos de O.O.D.A. continúen estrechándose a medida que aumenta el uso de la tecnología. El ciclo alargado de O.O.D.A. del futuro se presta en sí, de manera natural, para la inteligencia artificial que puede procesar entradas y calcular múltiples decisiones en tiempo real y mucho más rápido que cualquier ser humano. El impulso de fabricar armas "más inteligentes" y más rápidas puede verse claramente en la evolución de los aviones de combate (el USAF F-35 II y el Chengdu J-20 chino son sólo dos ejemplos), las "bombas inteligentes" (municiones guiadas con precisión como la Excálibur[7]) y en la mayor utilización de recursos asistidos por computadora, en la toma de decisiones en la planificación militar.[8]

Ante una mayor complejidad de la guerra moderna y un menor número de población apta y disponible para servir[9], la solución ha sido una mayor automatización de los actuales sistemas de armamento y un impulso por implementar sistemas de armas totalmente autónomos. Los sistemas actuales como el PHALANX (utilizado en los cruceros norteamericanos Aegis) permite que un sistema semiautónomo realice funciones esenciales de protección de buques, permitiendo que la tripulación restringida realice otras tareas esenciales[10]. El uso cada vez mayor de tales tecnologías, es el primer peldaño en la implementación de un sistema que tendrá la capacidad de seleccionar "objetivos y lanzar fuerza sin ningún aporte o interacción humana".[11] Como se mencionó anteriormente, la implementación de los AWS pudiera ser preocupante en muchos aspectos, sin embargo, este desarrollo tiene la favorable capacidad de reducir el daño imprevisto o colateral que acompaña a la guerra, de la manera en que se realiza actualmente.

1.2 ¿Qué son los Sistemas de Armas Autónomos?

Antes de profundizar en el debate sobre la implementación de los AWS, es importante entender lo que es un arma autónoma. Como es lógico,

---

7. Centro de Apoyo para la Adquisición del Ejército de los Estados Unidos (por sus siglas en inglés, "Proyectiles Excalibur de alta precisión de 155 mm".

8. Esto no debe interpretarse como el uso actual de computadoras *para* tomar decisiones de mando, en todo caso, como la dependencia de sistemas basados en computadoras para proporcionar más, mejor y/o más clara información a un comandante. Estos sistemas incluían todo, desde rastreo de carga mundial, rastreo de campo de batalla de unidades enemigas y amigas, monitoreo de sistemas electrónicos, etc. A medida que el mundo civil se ha vuelto más dependiente digitalmente, también lo ha hecho el ejército.

9. Consulte el documento temático No. 2 "Alcance y Reclutamiento" emitido por la Comisión de Diversidad de Liderazgo Militar.

10. Raytheon, "Phalanx, sistema artillero antimisil".

11. ICRC 2015, 6.

las comunidades académicas y diplomáticas, aún no se han decidido por una definición de los AWS que se tome en consenso. Las definiciones diplomáticas que se aceptan en la actualidad varían ampliamente: algunas incluyen armas que hoy se consideran automatizadas, aunque no autónomas, mientras que otras definiciones, únicamente incluyen sistemas completamente separados de la interacción humana. También existen definiciones que requieren la presencia de características o tecnologías específicas. Un ejemplo de lo anterior, es la definición que da el gobierno de los Países Bajos, la cual define los AWS como "un arma que, sin la intervención humana, selecciona y ataca objetivos que cumplen ciertos criterios predefinidos, que obedece la decisión humana de desplegar el arma, a sabiendas de que un ataque, una vez ejecutado, no puede detenerse por medio de la intervención humana".[12] Esta definición podría abarcar fácilmente armas que hoy en día no se consideran autónomas, tales como un misil de crucero[13]. Un misil de crucero está diseñado para buscar un objetivo específico programado (una huella térmica, designación láser de un soldado en el suelo o algún otro marcador designado previamente) y una vez que un humano haya dado la orden de desplegar el sistema, no se puede revocar.

El gobierno de Francia plantea la definición de los AWS en términos de "lo que no es"[14], estipulando:

> Las armas autónomas letales son sistemas totalmente autóno-mos...Los Sistemas de Armas Autónomos Letales (LAWS, por sus siglas en inglés) deben entenderse como aquello que implica una ausencia total de supervisión humana, lo que significa que no hay absolutamente ningún vínculo (comunicación o control) con la cadena militar de mando....La plataforma de lanzamiento de un LAWS sería capaz de moverse, adaptarse a su entorno ter-

---

12. Instituto de las Naciones Unidas de Investigación sobre el Desarme [UNIDIR, por sus siglas en inglés] 2017, p. 23

13. Este ejemplo también podría ampliarse a cualquier otra "munición guiada de precisión". Cabe señalar que, de acuerdo con la Convención de Ginebra, la ley actual ordena el uso de armas no indiscriminadas, lo que generalmente puede interpretarse en el sentido de que respalda el uso de municiones de precisión en lugar de las indiscriminadas y prohíbe "desplegar armas, proyectiles, materiales y métodos de guerra...los cuales indiscriminan de manera intrínseca violando el derecho internacional de los conflictos armados, siempre y cuando esas armas, proyectiles, materiales y métodos de guerra sean objeto de una prohibición integral y se incluyan en un anexo al presente Estatuto "(Artículo 8(2)(b)(xx) 1998 de la Corte Penal Internacional).

14. Instituto de las Naciones Unidas de Investigación sobre el Desarme [UNIDIR] 2017, p. 24.

restre, marino o aéreo y apuntar y disparar un efecto letal (bala, misil, bomba, etc.) sin ningún tipo de intervención o validación humana….Los LAWS probablemente poseerían capacidades de autoaprendizaje.[15]

La definición francesa difiere de la holandesa en que se requiere que los AWS (o LAWS) no tengan conexión con una cadena de mando (léase humano) militar, incluso en la planificación de la misión y la emisión final de órdenes para usar un Sistema de Armas Autónomo. Esta definición limitaría seriamente lo que podría llamarse un Sistema de Armas Autónomo, ya que es probable que exista alguna interacción humana significativa en algún punto de la "cadena de exterminio"., la definición francesa es tan estrecha que la hace prácticamente insostenible como una base sobre la cual se desarrollen discusiones diplomáticas prácticas y académicas.[16]

La definición de los Estados Unidos si bien adopta elementos de los enfoques funcionalistas utilizados por los franceses, es diferente porque distingue los sistemas autónomos de los semiautónomos. Estados Unidos (a través del Departamento de Defensa) define un Sistema de Armas Autónomo como,

> Un sistema de armas, que una vez activado, puede seleccionar y atacar objetivos sin más intervención que un operador humano. Esto incluye sistemas de armas autónomos supervisados por humanos que están diseñados para permitir que los operadores humanos anulen el funcionamiento del sistema de armas, pero puedan seleccionar y atacar objetivos sin más intervención humana después de la activación.[17]

Por lo tanto en la práctica, la definición norteamericana es más útil que la francesa o la holandesa, porque ofrece una descripción detallada de lo que es un Sistema de Armas Autónomo y lo que es más importante, excluye por implicación, los sistemas que no deberían contarse como los AWS.[18] Esta

---

15. Ibíd, p. 24.
16. Esto también puede decirse de la actual designación china de un AWS que tiene un nivel de autonomía que carece de "intervención humana y control durante todo el proceso de ejecución de una tarea" (Gobierno de China 2018).
17. Instituto de las Naciones Unidas de Investigación sobre el Desarme [UNIDIR] 2017, p. 30.
18. Como se mencionó, Estados Unidos brinda una definición de lo que determina como lo que no son los AWS, "Un sistema de armas que, una vez activado, está destinado a atacar solo objetivos individuales o grupos de objetivos específicos que han sido seleccionados

definición no incluye los sistemas disponibles hoy en día, los cuales podrían considerarse automatizados o semiautónomos[19] (PHALANX, C-RAM[20], etc.) ni los sistemas de "disparar y olvidar", que podrían incluir el misil de crucero previamente mencionado. También es importante señalar que la definición norteamericana permite que los AWS actúen sin la intervención de un operador humano, pero *no* excluye la interacción de un operador humano. Esto es significativo ya que se apega evidentemente con la directiva de la Norma 3000.09 del Departamento de Defensa de los Estados Unidos, que establece que: "Los sistemas de armas autónomos y semiautónomos deberán diseñarse para permitir que los comandantes y operadores ejerzan los niveles adecuados de criterio humano sobre el uso de la fuerza".[21] Esta directiva reguladora insinúa la naturaleza colaborativa que Estados Unidos prevé para la implementación de inteligencia artificial y los AWS. La definición de la norma de los Estados Unidos también "ubica el enfoque de lo que constituye la autonomía a nivel de *decisión* más que en la presencia o ausencia de una tecnología en particular».[22]

1.3 ¿Qué establece el Derecho Internacional Humanitario vigente respecto a los AWS?

Los conflictos militares modernos se rigen por un conjunto de normas y principios que generalmente se acuerdan como base para llevar a cabo una guerra. Estas normas y principios se basan en la larga historia de la teoría de la guerra justa. Antes del siglo XX, estas normas y principios no estaban codificados, sino eran más bien eran un conjunto de costumbres y prácticas

---

por un operador humano. Esto incluye: (a) sistemas de armas semiautónomos que utilizan la autonomía para funciones relacionadas con el enfrentamiento, que incluyen entre otras, pero no se limiten a conseguir, seguir e identificar objetivos potenciales; señalar objetivos potenciales a los operadores humanos; priorizar los objetivos seleccionados; sincronizar el disparo; o proporcionar una guía terminal para centrarse en objetivos seleccionados, siempre que se mantenga el control humano sobre la decisión de seleccionar objetivos individuales y grupos específicos objetivo para el enfrentamiento. (b) "Disparar y olvidar" o bloquear después de lanzar municiones autodirigidas que se basan en TTP (tácticas, técnicas y procedimientos) para tener más posibilidades de que solo los objetivos dentro del enceste que ha obtenido el buscador, cuando se active el buscador, sean esos objetivos individuales o grupos objetivo específicos los que hayan sido seleccionados por un operador humano" (UNIDIR, 2017, p. 31).

19. Sin embargo, debe considerarse que los sistemas como PHALANX y C-RAM se pueden situar en un entorno, el cual puede ser desde análogo hasta totalmente autónomo.

20. Oficina Ejecutiva del Programa: Misiles y Espacio, "Sistema de defensa contra ataques con cohetes, artillería y morteros (C-RAM, por sus siglas en inglés)".

21. Departamento de Defensa, Directiva 3000.09.

22. UNIDIR 2017 31.

tácitas[23] Por ejemplo, generalmente se consideraba una práctica "caballeresca" el rescatar a tantos marineros enemigos como fuera posible, una vez que se terminaba una batalla naval. Esta práctica no la exigía ningún tratado ni ningún acuerdo internacional formal, sino más bien fue una práctica aceptada que se realizó durante siglos de guerras navales. Aunque había sido una práctica común, con la proliferación de la guerra submarina, la práctica se abandonó. Después de la Segunda Guerra Mundial, durante los juicios de Nuremberg, los aliados acusaron al almirante Donitz de cometer crímenes contra la humanidad por la táctica de los nazis de hundir las naves enemigas y negarse a emerger a la superficie para rescatar a los sobrevivientes. Sin embargo, el enjuiciamiento fracasó, ya que se determinó que durante la evolución de la guerra naval, ya era una costumbre común para los submarinos, no recoger a los marineros supervivientes varados, debido al riesgo operativo extremo.

El Derecho Internacional Humanitario (IHL, por sus siglas en inglés) consistente en la Convención de Ginebra y sus protocolos adicionales no menciona a los AWS de manera explícita. Sin embargo, el hecho de que existan prohibiciones del IHL sobre ciertos tipos de armas, puede beneficiar en la elaboración de reglas que regulen a los AWS. La Convención sobre ciertas armas convencionales (CCW, por sus siglas en inglés) prohíbe el uso de determinadas formas de armas intrínsecamente indiscriminadas. Esta prohibición implica un estatus preferencial de armas de precisión o "inteligentes" sobre las indiscriminadas o "tontas". Entonces, para cumplir con la CCW, un Sistema de Armas Autónomo debe desarrollarse de tal manera que su uso no sea "intrínsecamente indiscriminado". Por lo tanto, ¿qué es un arma o un sistema de armas intrínsecamente indiscriminado? Un buen ejemplo sería una mina terrestre antipersona "tonta" o un gas tóxico. Se considera que el uso de ambos tipos de armas es indiscriminado, ya que al ser utilizadas, no pueden distinguir correctamente entre un objetivo militar legítimo y uno ilegítimo. La mina terrestre matará o mutilará a cualquiera que tenga la mala suerte de pisarla, incluso décadas después. Crear un Sistema de Armas Autónomo que pueda discriminar con precisión es una tarea difícil, pero no insuperable.

---

23. Si bien es cierto que algunos elementos del derecho internacional todavía se basan en normas y costumbres, existen actualmente reglas que se basan en tratados, como las que se especifican en los Convenios de Ginebra (1949) y en el Estatuto de la Corte Penal Internacional. Antes del establecimiento de órganos como la ICC, la mayoría de las naciones únicamente contaban con garantías de guerra o alianzas de defensa de apoyo mutuo para hacer cumplir las normas y costumbres aceptadas y algunas naciones, incluyendo Estados Unidos, no son parte de la ICC.

2 Objeciones contra los aws: argumentos a favor de su prohibición

Desde la invención de la ballesta en el siglo XIII[24], han surgido llamamientos para que se limite el armamento aceptable en la "guerra civilizada". Los avances tecnológicos han presionado para que las naciones busquen lo último en armas de vanguardia para obtener incluso la más mínima ventaja sobre su enemigo. Estos desarrollos han incluido la ametralladora, la mina terrestre y los gases tóxicos. Algunos de los proyectos, como las ametralladoras, se han mantenido dentro de los límites del material militar aceptable. Otros, como la mina terrestre, han sido regulados fuertemente y su uso se ha desalentado a nivel internacional[25]. La tercera categoría de armas, incluyendo los gases tóxicos, ha quedado expresamente prohibida bajo un tratado internacional.

A partir del 2013, la Campaña para detener a los robots asesinos ha promovido la prohibición total del desarrollo y empleo de los sistemas de armas autónomos letales[26]. Este grupo ha abogado a nivel nacional e internacional por una coalición de estados miembros de la ONU, organizaciones no gubernamentales, empresas y particulares con el explícito propósito de prohibir los Sistemas de Armas Autónomos letales. Al igual que a una cantidad de personas en el mundo académico, a la campaña le preocupa que el Sistema de Armas Autónomo llegue a cruzar el "umbral de lo moral", sacrificando la dignidad de la vida humana en aras de la eficiencia de la guerra automatizada. Los argumentos a favor de la prohibición de los "robots asesinos" pueden agruparse prácticamente en dos categorías, el argumento de la "responsabilidad" y el argumento de la "agencia".

2.1 El argumento de 'responsabilidad": ¿A quién se puede responsabilizar?

Una de las mayores preocupaciones de quienes están en contra del uso de los AWS es que podamos crear robots que puedan apuntar y matar huma-

---

24. Del derecho canónico emitido después del Segundo Concilio de Letrán: "Prohibimos bajo anatema ese arte asesino de ballesteros y arqueros, que es aborrecible para Dios, para ser empleado contra cristianos y católicos de ahora en adelante". (Encíclicas papales en línea, "El Segundo Concilio de Letrán").

25. Las minas terrestres antipersonales están explícitamente prohibidas en virtud del tratado de Quebec: las minas antitanque y antibuque siguen siendo aceptables. Son aceptables las minas que tienen una corta vida útil (aquéllas que son inertes después de X horas de despliegue).

26. "La Campaña para detener a los robots asesinos exige una prohibición preventiva e integral sobre el desarrollo, la producción y el uso de armas totalmente autónomas, también conocidas como sistemas de armas autónomos letales o robots asesinos" (Campaña para detener a los robots asesinos, https://www.stopkillerrobots.org/learn/).

nos sin que se pueda responsabilizar "debidamente" a un agente moral. Al problema de adjudicar debidamente la responsabilidad de una acción tomada por un Sistema de Armas Autónomo, algunas personas le han llamado una "brecha de responsabilidad".[27] Para mayor seguridad, si se puede rastrear una acción de un Sistema de Armas Autónomo directamente hasta la persona que autorizó la misión (por ejemplo, un comandante deshonesto que programó las órdenes para matar a civiles desarmados y a soldados enemigos heridos), por lo tanto, pareciera evidente que podamos atribuir con justicia la culpa de cualquier muerte que resulte, al comandante que autorizó la misión. Sin embargo, el problema surge cuando no podemos trazar directamente una línea desde la persona que autorizó el Sistema de Armas Autónomo, hasta el crimen de guerra que se perpetró. Esta es la "brecha de responsabilidad". Bonnie Docherty, una de las defensoras de la prohibición de los AWS considera que "no sería justo ni legalmente viable…responsabilizar a un comandante u operador [humano]".[28] Ella no es la única que cuestiona el hecho de no fincar responsabilidad al agente —el Sistema de Armas Autónomo— que cometió la acción moralmente problemática (o ilegal). En tanto que argumenta una brecha de responsabilidad, Robert Sparrow analiza dos posibilidades: transferir la culpa del Sistema de Armas Autónomo a los humanos (el programador y el oficial al mando) y dejar al Sistema de Armas Autónomo como el agente responsable.

En primer lugar, Sparrow argumenta que podríamos descargar, al menos en parte, la responsabilidad de un Sistema de Armas Autónomo descarriado sobre el programador o diseñador que construyó el dispositivo: "esto solo será justo si la situación previamente descrita ocurriera como resultado de la negligencia por parte del equipo de diseño/programación".[29] Sin embargo, Sparrow descarta rápidamente que se responsabilice al programador en aquellos casos donde no exista negligencia. La primera razón para descartar el hecho de culpar al programador es que "la posibilidad de que la máquina ataque los objetivos equivocados, puede ser una limitación aceptada del sistema".[30] Si la posibilidad de que la máquina pueda atacar a un objetivo no autorizado es un "efecto secundario" o una "limitación del sistema" y el programador comunica explícitamente esta limitación a cualquier usuario potencial, entonces no sería justo responsabilizar al programador. Sparrow argumenta que, en este caso, quienes todavía opten por implementar el

---

27. Scharre 2018, p. 261
28. Ibid, p 261.
29. Sparrow, 2007, p. 69.
30. Sparrow, 2007, p. 69.

sistema, con las limitaciones conocidas o los posibles efectos secundarios, tendrían que asumir el peso de la responsabilidad. Añade Posteriormente que "la posibilidad de que un sistema autónomo tome decisiones distintas a las previstas y apoyadas por sus programadores, es inherente a la afirmación de que es autónomo".[31] En este sentido, Sparrow señala que debido al diseño operativo del Sistema de Armas Autónomo y a la naturaleza compleja de sus posibles algoritmos y redes neuronales, ningún humano puede predecir en todos los casos, las decisiones de un Sistema de Armas Autónomo. Si este fuera el caso, nuevamente, sería injusto culpar al programador, ya que no pudo haber previsto todas las acciones del Sistema de Armas Autónomo.

Ya que no podemos hacer que el programador del Sistema de Armas Autónomo se responsabilice de sus acciones, entonces posiblemente podemos pedir cuentas al oficial al mando que ordenó su uso.[32] Señala: "Se acepta el riesgo de que el Sistema de Armas Autónomo pueda equivocarse cuando se toma la decisión de enviarlo a la acción. Este es el enfoque que prefieren las fuerzas militares que buscan desplegar los actuales AWS".[33] Sparrow sostiene que si tratamos a los AWS de la misma manera que tratamos a las armas "tontas" e "inteligentes" convencionales de hoy, parecería entonces que podemos sencillamente atribuir la culpa al comandante que ordenó su uso. Sin embargo, esta táctica no considera la naturaleza plena de la autonomía del arma. Sparrow considera que la naturaleza misma de la autonomía del arma significa que los comandantes no pueden controlar qué objetivos selecciona el Sistema de Armas Autónomo y por lo tanto, no deberían rendir cuentas por las elecciones del mismo: "Si las máquinas realmente eligen sus propios objetivos, entonces no podemos responsabilizar al comandante en jefe de las muertes que se causen".[34] Si el programador y el oficial al mando no pueden rendir cuentas, ¿se puede responsabilizar al propio Sistema de Armas Autónomo?

Sparrow sostiene que "la autonomía y la responsabilidad moral van de la mano".[35] Si llegamos a un punto en el que el Sistema de Armas Autónomo es totalmente capaz de tomar decisiones letales por sí solo (sin un humano

---

31. Ibid, p. 70.
32. Sparrow no define a qué nivel de mando uno deba rendir cuentas. Si, por ejemplo, el comandante de una compañía de infantería (un Capitán (O3) en el ejército y el cuerpo de Marines de los Estados Unidos) decide enviar un Sistema de Armas Autónomo a una población y mata a un niño, ¿quién debería ser responsable? ¿El capitán? ¿Su jefe, un comandante de batallón (teniente coronel)? O el comandante de brigada, el comandante de división, el cuerpo de Marines, etc. Por principio de cuentas ¿debe únicamente responsabilizarse a los de mayor rango por poner este dispositivo en la fuerza?
33. Sparrow, 2007, p. 70.
34. Sparrow, 2007, p. 71.
35. Ibid, p. 65.

en el circuito), entonces tendría que asumir la responsabilidad moral de sus acciones, lo que nos lleva al meollo del problema. "Es difícil tomar en serio la idea de que una máquina debería o podría, ser considerada responsable de las consecuencias de 'sus' acciones".[36] Suponiendo que responsabilizar a un agente por una mala acción implica un castigo para éste, Sparrow sostiene que para que "los actos sirvan como castigo, deben provocar el tipo de respuesta correcta en su objeto".[37] Entonces, ¿cuál sería el tipo de respuesta correcta de Sparrow? Según él, la única respuesta que se adecúa al castigo implica sufrimiento, por lo que para que un Sistema de Armas Autónomo sea castigado "debe poderse decir que éste sufra". [38]Pero esta noción de sufrimiento complica la manera de entender la funcionalidad y las capacidades del Sistema de Armas Autónomo como se interpretan e imaginan actualmente. Es poco probable que un programador pueda o vaya a incorporar en un sistema de este tipo, la capacidad de generar respuestas emocionales como el sufrimiento (o miedo) porque tales emociones contravendrían uno de los beneficios potenciales que éste brinda sobre los humanos, es decir, que a los sistemas no se les induce para cometer crímenes de guerra por ira, odio, sed de venganza, etc.[39] Dado que un Sistema de Armas Autónomo no tiene la capacidad de experimentar dolor físico o emocional, es probable que no pueda sufrir y por lo tanto, según Sparrow, no podría ser castigado.

En última instancia, Sparrow considera que a menos que podamos crear éticamente a un Sistema de Armas Autónomo que pueda ser "debidamente responsable",[40] no es ético desplegar estas armas en el campo de batalla. Señala que la capacidad de decidir quitar una vida debe quedar en manos de un agente que sea capaz de asumir la responsabilidad moral y del que pueda decirse legítimamente que va a ser castigado, en caso de que viole una de las Leyes de la Guerra.

2.2 El argumento de la "agencia": ¿Se debe castigar a la agencia humana hasta el extremo de la muerte?

Uno de los elementos cruciales de la guerra es la decisión de matar a un ser humano. Desde la época de los inicios de la guerra hasta la llegada de las

---

36. Ibid, p. 71.
37. Ibid, p. 71.
38. Ibid, p. 72.
39. Ronald Arkin argumenta que la falta de emociones específicas (miedo, ira, tristeza, etc.) de los AWS podría beneficiar su uso. Estos AWS no mostrarían las respuestas emocionales típicas que se ven en los humanos en el campo de batalla y por lo tanto, es más probable que tengan reacciones "correctas" de acuerdo con la ética que los rige.
40. Sparrow, 2007, p. 66.

armas de fuego, la mayor parte de estas muertes se daban a corta distancia y de persona a persona. Los combatientes enemigos podían verse a los ojos mientras luchaban por sus vidas. El teniente coronel Dave Grossman, en su libro "*On Killing*", estudia los efectos que ha tenido en nuestra capacidad colectiva de matar, el aumento en la distancia en la acción de matar. Cuando estamos cara a cara con nuestro enemigo, ellos son humanos y podemos entendernos al mismo nivel. Consecuentemente, el acto de matar es más íntimo y más brutal. Cuando matamos a distancia, nuestro enemigo pareciera ser un poco menos humano y, por lo tanto, es más fácil justificar su muerte. La mayor distancia entre los combatientes y el acto de matar es eliminar la decisión de matar a un agente humano y permitir que esa decisión la tome un agente artificial. Alex Leveringhaus sostiene que "el reemplazo de la agencia humana con la 'agencia artificial' de las máquinas en una guerra, es sumamente problemático".[41] El debate fundamental es entonces, si deberíamos renunciar a la agencia humana en favor de una artificial.

Leveringhaus afirma que el primer problema que se presenta al ceder la hegemonía del agente humano sobre la decisión de matar, es que se pierde la "equivalencia moral de los soldados". El principio de equivalencia moral, formulado por Michael Walzer, establece que desde la perspectiva de las leyes de la guerra, cada grupo de soldados (los agresores y los defensores) tiene el mismo valor moral, por lo que todos tienen igual derecho de usar la fuerza para matar al enemigo y para defenderse.[42] Esta equivalencia moral se mantiene, según Walzer, independientemente de la justicia de la guerra que se libra. Todos tienen el derecho moral a luchar. Cuando una parte de la igualación se reemplaza con un Sistema de Armas Autónomo, ya no existe entonces una equivalencia moral, debido a que éste no tiene el derecho moral a la autodefensa y como tal, pierde su igualdad ante la oposición.

El segundo problema que aborda Leveringhaus, es la falta de capacidad del Sistema de Armas Autónomo para emitir un "juicio moral". Esta falta de capacidad es de extrema importancia cuando el sistema determina el nivel de fuerza a utilizar porque "...la aplicación del criterio de proporcionalidad en el IHL implica emitir *juicios morales*".[43] Si un Sistema de Armas Autónomo no puede emitir un juicio moral sobre la proporción correcta de fuerza que se requiere en una determinada situación, ¿debe ser capaz en primer lugar, de tomar la decisión moral definitiva de quitar una vida? Leveringhaus señala que

---

41. Leveringhaus, 2016, p. 2.
42. Walzer, 2015, p. 34.
43. Leveringhaus, 2016, p. 2.

"no", y argumenta que la capacidad de matar sin la capacidad de deliberar sobre las consecuencias morales de esa acción es básicamente, una falta de respeto a los derechos humanos y a la dignidad del individuo que está siendo atacado.

El punto decisivo del argumento de Leveringhaus es la controversia de que al usar un Sistema de Armas Autónomo para matar a otro ser humano, estamos eliminando cualquier posibilidad de misericordia de la cadena de exterminio y por lo tanto, nos distanciamos moralmente del acto de matar de manera que no se respeta la dignidad de la persona que se mata. En la cadena de exterminio, la misericordia significa que en cualquier momento, un soldado puede optar por *no* apretar el gatillo. Leveringhaus afirma: "Los robots asesinos, como agentes artificiales, carecen del componente central de una agencia humana que es la capacidad de hacer lo contrario: no disparar al objetivo".[44] Esta falta de capacidad para *no* matar a un combatiente autorizado, es por lo tanto y por su misma naturaleza, irrespetuosa de la dignidad inherente de todo ser humano. "El enemigo en calidad de blanco lógico no tiene derecho a que los soldados atacantes no lo maten, pero ciertamente, la capacidad humana para tener piedad con, sentir compasión por o empatía con otros humanos, incluso si éstos pertenecen a un país contrario, es de relevancia moral y digna de protección".[45] El problema que Leveringhaus argumenta con un Sistema de Armas Autónomo que ejecuta una acción letal sobre un humano, es que carece fundamentalmente de un sentido de compasión y comprensión del valor de la vida humana. Por lo que escribe: "Considero que retener la agencia humana al grado de aplicar la fuerza, protegiendo en esta forma la libertad de no apretar el gatillo, presionar el botón o lanzar una granada, es fundamental para que se mantenga nuestra humanidad, precisamente en la situación que más la desafía: la guerra".[46] Si un Sistema de Armas Autónomo no tiene la opción de no matar a un enemigo, entonces carece de la capacidad de mostrar misericordia, la cual se requiere para respetar la dignidad humana. Leveringhaus cierra con un mensaje inquietante, que opaca el optimismo que se ha visto en muchos desarrolladores e investigadores de tecnología de armas avanzadas "Los robots asesinos no nos rescatarán de la condición humana".[47]

---

44. Leveringhaus, 2016, p. 9. Leveringhaus utiliza el término robots asesinos en vez de Sistema de Armas Autónomos. Esta parece ser una táctica emotiva para convencer al lector del dilema moral que presenta el uso de tales dispositivos. Considero que esto distrae de la naturaleza objetiva de su argumento y presenta en cambio, un argumento emotivo y más débil.
45. Ibid, p. 10.
46. Ibid, p. 10.
47. Ibid, p. 15.

3. Contraargumentos

Existe una relación necesaria entre la muerte y la guerra, como lo señala J. Glenn Gray: "en la guerra, la muerte regularmente la causan los miembros de mi propia especie que buscan activamente mi fin, a pesar del hecho de quizás nunca me hayan visto y no tengan motivo para una enemistad a muerte".[48] Este hecho nos lleva a preguntarnos: ¿cómo podemos entonces mitigar el sufrimiento de quienes participan activamente en la guerra y el de los espectadores inocentes que han quedado atrapados en su furia? Parte de la respuesta *puede* estar en la implementación de la inteligencia artificial y los sistemas de armas autónomos en el campo de batalla del mañana. En lo que resta de esta tesis, argumentaré, al igual que lo han hecho muchos otros en los sectores de seguridad nacional y defensa[49], que es muy posible que veamos a los AWS operando en conjunto con los soldados del mañana. Si bien es cierto que existen muchas funciones que podrían transferirse más fácilmente a un sistema autónomo (como conducir convoyes logísticos por rutas peligrosas o procesar trámites de recursos humanos), dentro del ejército existen tareas que es poco probable que alguna vez se automaticen por completo. En cambio, es factible que veamos una combinación de humanos y máquinas acoplados de tal manera que aprovechen al máximo la inteligencia, durabilidad, fuerza y potencia del soldado humano. Sostendré que cada uno de los argumentos a favor de una prohibición que se han presentado hasta ese punto, no brindan una razón suficiente para la implementación de dicha prohibición. Lo que, en todo caso, pueden apoyar lógicamente es la implementación de un sistema de regulación, mediante el cual las partes internacionales puedan monitorear y guiar el desarrollo de dichos sistemas, de manera que continúen siendo compatibles con el IHL y estén permitidos moralmente.

3.1 Respuesta al argumento de la 'responsabilidad"

Aunque a simple vista el argumento de Sparrow puede ser convincente, en algunos puntos presenta supuestos con débil fundamento al tiempo que ignora las cadenas causales de responsabilidad como se interpretan actualmente en el ejército. Abordo primero la opinión de Sparrow sobre la posibilidad de culpar al programador del AWS y al oficial al mando que implementa el sistema y posteriormente, trato el argumento de Sparrow de que sería imposible castigar a un Sistema de Armas Autónomo.

---

48. Gray 1959, p. 100.
49. Consulte el informe técnico del general de división Mick Ryan (ejército australiano) "Equipo humano- máquina para las fuerzas terrestres del futuro. https://csbaonline.org/uploads/documents/Human_Machine_Teaming_FinalFormat.pdf.

En términos generales, Sparrow está en lo correcto al ser cauto en el hecho de adjudicar responsabilidad moral al programador del Sistema de Armas Autónomo. Esta adjudicación equivaldría probablemente a responsabilizar moralmente al fabricante de un rifle por su uso durante un tiroteo escolar; si bien al hacerlo puede mitigar los sentimientos con respecto al uso que de esa manera se le da al arma, no ayuda a comprender quién es moralmente responsable. Sparrow argumenta que podríamos responsabilizar a un programador si la fechoría se debió a alguna negligencia en la programación, de la misma manera en que un fabricante es responsable hoy, por las fallas de sus productos que resultan en daños o muerte al usuario final. Sin embargo, lo que no debe suceder, es que se responsabilice a un programador porque consideramos que el uso de su producto sea moralmente ofensivo. Sobre la cuestión de responsabilizar al programador, coincido con Sparrow en que solo deberíamos responsabilizar a alguien si cometió un error que fue de cierta manera, negligente.

Sparrow señala que no debemos responsabilizar a los comandantes de las acciones de los AWS bajo su mando, porque este sistema es completamente autónomo y que, como tal, no podemos estar seguros de qué acciones o motivaciones tomarán los AWS para ese efecto. Lo anterior, hace caso omiso de algunos de los principios básicos de liderazgo y de responsabilidad que son fundamentales para la cultura militar norteamericana actual.

El concepto de responsabilidad es un principio importantísimo de la cultura militar. Todos los miembros del servicio están investidos de un cierto nivel de responsabilidad de acuerdo con su rango y posición. Todos tienen la responsabilidad primordial de apegar su conducta a la ley, a la regulación militar y a la tradición. A medida que uno asciende en la estructura de rango de la división a la cual está adscrito, se confieren mayores niveles de responsabilidad, que incluyen deberes tanto para los recursos del personal como materiales. La cúspide de la responsabilidad militar se logra obteniendo el puesto de "comandante". Dependiendo de la división, un comandante será responsable en los diferentes niveles, del personal y del material (conforme al tamaño de la unidad), pero los principios básicos continúan siendo los mismos. El manual sobre liderazgo del Ejército de los Estados Unidos[50] especifica que "el mando incluye la autoridad y la responsabilidad de utilizar eficazmente los recursos disponibles y de planificar el trabajo de organizar, dirigir, coordinar y controlar las fuerzas militares para la realización de las

---

50. Publicación en Referencia de la Doctrina Militar 6-22 Liderazgo militar.

misiones asignadas".[51] La parte importante en este punto, es la responsabilidad que tiene un comandante. Un comandante es responsable de todas las acciones que sus soldados tomen o dejen de tomar en un determinado momento. Los comandantes del ejército norteamericano aceptan, a través de su asignación en un puesto de rango superior, la carga de responsabilidad por las acciones de sus subordinados. Por ende, los comandantes serían al menos parcialmente responsables de las fallas y de la actividad problemática de los AWS, incluso si el evento se diera sin un control humano directo.

El estándar Yamashita se ha establecido como un precedente legal a partir de la Segunda Guerra Mundial. En los juicios militares que precedieron al fin de la guerra en el Pacífico, el general Tomoyuki Yamashita fue juzgado por los crímenes en contra de la humanidad, perpetrados por las tropas bajo su mando. El general Yamashita argumentó que no podía haberse enterado de todas las atrocidades que se estaban cometiendo ni podía esperarse que ejerciera alguna forma de control directo sobre sus tropas ampliamente dispersas, para evitar tales actos. El tribunal consideró este argumento poco convincente y señaló:

> La ley de la Guerra impone sobre un comandante del ejército el deber de tomar aquellas medidas apropiadas que estén dentro de su autoridad, para controlar las tropas bajo su mando con el fin de evitar actos que se consideren violaciones de la ley de la Guerra y mediante los cuales es probable que se vigile la ocupación del territorio hostil por tropas militares no controladas y que él pueda ser acusado de responsabilidad personal por no tomar dichas medidas cuando se presentaron las violaciones.[52]

El veredicto que se dictó en el caso Yamashita establece rotundamente que los comandantes, a cualquier nivel, tienen el deber de evitar que sucedan atrocidades en las unidades bajo su mando. No obstante, existe una réplica que establece que: "Un comandante es responsable principalmente de las acciones de sus tropas, pero no podemos responsabilizarlo totalmente de las acciones de un "Sistema de Armas Autónomo que fue diseñado en forma no deliberada y del cual básicamente se desconoce su proceso de toma de decisiones. "Mi respuesta es que no consideremos responsables únicamente a los comandantes, por lo menos en parte, de las acciones de sus subordinados,

---

51. ADRP 6-22, 2012, p. 1-3
52. En referencia a Yamashita.

independientemente del proceso de toma de decisiones de los mismos, sino que también consideremos responsables al comandante por promover un entorno donde dichas opciones son vistas como válidas. Primero, el ejército básicamente responsabiliza a sus oficiales al mando, de las acciones de todos aquéllos que estén a su cargo, *independiente* de si pueden o no controlarlos físicamente. Analicemos por ejemplo la reciente avalancha de accidentes navales relevantes de la 7ª Flota Naval de los Estados Unidos (apostada en Japón). Los capitanes de ambos navíos fueron encontrados responsables (por lo menos uno de ellos fue puesto en manos de los fiscales por homicidio imprudencial), aunque no estuvieron físicamente al mando del timón e incluso en el puente de mando al momento del incidente.[53] La Fuerza Naval determinó que fueron negligentes en su tarea de asegurar que el barco operara de manera apropiada. La Marina también determinó que a bordo de estos navíos y a nivel de mando de flota (cuartel general de la flota), los comandantes *promovieron un entorno* donde las normas laxas y fáciles, eran vistas como aceptables[54]. Si sobre la estructura legal militar vigente, consideramos de nuevo el Sistema de Armas Autónomo, resulta lógico asumir que si se le permitió cometer un crimen de guerra o *no se le evitó* que lo hiciera, eso podría ocasionar que se considerara responsable al comandante, tanto legal como moralmente.

Si estamos dispuestos a responsabilizar de manera colectiva a un comandante, por lo menos parcialmente, por la conducta de su tropa, quien está en sí constituida por los mismos agentes autónomos, entonces no existe un motivo legal o moral para *no* considerarlos responsables con el mismo grado de responsabilidad de las acciones o la falta de acciones de un Sistema de Armas Autónomo. Sparrow considera que sería injusto responsabilizar a un comandante, ya que éste probablemente no pueda predecir la conducta del Sistema de Armas Autónomo, sin embargo, en este punto surge la pregunta sobre si el comandante puede predecir la conducta de sus tropas en el campo de batalla. Los comandantes entrenan de manera regular y activa a sus soldados para que sus acciones puedan ser *más* predecibles durante una situación estresante, pero esto no excluye la posibilidad de que un soldado humano pueda cruzar el límite y cometer un crimen de guerra. El roboticista Ronald Arkin apunta:

---

53. También debe observarse que como resultado de estos incidentes, fueron obligados a renunciar los comandantes de mayor rango, incluyendo al capitán de la 7ª flota.
54. Ver los informes de la Marina de los Estados Unidos tanto en el accidente del USS Fitzgerald como en el USS John S. McCain: https://www.secnav.navy.mil/foia/readingroom/HotTopics/CNO%20USS%20Fitzgerald%20and%20USS%20John%20S%20McCain%20Response/CNO%20USS%20Fitzgerald%20and%20USS%20John%20S%20McCain%20Response.pdf.

"De manera personal, yo no confío en la perspectiva de apartarse de la regla (La Ley de la Guerra (LoW) o de las Reglas de Enfrentamiento (RoE) por el agente autónomo (AWS) en sí, por lo que obliga la cuestión sobre si existe algún tipo de responsabilidad. Sin embargo, existe la posibilidad de que un humano asuma la responsabilidad por tal divergencia, en caso de que alguna vez se considerara apropiada."[55] En este sentido, Arkin argumenta que cuando diseñamos y construimos un Sistema de Armas Autónomo, nunca debemos permitirle la capacidad de decidir por su cuenta, apartándose de las las LoW o RoE (lo cual sería su programación básica) y de preferencia, dejar esa responsabilidad únicamente en manos de un humano. De ser así, esto transferiría la responsabilidad de los Sistemas de Armas Autónomos, violando sus LoW o RoE , sobre un humano que tome decisiones (específicamente, un oficial al mando de algún nivel). [56] Si un comandante humano, no obstante, lejos del punto de la decisión final de matar, decidió enviar a un Sistema de Armas Autónomo a una situación donde se sabe que existe la posibilidad de que suceda demasiado daño colateral, en este caso pareciera ser moralmente correcto, responsabilizar al comandante cuando se presentan los incidentes.

En este punto, alguien podría preocuparse y con justa razón por el hecho de que no he aportado las bases suficientes o los fundamentos convincentes para afirmar que el estándar Yamashita nos proporciona la suficiente *justificación* moral para sustentar la responsabilidad en el cargo de un comandante. Argumento que, en vez de buscar una justificación de fondo, debemos abordar este problema reconociendo que el estándar Yamashita ofrece una razón que se puede *justificar* moralmente para responsabilizar a un comandante (incluso quien supervisa el uso de los AWS). ¿Cuál es la razón para que este tipo de doctrina de responsabilidad puede tener una justificación moral? Deseamos conminar a los comandantes en el campo, en época de guerra, para que se esmeren en todo lo posible por fomentar un entorno que opere dentro de y respete la Ley de la Guerra, las leyes internacionales humanitarias vigentes y las Reglas de Enfrentamiento para esa área de

---

55. Arkin, 2009, 40.
56. Creo que esto podría ser similar al uso de un determinado oficial en un conflicto actual en el que esté involucrado E.U. En este tipo de situaciones, cuando se ha determinado un objetivo, regularmente se le pide a un superior (con frecuencia a un oficial general) que valide el objetivo y autorice el combate. Este oficial generalmente cuenta con un abogado presente que le proporciona asesoría legal en la situación, pero al final la responsabilidad es de quién toma la decisión. Esto pudiera ser igual a hecho de autorizar a un Sistema de Armas Autónomo para que se desvíe de su programación previa de las LoW/RoE, si un comandante así lo decide, por lo que ellos deben autorizar y aceptar plena responsabilidad por esa acción.

operación. El estándar Yamashita (o las normas Medina actualizadas) nos ofrece una vía que puede ser *justificable* moralmente para lograr esa meta. Funciona como un recordatorio para los comandantes (a través de la cadena de mando) de que ellos son *personalmente* responsables de las acciones de sus subordinados. No obstante, esto no significa que sean *totalmente* responsables de los actos (o la falta de los mismos) de los subordinados, pero si comparten la parte de responsabilidad que *les corresponde.*[57]

El problema definitivo con el argumento de Sparrow es su renuncia en considerar responsable por sus delitos a un Sistema de Armas Autónomo, como agente moral, ya que uno no puede castigarlo de manera legítima porque no puede sufrir y ya que no puede sufrir, no va a ser castigado. Al parecer, basa su argumento del castigo en la idea de la justicia retributiva. El problema es que Sparrow afirma que la justicia retributiva es el rumbo adecuado a seguir (de manera explícita con los AWS y de manera implícita con los humanos). Afirma que "para que cualquiera de estas acciones (diferente tipo de castigo) sirva como castigo, debe provocar el tipo de respuesta apropiada en su objeto...ser capaz de ser castigado, por lo tanto, (la cosa o persona a ser castigada) puede decirse que sufre". [58] Este deseo por el sufrimiento puede rechazarse al adoptar una de las otras posibles afirmaciones morales de vanguardia para el castigo, de que se dispone en la literatura. Podríamos, por ejemplo, querer una forma de castigo más comunicativa, que tenga la intención de comunicar la naturaleza inaceptable de un acto a otro Sistema de Armas Autónomo. También podríamos optar por un enfoque de rehabilitación para el castigo, en el cual volviéramos a programar o entrenar a los AWS para que aprendan que la acción previa fue mala o no deseada. Si insistimos en un sistema retributivo, como lo pide Sparrow, entonces él estaría en lo correcto; sería imposible castigar a los AWS. Sin embargo, no existe una razón para pensar que Sparrow esté en lo correcto en este aspecto.

Con respecto a tener la responsabilidad moral de la muerte de un soldado enemigo, Sparrow afirma: "lo menos que debemos a nuestros enemigos es admitir que sus vidas valen lo suficiente para que alguien deba aceptar la responsabilidad por sus muertes".[59] Sparrow requiere que se pueda responsabilizar a los AWS como individuos, cuando pareciera que el enfoque debe

---

57. Creo que es importante que tengamos un debate sobre "la parte de responsabilidad que corresponde" pero esto queda fuera del ámbito de esta tesis.
58. Sparrow 2007, 72
59. Ibid, 67.

estar sobre el comandante que decide usar el arma o el político que inicia la guerra. Si el Sistema de Armas Autónomo funciona de manera legítima, no habrá entonces ninguna obligación de responsabilizar a los individuos -humanos o a los AWS- por matar de manera legitima en la guerra.[60]

Por otra parte, ¿cómo tratamos a un Sistema de Armas Autónomo que "se volvió malvado" y cometió un crimen de guerra? Sostengo que en vez de castigarlo, debemos analizar las circunstancias bajo las cuales se dio el incidente. Un evento nunca será igual a otro, a tal grado de establecer una afirmación genérica o un principio universal respecto a quien se debe culpar por lo que no es correcto. En todo caso, debemos analizar la decisión que se tomó para utilizar el arma (¿se estimó un alto grado de posibilidad de exceso de daño colateral? y la otra decisión por parte del comandante, junto con la información importante de que se disponía en ese momento, para atribuir responsabilidad en los lugares adecuados. Al final, si se puede demostrar de manera concluyente que un comandante e incluso un Sistema de Armas Autónomo hicieron todo lo posible por evitar una atrocidad, pero se dio (por ejemplo, una bomba perdida), entonces *tampoco debemos* hacerlos responsables (aplicando posiblemente la doctrina del doble efecto).

Sparrow contestaría que si nos apegamos a este plan, crearemos una brecha de responsabilidad y la única solución adecuada en esta situación, sería no usar un Sistema de Armas Autónomo como primera opción. Ante esto, sostengo que Sparrow está equivocado. Si como se mencionó previamente, aplicamos estándares tales como el Yamashita (o Medina) podemos ubicar el nexo de responsabilidad moral sobre el oficial al mando en aquellos casos donde no podamos demostrar evidentemente que el Sistema de Armas Autónomo hizo un movimiento ilegal (o inmoral). Estaríamos entonces frente a dos opciones, ya sea la opción a)" castigar" al Sistema de Armas Autónomo basándose en una diferente moral (comunicativa, rehabilitadora, etc.), o b) castigar al oficial al mando (a cualquier nivel que se considere apropiado, que pudiera no ser el de menor rango) usando los estándares Yamashita/Medina.

Como ha quedado demostrado hasta la fecha, el argumento de la responsabilidad fracasa, basándose en los precedentes de las actuales leyes internacionales, las normas de liderazgo militar norteamericano y la reconsideración

---

60. Por supuesto que alguien como McMahan no estaría de acuerdo y diría que si esos soldados o quizás AWS, que participan en una guerra injusta *son* responsables de manera individual por la muerte de un soldado enemigo porque ese otro soldado (supuestamente justo) no es un objetivo válido (Mc Mahan 2011, 14).

de la idea del castigo. En vez de proporcionar una evidencia convincente de que la comunidad internacional prohibir debe estrictamente el desarrollo y uso de los AWS, este argumento más bien nos convence de regular el desarrollo y uso de los mimos.

3.2 Respuesta al argumento de la 'agencia"

El argumento más contundente que se ha abordado hasta ese punto, sostiene que no se le debe pasar a un agente artificial, el control de la decisión de matar a un ser humano. Esto no debe suceder, ya que un agente artificial no tiene la capacidad de mostrar piedad al momento de la acción letal y porque de manera intrínseca, el hecho de que una persona sea asesinada por la decisión de un robot autónomo, es una falta de respeto para la dignidad humana. Ambas partes de este argumento son básicamente erróneas.

Leveringhaus insiste en que debemos permitir la opción de *no* seguir una orden legítima de matar al enemigo en el campo de batalla, básicamente la opción de *no* disparar a un auténtico combatiente y en todo caso, practicar la misericordia. Afirma que comparado con la agencia artificial, lo que hace valiosa a la agencia humana en la guerra y en la vida diaria, es la posibilidad de involucrarse en un curso alterno de acción".[61] Leveringhaus considera realmente que en un campo de batalla, uno debe ser totalmente apto para tomar la decisión de no matar cuando se enfrenta a la opción que le permite ejercer la fuerza letal. El asume que si un Sistema de Armas Autónomo está programado con sus órdenes, con los parámetros de la misión y con los parámetros de las Leyes de la Guerra y las Reglas de Enfrentamiento, atacará sencillamente a todo enemigo que se encuentre. Considero que esta suposición, no es necesariamente cierta. Si seguimos el consejo de Arkin respecto al "gobernador ético", un Sistema de Armas Autónomo que fuera diseñado adecuadamente, primero predeterminará las medidas no letales, ya sea para evadir o para contener al enemigo, y no podía determinar de inmediato las acciones letales. Si requerimos que se construya un algoritmo sobre este modelo, entonces las acciones letales se darían únicamente si fueran obligatorias. Supongamos por ejemplo que existe un Sistema de Armas Autónomo patrullando junto con un escuadrón de soldados de la infantería norteamericana, podríamos establecer como una de las RoE: "si un miembro de nuestro escuadrón está en peligro inminente de ser capturado, entonces tú estás *obligado* a usar la fuerza adecuada de manera proporcional para evitar su captura". Si algún

---

61. Leveringhaus 2016, 9

miembro de la patrulla no se encuentra en peligro inminente de ser capturado, entonces el Sistema de Armas Autónomo debe predeterminar hacia una acción no letal, excepto que deba satisfacer otro criterio reglamentario que se hubiera definido previamente.

Al Sistema de Armas Autónomo como recurso, debe obligársele[62] a seguir las órdenes *legítimas* y *válidas,* pero también a no seguir las órdenes ilegitimas y no válidas. Lo segundo es tan importante como lo primero para evitar crímenes de guerra en el campo de batalla. Lo anterior también pareciera servir como "control de conducta ética" de Arkin".[63] En este sentido, señala: "especialmente en el caso de los robots del campo de batalla (pero también para un soldado humano), no queremos que el agente pueda deducir sus propias convicciones respecto a las implicaciones morales del uso de la fuerza letal, sino más bien que sea capaz de aplicar aquéllas que hayan sido deducidas previamente por humanidad, conforme lo prescrito por las LoW y las RoE".[64]

Por lo tanto y de acuerdo con Leveringhaus, una de las características determinantes que separan a los agentes humanos y a los artificiales, es nuestra capacidad (humana) para mostrar misericordia hacia nuestros enemigos. Para Leveringhaus, "la capacidad humana para tener misericordia con, sentir piedad por o empatizar con otros humanos, incluso si éstos pertenecen a un país opositor, es por supuesto de trascendencia moral y digna de protección". [65] Sin embargo, ¿qué sucede entonces, si esta piedad no tiene la capacidad de hacer lo contrario? Pareciera que para Leveringhaus, la clave está en que podemos empatizar con nuestro enemigo; reconocer su humanidad y de esa manera, abstenernos de hacerles daño cuando se pueda o sea apropiado hacerlo; "pudo haber sido que esos soldados que no mataron lo hicieran porque reconocieron la humanidad del enemigo y se dieron cuenta de la gravedad de la decisión de apretar el gatillo".[66] ¿Podríamos, no obstante, estar confundiendo lo que constituye una genuina piedad en el campo de batalla? ¿El hecho de decidir no matar a un combatiente enemigo y permitirle vivir un día más (incluso probablemente en cautiverio), implica no reconocer su humanidad? Se argumentaría que la decisión de no matar, basada en la falta

---

62. En este punto debemos definir las obligaciones de los AWS simplemente conforme a su programación para seguir las reglas escritas dentro de su código, pero de ser posible, esto puede ampliarse para incluir una visión más extensa de las obligaciones morales.
63. Arkin, 2009, 66-67
64. Ibid, 117.
65. Leveringhaus 2016, 9-10
66. Leveringhaus 206, 10.

de necesidad militar de su muerte, es una forma apropiada de compasión y de misericordia que pudiera implementarse en el campo de batalla del mañana. Lo anterior nos colocaría en primera fila, al reducir el número de matanzas y de muertes desafortunadas que ocurren a consecuencia de otra acción intencionada. De igual manera, se debe reconocer que como están las cosas actualmente, los humanos no cuentan con un buen historial, mostrando compasión a gran escala en el campo de batalla (aunque esto se dé a nivel personal). Es frecuente que la maquinaria de propaganda de un país invente al enemigo en un "otro" o en algún otro ser que elimine su humanidad, haciéndolo así más fácil de matar (recuerdo cómo se llamaba a los alemanes "hunos" durante la Segunda Guerra Mundial o "vietcongés" a los vietnamitas). Si somos capaces de crear un Sistema de Armas Autónomo bajo una estricta regulación internacional, que se apegue a la ley internacional y respete la vida de una persona (matando únicamente a aquéllos que se considere permitido matar legalmente y conforme a las necesidades militares), podríamos mostrar *mayor* misericordia en el campo de batalla de la que hasta ahora hemos hecho.

En este punto, puede presentarse una posible réplica a mi objeción junto a las vías de factibilidad. ¿Resulta lógico pensar que podemos programar de manera factible un Sistema de Armas Autónomo "para que muestre misericordia" hacia los combatientes enemigos siempre que sea posible? Esta es una vía de argumentación sólida que debemos continuar abordando durante el desarrollo de dichos sistemas. Se podría argumentar que podemos "simplemente"[67] escribir en el algoritmo rector del Sistema de Armas Autónomo que "siempre que usted se encuentre con un soldado enemigo que no presente una amenaza directa para usted o para cualquier soldado humano en las cercanías directas, muestre misericordia no usando una acción letal para neutralizarlo". Esto sería tan solo una táctica posible, pero que se debe analizar a fondo. Retomando de nuevo a Ronald Arkin y a su proyecto teórico sobre construir un algoritmo que rija ese tipo de máquina, pareciera que a falta de una opción no-letal como primer curso de acción, estaría intrínseca la misericordia. En vez de que un soldado humano optara por no matar al enemigo (utilizando supuestamente medidas no letales para capturarlo y no solo dejándolo ir en libertad), tendríamos un Sistema de Armas Autónomo tardo para capturar al soldado enemigo usando tácticas no letales y humanas.[68]

---

67. Lo que confirma totalmente que esto no sería una tarea fácil.
68. Se negaría todo este proyecto si el Sistema de Armas Autónomo usó tácticas no letales pero *inhumanas*. Tácticas como éstas (quizás apalear al enemigo hasta quedar inconsciente)

El argumento final de Leveringhaus analiza la necesidad de preservar la dignidad humana en la decisión de matar. Leveringhaus afirma que esta dignidad únicamente se mantiene, si un agente humano toma la mejor decisión al momento de la muerte. Esto parece esquivar el tema sobre si se requiere la decisión de matar de un agente humano para mantener la dignidad y mi respuesta sería que no. Paul Scharre hace hincapié, al señalar:

> Cuando desde la perspectiva del soldado al ser matado en el campo de batalla, se considera esto (la muerte digna) es una crítica poco común y casi descabellada de las armas autónomas. No existe una tradición legal, ética o histórica de los combatientes que les permita a sus enemigos el derecho de morir con una muerte digna en la guerra. No hay nada digno en ser abatido por una ametralladora, volado en pedazos por una bomba, quemado vivo en una explosión, ahogado en un barco que se hunde, sofocándose lentamente de una herida de bala en el pecho, o cualquier otra manera horrible de morir en la guerra.[69]

El deseo de que solo se den muertes dignas en la guerra parece ser un sutil intento de esterilizar el combate al decir, "por lo menos el enemigo tuvo una muerte digna". Aunque para la mayoría no resulte cómodo, debemos reconocer que a nivel básico, la guerra se define por la muerte y la acción de matar. Por lo tanto, nuestro meta debe ser reducir la cantidad de matanzas y de sufrimiento infringido sobre las personas (tanto combatientes como no combatientes); sin embargo, exigir que la "muerte con dignidad" sea un requisito, rechaza la agresividad de la guerra. Es totalmente aceptable que se exija que los países vayan a la guerra únicamente cuando dicha acción se justifique moralmente o que por lo menos así sea, pero exigir que solo maten de manera digna resulta ideal en extremo y al mismo tiempo, hace caso omiso de la cruel realidad de la más mortífera de las relaciones humanas.

En la guerra podría esperarse que la muerte más digna[70] fuera aquella que causara el menor sufrimiento posible. Una muerte "limpia" por así decirlo, que extinga de manera rápida y efectiva la vida de un combatiente, sin causarle dolor y sufrimiento permanentes pudiera ser lógicamente, la más deseada. Lo anterior, no debe considerarse como una forma de subestimar

---

parecen ser tan moralmente sospechosas como dispararle a cada sujeto enemigo que uno se encuentre (que no representen una amenaza real)

69. Scharre 2018, 288.

70. Si acaso fuera realmente posible esperar tal cosa en un combate.

la importancia de la muerte en el campo de batalla a algún tipo de sistema de masacre con eficiente crueldad parecido a un matadero, sino más bien como un deseo de terminar las hostilidades a la brevedad posible, sin dolor ni sufrimiento innecesarios. Como lo menciona Paul Scharre (basado en su propia experiencia personal en la guerra), resulta absurdo insistir que la muerte en "manos" de una máquina sería, de alguna manera, menos digna que las distintas y diversas maneras en que uno puede morir en la guerra moderna.

En vez de preocuparse por una "dignidad percibida en la manera de morir" (ya que no queda claro si uno pudiera ser capaz de tener una muerte digna) debemos enfocarnos en reducir el sufrimiento en la guerra. Los sistemas de armas autónomos ofrecen una posible manera de lograrlo. Como lo argumento en la siguiente sección, nuestra meta en la guerra debe ser reducir el dolor y el sufrimiento innecesarios. Por lo tanto, debemos diseñar AWS encaminados a lograr esta meta y rechazar como tal, la afirmación de Leveringhaus de que la muerte por los AWS es intrínsecamente indigna.

4. Los aws como opción logica en la evolución de la guerra

El propósito de cualquier fuerza moralmente honesta debe ser limitar las muertes de los no combatientes y de los civiles en el campo de batalla. El IHL requiere que los ejércitos de cada estado, independientemente de que haya o no haya ratificado los Tratados de Ginebra, tengan el cuidado y las precauciones razonables de no matar o lastimar a las personas de las clases protegidas y de no causar daños innecesarios ni destruir propiedades (especialmente de las clases protegidas). En este aspecto, los ejércitos a nivel mundial, han desarrollado "armas inteligentes". Los sistemas de armas autónomos son el paso más lógico a seguir de estas armas inteligentes que como mínimo, tienen un beneficio doble sobre las supuestas "armas tontas" 1) pueden ser dirigidos hacia un blanco en específico (regularmente con márgenes de error de unos cuantos metros) y 2) ofrecen beneficios en términos económicos. Ahora bien, estas dos razones influyen en el deseo de limitar el daño colateral innecesario en la mayor medida posible. Si se puede apuntar a un área, con un margen mínimo de error, podemos entonces usar pocas armas para neutralizar la amenaza, limitando así la exposición al peligro tanto para los civiles como para las propiedades circundantes. Este cálculo se apega a la arquitectura fundamental que Arkin insta que incluyan en su diseño quienes investigan y desarrollan los AWS.[71] Este diseño presionaría hacia una "masacre efectiva en el campo de

---

71. A+B+C+D= Masacre en el campo de batalla. A= Combatientes planeados, B= Fuerzas amigables no planeadas C= No Combatientes planeados, D= No Combatientes

batalla" o al grado mínimo posible de daño colateral. Segundo, en términos económicos, las armas inteligentes ofrecen mayor beneficio comparadas con las armas "tontas". Esto pareciera contradecir a la lógica, debido a que muchas de las armas inteligentes cuestan cientos de miles e incluso millones de dólares por pieza. La lógica es que si puedo lograr la misma misión con pocas armas (que pueden costar más si se adquieren en forma individual) que con algunas municiones "tontas" relativamente baratas (que en conjunto pueden costar más que el arma inteligente); por lo tanto, usar el arma inteligente ofrece más beneficios en términos económicos. Lo anterior parece tener sentido. Si puedo usar un sólo misil guiado para deshacerme de un enorme búnker, fuertemente resguardado, que anteriormente hubiera requerido de 200 bombas no dirigidas, entonces debo usar obviamente, el único misil guiado inteligente. Si este caso aplica con armas como los misiles y las bombas lanzadas desde el aire, entonces también sostiene que si un Sistema de Armas Autónomo puede hacer el trabajo de diez soldados humanos, por lo tanto, su uso resulta más viable económicamente. Si un Sistema de Armas Autónomo puede ayudar a que los ejércitos reduzcan los costos económicos, así como el sufrimiento de los no combatientes, existen por lo tanto, motivos de consideración para concluir que el curso razonable a seguir, es el desarrollo y uso de dichos sistemas.

Arkin y otras personas consideran que el uso de los AWS (y en general de IA) en el campo de batalla pudiera ser el rumbo moral a seguir debido a un conjunto de características inherentes a su naturaleza. Primero, el AWS puede actuar de manera conservadora.[72] Un Sistema de Armas Autónomo puede (y posiblemente deba ser programado) para ser determinado hacia una acción no letal. Lo anterior se debe principalmente a la falta de una necesidad de supervivencia. [73] Al renunciar al deseo innato de mantenerse vivo y libre de daño, un Sistema de Armas Autónomo puede tomar acciones no letales más desafiantes (tales como salir de un área peligrosa que fuera difícil para un humano) o sacrificándose en sí, por el buen cumplimiento de la misión con el propósito de desviar la atención del enemigo del resto de su unidad. Un Sistema de Armas Autónomo no se dejaría confundir por las emociones y los consiguientes pronósticos de auto realización que turban comúnmente el criterio de los agentes humanos.[74] Los crímenes

---

No Planeados. El objetivo debería ser maximizar A, mientras eliminamos B & C y nos aseguramos de que D esté lo más cerca posible de 0 (Arkin 2009, 128)
72. Arkin 2009, 29
73. Ibid, 29
74. Ibid, 30

de guerra se cometen frecuentemente en el ardor de la batalla cuando las emociones están en su máximo nivel y cuando el miedo o el enojo nublan el juicio. Conforme lo comenta J Glenn Gray, un soldado "se convierte en un luchador, un Homo furens". [75] Si se crea un Sistema de Armas Autónomo sin tales emociones que turben el juicio, como sería el mejor curso lógico y moral, ya no sería, por lo tanto, un "esclavo" del miedo o del enojo, ni actuaría agresivamente porque otro Sistema de Armas Autónomo o un miembro del escuadrón humano fueron asesinados en una población local. Básicamente, podría ser un mejor agente ético y moral de lo que nosotros somos en la batalla. En consecuencia, Arkins señala: "No considero que un sistema autónomo no tripulado pueda ser totalmente ético en el campo de batalla, sin embargo, estoy convencido de que puede desempeñarse de manera más ética que los soldados humanos".[76]

Si como Arkin afirma, podemos diseñar un Sistema de Armas Autónomo con la capacidad para actuar mejor tanto ética como moralmente (o al menos a la par) comparado con los soldados humanos; por lo tanto, el rumbo más racional que se debe tomar, es desarrollar ese sistema. Si un Sistema de Armas Autónomo puede por lo menos ser tan ético y moral como el mejor de nosotros en la guerra, tenemos entonces, razones morales convincentes para construir dicho dispositivo. Primero, se disminuiría el número de nuestros propios soldados que se requieren que estén de alguna forma, frente al peligro. En este punto se reconoce, que no todos los soldados humanos pueden ser reemplazados por los AWS, más sin duda, se podría reemplazar a un buen número de ellos. Si puedo desplegar un sistema autónomo que pueda bajar en una autopista cargada de artefactos explosivos improvisados (IED, por sus siglas en inglés) para entregar mis suministros, sin arriesgar las vidas de los camioneros, entonces estoy obligado moralmente a hacerlo. Por el contrario, si decido no tomar dicha acción cuando dispongo de tecnología, entonces, estoy de hecho, actuando de manera inmoral. Segundo, si un Sistema de Armas Autónomo puede tomar mejores decisiones éticas y morales que los humanos en el campo de batalla, entonces estoy obligado a desplegar dicho sistema. Si, y éste es un gran si, dicho sistema puede ser construido y estar a mi disposición como comandante y si puede tomar decisiones que sean moral y éticamente más correctas (tales como diferenciar objetivos adecuadamente, evitar el exceso de muertes de

---

75. Gray 1959, 27
76. Arkin 2009, 31.

los objetivos, reducir el daño colateral) que los humanos, entonces estoy moralmente obligado a desplegar ese sistema. Este despliegue no libera a los comandantes que decidan usarlo (en este aspecto, probablemente de mayor rango que los comandantes de compañía y de batallón a nivel táctico [77]) del peso moral de matar, ni los absuelve de cualquier daño colateral excesivo que se relacione.[78] Tal y como Arkin lo mencionó, no existen muchas probabilidades de que, incluso con la mejor tecnología, podamos reducir de manera eficaz el daño colateral a cero. Sin embargo, como comando, estaría moralmente obligado a desplegar un Sistema de Armas Autónomo que pudiera tomar mejores decisiones morales que los humanos, quienes por lo demás, estarían usando la fuerza letal.

Al final, el curso de acción razonable para desarrollar y desplegar un sistema de armas es lo que pueda reducir la cantidad de masacre en el campo de batalla. Esta perspectiva no busca de forma alguna, sanear la guerra, ya que los combatientes reales seguirán muriendo y como lo señala Levering-haus, "el objetivo enemigo real como tal, no espera que no lo maten los soldados que lo atacan".[79]

5. Propuesta: un esquema para regular los aws

Considerando que ya he abordado los argumentos más persuasivos que se han utilizado en contra del uso de los AWS en el campo de batalla del mañana y argumentado los motivos por los que estamos obligados moralmente a utilizar tales armas, se requiere crear un sistema teórico de gobernanza que pueda regular el desarrollo y despliegue de esos sistemas a nivel internacional. Como se señaló anteriormente, no existe actualmente

---

77. En el ejército de EUA, una compañía es la unidad estándar de menor tamaño con un comandante designado (aunque hay unidades más pequeñas llamadas destacamentos, pero son excepciones a la regla). Las compañías varían en fuerza con personal desde 50 hasta más de 300. Una compañía es entonces, la unidad táctica de nivel básico a la cual le otorgamos liderazgo y responsabilidad. Una compañía es comandada por un capitán (0 a 3) que, si no tiene experiencia de reclutamiento previa, tiene entre 4-6 años en servicio. Un batallón (por lo menos uno estándar) está conformado por cinco a siete compañías y generalmente tiene un personal de 700 a 1500 dependiendo de cómo esté integrado y de la misión estipulada para la unidad. Se considera que un batallón está todavía a nivel táctico. Un batallón está generalmente bajo el mando de un teniente coronel (O 5) con aproximadamente 17 a 19 años de servicio.
78. Es físicamente imposible limitar TODO el daño colateral cuando la guerra se lleva a cabo donde viven personas. Este es un hecho aceptado. Sin embargo, la meta es REDUCIR o LIMITAR la cantidad de daño colateral. De esta forma, el daño colateral en exceso es visto como un crimen de guerra, mientras que el daño colateral incidental no.
79. Leveringhaus 2016, 10.

un Derecho Internacional Humanitario que se enfoque específicamente en el desarrollo y despliegue de los AWS. Esta sección aspira a ser el punto de partida para esa discusión y con ese fin, recomiendo tres áreas amplias de interés para el desarrollo y despliegue de los AWS. Estas tres áreas incluyen las dudas más apremiantes que uno pueda tener con respecto a los AWS. Ciertamente, lo anterior no comprenderá todas las posibilidades en el uso del sistema, ya que más bien tiene como fin, servir como una infraestructura teórica, lo suficientemente amplia, para guiar la elaboración de la ley internacional. Las tres áreas que enfatizo en este esquema teórico incluyen 1) despliegue apropiado de los AWS, 2) cumplimiento con el IHL actual y futuro y 3) establecimiento de una cadena de responsabilidad.

En primer lugar, el problema es: ¿cuándo resulta apropiado desplegar dicho sistema? El IHL debe establecer algunas leyes en las que se estipule que no debe desplegarse ningún Sistema de Armas Autónomo por ningún ejército o nación, únicamente hasta que los expertos técnicos relacionados con el mismo, hayan certificado que el sistema ha sido programado para adaptar su conducta con el IHL y que cualquier comandante que despliegue ese sistema, sin estar certificado, sea castigado independiente de que el sistema cometa realmente crímenes de guerra. Este requisito no sería ajeno para los ejércitos en la actualidad, ya que deben pasar por el mismo tipo de proceso de certificación para asegurarse de que los sistemas de armas estándar o convencionales (por decir, un tanque) sean diseñados y funcionen dentro de los límites legales. Una vez que un ejército o una nación ha pasado este umbral, debe entonces tomar otra decisión, la cual consiste en dos partes separadas, pero casi iguales 1) cuándo usar fuerza no letal contra fuerza letal (despliegue táctico/operativo) y 2) cuándo desplegar un Sistema de Armas Autónomo (despliegue estratégico). A continuación, abordo cada uno de estos problemas.

La decisión de utilizar un Sistema de Armas Autónomo en una situación táctica, significa únicamente, que el comandante en la base decide usarlo para una determinada misión. Se acepta por lo general, que estos comandantes operen a "nivel táctico" y tengan la libertad de decidir sobre el uso directo de tropas y armamento necesarios para lograr cierta misión u orden. En este sentido, un comandante de compañía tendría la autoridad de mando para decidir emplear el vehículo aéreo no tripulado de la compañía, con el fin de tener un mayor espacio v́ ;ual, sin embargo, no tendría autoridad para dirigir un recurso de nivel estratégico (como un satélite) para lograr su misión. No obstante, cuando se habla de un Sistema de Armas Autónomo, un comandante de nivel táctico (incluso hasta un comandante de Brigada que generalmente está al mando de una tropa aproximada de 5,000) debe tener la responsabilidad de mando y la autoridad para decidir si es apropiado usar ese tipo de arma. Por ejemplo, si un comandante de compañía es responsable de proteger a un pueblo, en ese momento debe tomar la decisión (tal vez consultando con órdenes de nivel superior) sobre el uso de un arma o una táctica específicos. Lo mismo aplica para un Sistema de Armas Autónomo. Para controlar el uso apropiado de fuerza, el Derecho Internacional Humanitario debe especificar que el uso táctico de un Sistema de Armas Autónomo debe garantizar que se va a reducir al mínimo, el posible daño colateral como resultado de su uso.

En segundo lugar, se abordará la cuestión respecto al despliegue estratégico del Sistema de Armas Autónomo y por despliegue estratégico me refiero, a si es moral o legalmente aceptable usar dicha arma en una determinada guerra o conflicto. Para solucionar esta inquietud, parece bastante sencillo legislar que el uso del AWS deba coincidir con los principios de la Teoría de la Guerra Justa y con el IHL, ¿habría más probabilidades de que el despliegue de un Sistema de Armas Autónomo no causara daños colaterales en exceso al ser desplegado en el escenario X en comparación con el escenario Y? Considerando, por ejemplo, el nivel de perfeccionamiento tecnológico en su momento, pudiera no ser ético desplegarlo en un escenario de combate urbanizado en extremo (Por ej. Singapur) cuando se compara con un escenario de combate rural o lejano (Por ej. la estepa rusa). Esta regulación debe establecer que el despliegue por cualquier nación o ejército, de un Sistema de Armas Autónomo, es inadmisible en un escenario de combate donde sea mayor la probabilidad del exceso de daño colateral, del que pudiera esperarse por el uso de fuerzas humanas. Por ejemplo, si su simple uso en un escenario ocasionara probablemente, el uso indiscriminado de fuerza debido a que el Sistema de Armas Autónomo (y posiblemente, un humano) tendría una dificultad enorme para diferenciar de manera adecuada entre los combatientes y los no combatientes, por lo tanto, su uso constituiría un crimen de guerra, incluso si no se equivocara al diferenciar a los verdaderos combatientes. No existe motivo alguno para considerar que, cuando un Sistema de Armas Autónomo se equivoca, no elaboraríamos algún tipo de evaluación de responsabilidad, aunque finalmente, a quien decidamos culpar por el error, pueda tener una apariencia distinta de la actual. Si un soldado comete un error en nuestros días, (un error que resulte en un crimen de guerra), ese individuo soldado y su cadena de mando pueden ser así, considerados responsables.[80]

---

80. Esto ciertamente supondría que el error fue algún tipo de acción deliberada o que se produjo por algún tipo de negligencia grave, los detalles en este punto no son particular-

Por lo tanto, la segunda amplia categoría de regulación debe incluir alguna estipulación con el fin de que "un Sistema de Armas Autónomo no pueda ser desplegado, en caso de que, debido a su diseño, no pueda apegarse a los principios básicos de la Teoría de la Guerra Justa y a los actuales o futuros preceptos del IHL". Como se mencionó anteriormente, emplear un sistema que pueda considerarse responsable por medio de su programación, sería intrínsicamente incorrecto tanto moral como legalmente. A dicho sistema le puede faltar la capacidad de que se le audite de cierta forma (como tener un registro de incendio o de desempeño para poder revisar todas las formas en que dicho sistema se involucró), o puede simplemente determinar el uso de la acción letal como primera respuesta apropiada. Aunque no sería propio del IHL ordenar la tecnología precisa que pudiera o no usarse, algo parecido al gobernador ético de Arkin, sería el mejor ejemplo de un tipo de sistema que pudiera cumplir con esta regulación teórica. Cualquier sistema que, como tal, cumpla con el propósito de la regulación y pueda de esta forma, apegarse a la Teoría de la Guerra Justa y a la IHL debe considerarse como aceptable.

La última área de enfoque para esta ejemplificación futura del IHL, es que debería existir una cadena de responsabilidad establecida. El futuro IHL debe prever que "en caso de que se despliegue un Sistema de Armas Autónomo, un comandante o líder político debe asumir la responsabilidad moral y legal por la decisión estratégica de emplear ese sistema de armas". La ley también debe estipular que a nivel táctico, "un comandante que decida utilizar dicha arma es responsable tanto moral como legalmente por todo lo que la misma haga o deje de hacer". Quienes se oponen a esas regulaciones podrán argumentar que se impone una carga demasiado pesada en los mandos militares, a lo que respondo: la carga debe ser pesada, ya que esto impide el libre uso de dichos sistemas en situaciones en las que es posible, ya sea infringir las Leyes de la Teoría Justa o el IHL, o en su defecto, aumentar el daño colateral a niveles que no sean aceptables. Las regulaciones pueden tener un posible efecto positivo de limitar el uso de los AWS únicamente en aquellas situaciones donde los resultados se puedan controlar de manera razonable o en situaciones donde la probabilidad de daño colateral sea baja. (Por ejemplo, la regulación puede disuadir el uso de los AWS en entornos urbanos con población densa, pero puede aumentar su uso en áreas virtualmente despobladas, como en mar abierto).

Aunque existe una ventaja al elaborar una ley internacional que aliente al desarrollo y al uso moralmente correcto de los AWS, debe existir un

mente importantes ya que el caso aún se mantiene íntegro.

mecanismo apropiado para obligar a su cumplimiento. Tal mecanismo puede ser como el que estableció la ICC o una nueva forma de observancia a nivel internacional. Las regulaciones legales que he propuesto, no dependen de ningún método de observancia en particular y son compatibles con una forma de mecanismo de cumplimiento creada recientemente para "obligar" a las naciones a desarrollar sus propios AWS, de tal manera que cumplan con las regulaciones. No me corresponde decidir la manera en que debe funcionar este mecanismo, en todo caso, abogar por un sistema que pueda, de acuerdo con sus posibilidades, evitar los crímenes de guerra *antes* que se cometan.

6. Conclusion

El avance humano es análogo a una máquina en movimiento continuo. Sin un comienzo definido y sin un fin aparente, avanzamos sin cesar, al igual que el desarrollo de maneras mejores y más efectivas de matarse entre sí. Desde los inicios de la existencia humana, cuando el hombre se dio cuenta que el hatlatl le permitía lanzar su jabalina más lejos que su oponente, hasta los avances modernos en el campo de la inteligencia artificial, la presión por encontrar la siguiente arma más poderosa, avanza de manera inexorable. El momento de actuar es hoy, con el fin de formar un órgano de regulación que configure la manera en que nosotros, como especie, desarrollemos y despleguemos lo que indudablemente, es el subsiguiente tipo de sistema de armas.

He presentado dos de los argumentos más persuasivos en contra del uso de los sistemas de armas autónomos, a manera de argumentos de responsabilidad y de agencia. Aunque ambos argumentos persuaden de manera superficial, ninguno ofrece las bases suficientes (ya sea de manera individual o colectiva) para inclinar la balanza hacia una absoluta prohibición sobre el uso de esta incipiente tecnología. En todo caso, ambos (y los demás argumentos) ofrecen un motivo persuasivo en cuanto al porqué es necesario impulsar *regulaciones* internacionales sobre el desarrollo y el despliegue moralmente apropiado de dichos sistemas. Asimismo, he argumentado que el desarrollo y despliegue adecuados de un sistema de armas autónomos es la opción razonable, únicamente si se pueden cumplir nuestros estrictos estándares morales de conducta. Por lo tanto, el propósito es reducir el horror que se da en la guerra. Como Sherman lo señaló: "la guerra es el infierno" pero debemos hacer todo lo posible para que sea un inferno tolerable.

El temor a lo desconocido es un instinto profundamente arraigado en los humanos. Las películas de ciencia ficción no han contribuido para calmar los temores de que, si continuamos con nuestra ruta de avances tecnológicos, los robots derribarán el yugo de su "opresión" y se convertirán en sus amos. Este temor, aunque pudiera ser generalizado, no es una base firme para decisiones morales o legales.

Agradecimientos

Me gustaría agradecer al profesorado y al personal del Departamento de Filosofía, especialmente al Dr. Andrew Altman y al Dr. Andrew I. Cohen: la presente tesis no hubiera sido posible sin su empeño. También agradezco a todos los profesores con los que he tenido el privilegio de tomar clases: gracias por aguantarme. Igualmente quiero dar las gracias a aquéllos en el ejército norteamericano que vieron una chispa en mí y pensaron que era digno de la tarea. Gracias a todos.

Referencias

Arkin, Ronald. *Governing Lethal Behavior in Autonomous Systems.* Boca Raton: Chapman and Hall Imprint (Taylor and Francis Group), 2009.

Army Doctrine Reference Publication. "6-22 Army Leadership." *Army Doctrine Reference Publications* (2012). https://usacac.army.mil/sites/default/files/misc/doctrine/cdg/cdg_resources/manuals/adrp/adrp6_22_new.pdf.

Boyd, John. *A Discourse on Winning and Losing.* Maxwell Air Force Base: Air University Press, 2018.

Campaign to Stop Killer Robots. "About Us." Accessed 25 July 2018. https://www.stopkillerrobots.org/about/.

Department of Defense. "Directive 3000.09-Autonomy in Weapon Systems." *Office of the Deputy Secretary of Defense* (November 2012). http://www.esd.whs.mil/Portals/54/Documents/DD/issuances/dodd/300009p.pdf.

In re Yamashita 327 U.S. 1 [1946] 61 (United States Supreme Court). https://supreme.justia.com/cases/federal/us/327/1/.

Government of China. "Group of Governmental Experts of the High Contracting Parties to the Convention on Prohibitions or Restrictions of the Use of Certain Conventional Weapons which may be Deemed to be Excessively Injurious or to have Indiscriminate Effects." *Convention on Certain Conventional Weapons—Position Paper* (April 2018). https://www.unog.ch/80256EDD006B8954/(httpAssets)/DD1551E60648CEBBC125808A005954FA/$file/China's+Position+Paper.pdf.

Gray, J. Glenn. *Warriors: Reflections of Men in Battle.* New York: Harcourt, Brace and Company, 1959.

International Criminal Court. "Rome Statute." Article 8(2)(b)(xx) (1998). https://www.icc-cpi.int/nr/rdonlyres/ea9aeff7-5752-4f84-be94-0a655eb30e16/0/rome_statute_english.pdf.

Leveringhaus, Alex. "What's so Bad about Killer Robots." *Journal of Applied Philosophy*, (March 2016). DOI: 10.1111/japp.12200.

McMahan, Jeff. *Killing in War.* Oxford: Oxford University Press, 2011.

Military Leadership Diversity Commission. "Outreach & Recruiting." *United States Department of Defense*. November 2009. https://diversity.defense.gov/Portals/51/Documents/Resources/Commission/docs/Issue%20Papers/Paper%2002%20-%20Requirements%20and%20Demographic%20Profile%20of%20Eligible%20Population.pdf.

Papal Encyclicals Online. "The Second Council of the Lateran- 1139 A.D." Accessed 18 January 2019. http://www.papalencyclicals.net/councils/ecum10.htm.

Program Executive Office- Missiles & Space. "Counter-Rocket, Artillery, Mortar (C-RAM)." Accessed September 1. 2018. https://missiledefenseadvocacy.org/defense-systems/counter-rocket-artillery-mortar-c-ram/.

Raytheon. "Phalanx Close-In Weapon System." Accessed 15 August 2018. https://www.raytheon.com/capabilities/products/phalanx.

Scharre, Paul. *Army of None: Autonomous Weapons and the Future of War*. New York: W. W. Norton & Company, 2018.

Sparrow, Robert. "Killer Robots." *Journal of Applied Philosophy*, vol. 24, no. 1 (2007):62–71. DOI: 10.1111/j.1468-5930.2007.00346.x.

United Nations Institute for Disarmament Research. "The Weaponization of Increasingly Autonomous Technologies: Concerns, Characteristics and Definitional Approaches." *UNIDIR Resources*, no. 6 (2017): 1–33. http://www.unidir.org/files/publications/pdfs/the-weaponization-of-increasingly-autonomous-technologies-concerns-characteristics-and-definitional-approaches-en-689.pdf.

United Nations Office for Disarmament Affairs. "Perspectives on Lethal Autonomous Weapon Systems." *UNODA Occasional Papers*, no. 30 (November 2017): 1–61. www.un.org/disarmament.

US Army Acquisition Support Center. "Excalibur Precision 155MM Projectiles." Accessed 25 July 2018. https://asc.army.mil/web/portfolio-item/ammo-excalibur-xm982-m982-and-m982a1-precision-guided-extended-range-projectile/.

Interdiction des Systèmes d'armes Létales Autonomes[1]
Une Analyse Critique

Hunter Cantrell

Liste Des Abréviations

SALA- Système(s) d'armes (létales) autonomes
CPI- Cour pénale internationale
DHI- Droit humanitaire international
DG- Droit de la guerre
RE- Règles d'engagement

I. Introduction

Une augmentation de l'emploi des systèmes d'armes entièrement autonomes –que d'aucuns annoncent comme imminente[2]—a suscité l'appel
à une campagne pour cesser le recours aux « robots tueurs ». Cet appel a
jusqu'à présent été soutenu par vingt-trois nations[3], et n'a cessé de gagner en
légitimité depuis le début de la campagne intitulée *Campaign to Stop Killer
Robots*[4] en 2013[5]. Cette initiative est motivée en partie par la crainte d'une
perspective selon laquelle tous les attributs du soldat humain, y compris
la notion de vie et de mort, seraient retirés du champ de bataille pour y
être remplacés par une forme d'intelligence artificielle meurtrière. Il y

---

1. *Je dédie ce travail à mon épouse tant aimée, Tiffany, et à mes deux merveilleux fils, Holden et
Bryson. Sans vous, je ne serais rien.*
2. Ce qui soulève la question du consensus concernant l'imminence de la situation qui
pourrait s'échelonner sur 5, 10, 50, 100 ans. Ce manque de clarté est commun dans le
domaine des nouveaux systèmes d'armes létales autonomes.
3. A noter que l'ensemble des pays qui se sont joints à cette campagne n'ont probablement
pas les capacités technologiques, les infrastructures ou les besoins militaires pour construire
de tels équipements. Algérie, Argentine, Bolivie, Brésil, Chili, Costa Rica, Cuba, Equateur,
Egypte, Ghana, Guatemala, Irak, Mexique, Nicaragua, Ouganda Pakistan, Panama, Pérou,
Venezuela, Zimbabwe, ainsi que le Vatican et la Palestine ont participé à cette campagne.
4. Campaign to Stop Killer Robots, "About Us."
5. Les participants à cette initiative se réunissent annuellement depuis 2013 au bureau des
Nations Unies à Genève.

a toutefois peu de raisons de penser qu'il s'agisse d'une crainte réaliste, contrairement aux représentations apocalyptiques imposées par l'industrie cinématographique d'Hollywood, en particulier l'image de nombreux Terminators errant dans les villes.

Il existe néanmoins des perspectives éclairées s'insurgeant contre le développement et la mise en place de systèmes d'armes entièrement autonomes. Ces positions appartiennent à deux grands types d'argumentation : l'un s'attache à l'argument dit « de la responsabilité », l'autre répondant de l'argument dit « de l'agent responsable ». D'une façon générale, la *responsabilité* se définit par la chaîne de responsabilité nécessaire à l'utilisation des systèmes d'armes létales autonomes (SALA) dont les acteurs devraient endosser toute responsabilité en cas de dysfonctionnement. D'autre part, l'*agent responsable* entend mettre en question la substitution du jugement humain par celui d'une entité artificielle dans le cadre d'une action destinée à entraîner la mort ; il en étudie également les implications pour la dignité humaine et la possibilité accordée à une éventuelle grâce.

Ce mémoire entend proposer une évaluation de ces deux arguments en tant qu'ils ne suffisent pas à justifier une interdiction pure et simple des SALA. Par ailleurs, ce travail de recherche soutient que les arguments sus-cités parent au maintien d'un cadre juridique fondé sur le droit international humanitaire actuel qui visera à *réglementer*, et non à *interdire*, le développement et l'emploi des SALA. Dans ces pages, le recours aux SALA est défendu en tant que choix rationnel pour les dirigeants militaires et politiques. Y est également décrit un potentiel cadre juridique, fondé sur l'actuelle convention de Genève et le droit humanitaire international, afin de réglementer l'usage des SALA.

1.1 Pourquoi il est essentiel de parler des systèmes d'armes autonomes

La démocratisation du recours aux systèmes d'armes autonomes est une prochaine étape dans l'usage des technologies militaires modernes. Alors qu'on constate une rapidité accrue dans les prises de décision militaires, rapidité largement attribuable aux prouesses croissantes de l'informatisation, la capacité de l'esprit humain à suivre cette tendance reste à la traîne. La boucle OODA en est un excellent exemple. Le concept a été inventé par le colonel John Boyd, pilote de l'US Air Force et stratège de la puissance aérienne américaine.[6] L'acronyme recense quatre processus, OODA sig-

---

6. Boyd 1987, 383.

nifiant « observer, s›orienter, décider et agir ». Le principe de cette boucle démontre que si un pilote de chasse parvient à pénétrer dans la boucle OODA de l'ennemi, il est alors en mesure de descendre son appareil. La boucle OODA est donc un processus décisionnel très rapide par lequel une personne — ou, à l'avenir, une machine ? — sera en mesure de prendre l'initiative d'une action donnée. Il est probable que les boucles OODA continueront de se resserrer à mesure que s'imposeront de nouveaux progrès technologiques. Dans l'avenir, le resserrement de la boucle OODA pourra se prêter à une intelligence artificielle capable de traiter de nombreuses données de calcul de décisions simultanément en temps réel, c'est-à-dire beaucoup plus rapidement que ne pourrait le faire un humain. On peut déjà remarquer un élan de fabrication d'armes plus « intelligentes » et plus rapides en observant l'évolution des avions de chasse (dont deux exemples parmi tant d'autres, l'US Air Force F-35 II américain et le Chengdu J-20 chinois), de même que l'évolution des « bombes intelligentes » (obus de précision Excalibur à guidage GPS et inertiel[7]), ainsi que par le niveau d'utilisation accru d'outils de prise de décision assistée par ordinateur dans la planification militaire.[8]

L'automatisation accrue des systèmes d'armement actuels et la volonté de recourir à des armes entièrement autonomes ont quelque peu remédié à la complexité accrue de la guerre moderne et à la baisse du nombre des engagés déclarés aptes au service dans l'armée.[9] C'est le cas du système d'arme rapproché PHALANX (sur les croiseurs américains Aegis) qui confie à un système semi-autonome des fonctions essentielles de protection antimissile des navires en dernière ligne de défense, libérant ainsi un équipage limité en nombre qui sera affecté à d'autres tâches.[10] L'utilisation croissante de ces technologies est une première étape dans la mise en place de systèmes capables de sélectionner des « cibles et [de recourir] à la force

---

7. US Army Acquisition Support Center, "Excalibur Precision 155MM Projectiles."
8. Il ne s'agit pas là de confier des décisions stratégiques aux ordinateurs et autres calculateurs électroniques, mais de mettre l'informatique au service de la hiérarchie militaire en mobilisant des renseignements toujours plus nombreux, plus exacts et plus clairs. Ces systèmes informatiques comprennent des possibilités très diverses dont la localisation automatisée de cargaisons expédiées à l'international, ainsi que de lieux de bataille amis et ennemis, les systèmes de surveillance et de détection, etc. Si tant est que certaines inventions technologiques sont à l'origine de dépendances au numérique dans le civil, c'est également le cas dans l'armée.
9. Voir the Military Leadership Diversity Commission Issue Paper #2 "Outreach & Recruiting."
10. Raytheon, "Phalanx Close-In Weapon System."

sans aucune intervention ou interaction humaine ».[11] Comme nous l'avons vu précédemment, le déploiement des SALA est théoriquement inquiétant de nombreux points de vue, mais cette évolution technologique a également le bénéfice potentiel de réduire les imprévus ou les dommages collatéraux inhérents à la guerre telle qu'elle est pratiquée actuellement.

1.2 Description des systèmes d'armes autonomes

Avant de se pencher sur le débat concernant le recours aux SALA, il est essentiel de comprendre exactement ce qu'est une arme autonome. Il n'est pas étonnant que les milieux universitaires et diplomatiques ne se soient pas encore accordés sur une définition opératoire des SALA. Ainsi les définitions diplomatiques acceptées jusqu'ici varient-elles considérablement : certaines incluent des armes aujourd'hui considérées comme automatisées, mais non autonomes, alors que d'autres prennent seulement en compte les systèmes ne nécessitant aucune intervention humaine décisive. Certaines autres définitions existantes requièrent la présence de fonctionnalités ou de technologies spécifiques. Un exemple assez parlant est celui du gouvernement néerlandais qui donne la définition suivante : un SALA est « un armement qui sélectionne des cibles et engage la force de manière autonome par rapport à certains critères définis à l'avance, et à la suite d'une décision prise par un opérateur humain de déployer l'arme, en sachant qu'une fois lancée, l'attaque ne peut pas être interrompue par une intervention humaine ».[12] À savoir que cette définition pourrait tout à fait s'appliquer à des armes qui ne sont actuellement pas considérées comme totalement autonomes, tels les missiles de croisière.[13] En effet, le missile de croisière, conçu pour frapper une cible spécifique programmée (signature thermique, désignation par laser d'un soldat au sol ou autre cible prédéfinie), ne devient totalement autonome qu'une fois lancé, par un opérateur humain ayant donné l'ordre de déployer le système, et ne peut donc pas être rappelé.

---

11. ICRC 2015, 6.

12. United Nations Institute for Disarmament Research [UNIDIR] 2017, 23

13. Cet exemple peut également s'appliquer à d'autres armements dotés de munitions à guidage de précision. Il est important de remarquer que les lois en vigueur selon les Conventions de Genève interdisent l'utilisation d'armes aveugles, ce qu'on peut interpréter comme un aval accordé à l'emploi des armes à guidage de précision. En outre, les termes de ces conventions prohibent « le fait d'employer les armes, projectiles et méthodes de guerre […] (visant à) frapper sans discrimination en violation du droit international des conflits armés, à condition que ces armes, projectiles, matières et méthodes de guerre fassent l'objet d'une interdiction générale et qu'ils soient inscrits dans une annexe au présent Statut » (Cour pénale internationale, Article 8 (2)(b)(xx) 1998).

Le gouvernement français donne sa propre définition du SALA par « la négative »[14] :

> Les armes létales autonomes sont des systèmes entièrement autonomes…Les SALA doivent s'entendre comme impliquant l'absence totale de surveillance humaine, ce qui signifie qu'il n'y a absolument aucun lien (communication ou contrôle) avec la chaîne de commandement militaire.…La plate-forme de livraison d'un SALA est techniquement en mesure de se déplacer, de s'adapter à des environnements terrestres, marins ou aériens et de cibler et de tirer un effecteur mortel (balle, missile, bombe, etc.) sans aucune intervention ou validation humaine.…Le SALA possédera très probablement des capacités d'auto-apprentissage.[15]

La définition des SALA proposée par les Pays-Bas diffère de celle de la France qui affirme que ces systèmes d'armement ne sont pas liés à la chaîne de commandement militaire (c'est-à-dire à un opérateur humain), y compris dans la planification de mission et la prise de décision de recours à l'un de ces systèmes. Cette définition limite considérablement la notion même de SALA, car une opération humaine décisive intervient très probablement à un moment précis dans la « chaîne de frappe ». La définition donnée par la France est donc si étriquée qu'elle en devient pratiquement inutilisable en tant que base à des consensus diplomatiques et académiques concrets.[16]

Bien que la définition donnée par les États-Unis aux SALA inclue certains éléments empruntés à la perspective fonctionnaliste française, elle s'en détache également en distinguant les systèmes d'armes létales entièrement autonomes des semi-autonomes. Ainsi, les États-Unis (par le biais du Département de la Défense) donnent aux SALA la définition suivante :

> Un système d'armes qui, une fois activé, peut sélectionner des cibles données et engager la force sans autre intervention d'un opérateur humain. Cela inclut les systèmes d'armes autonomes supervisés par l'homme et conçus pour permettre aux opérateurs humains de se substituer au fonctionnement du système d'armes,

---

14. United Nations Institute for Disarmament Research [UNIDIR] 2017, 24
15. Ibid, 24.
16. C'est également la perspective de la Chine qui considère les SALA comme ayant un niveau d'autonomie qui manque « d'intervention humaine et de contrôle durant le processus d'exécution d'une mission donnée » (gouvernement chinois, 2018).

mais qui peuvent sélectionner des cibles et engager la force sans autre intervention humaine après l'activation.[17]

La définition états-unienne est alors plus utile en pratique que les définitions française ou néerlandaise, car elle propose un compte-rendu détaillé des SALA en excluant implicitement des systèmes qui ne devraient pas être considérés comme tels.[18] Ainsi, les systèmes en place aujourd'hui qui pourraient être considérés comme automatisés ou semi-autonomes[19] (PHALANX, C-RAM[20], etc.) n'en font pas partie, de même que les systèmes « Tire et oublie », qui pourraient inclure le missile de croisière évoqué plus haut. Il est également important de souligner que selon la définition américaine un SALA peut agir sans l'intervention d'un opérateur humain, mais *en aucun cas* n'empêche l'intervention d'un opérateur humain. C'est d'autant plus important car cette distinction est clairement conforme à la directive 3000.09 du Département de la Défense (DoD) américain, stipulant que « les systèmes d'armes autonomes et semi-autonomes doivent être conçus pour permettre aux responsables militaires et aux opérateurs d'exercer des niveaux appropriés de jugement humain quant au recours à la force ».[21] Cette directive indique que les États-Unis envisagent une relation complémentaire entre le jugement humain et le recours à l'intelligence artificielle et aux SALA. Cette politique « met également l'accent sur ce

---

17. United Nations Institute for Disarmament Research [UNIDIR] 2017, 30.

18. Comme il a été mentionné plus haut, les Etats-Unis donnent une définition de ce qui n'entre pas dans la dénomination de SALA, en l'occurrence : « un système d'arme qui, une fois activé, ne peut engager la force que de cibles ou de groupes de cibles préalablement programmées par un opérateur humain. Cela recouvre : (a) les systèmes d'armes semi-automatiques autonomes pour les fonctions d'engagement de la force, y compris, mais sans limitation imposée à l'acquisition, la poursuite et l'identification de cibles éventuelles, la facilitation du repérage visuel de cibles éventuelles pour l'opérateur humain, le classement des cibles sélectionnées par ordre de priorité, le minutage de la mise à feu, ou la mise à disposition du guidage terminal pour la focalisation sur des cibles visées, pourvu qu'un contrôle humain parraine la décision de sélectionner des cibles isolées ainsi que des groupes de cibles sur lesquelles engager la force. (b) Mode « Fire and Forget », soit « Tire et oublie » ou verrouillage de la cible après le lancement qui retient les munitions en s'appuyant sur le TTP (tactiques, techniques et procédures) afin d'optimiser la probabilité que seules les cibles dans la liste d'acquisitions du programmeur quand celui-ci active le système sont les cibles individuelles ou groupe de cibles sélectionnées par un opérateur humain » (UNIDIR 2017, 31).

19. Il faut toutefois préciser que les systèmes PHALANX et C-RAM peuvent aussi être enclenchés sur un mode totalement autonome.

20. Program Executive Office- Missiles & Space, "Counter-Rocket, Artillery, Mortar (C-RAM).

21. Department of Defense, Directive 3000.09.

qui constitue l'autonomie au niveau *décisionnaire* plutôt que sur la présence ou l'absence de recours à une technologie particulière ».[22]

1.3 Le droit international humanitaire actuel et les SALA

Les conflits militaires modernes sont régis par un ensemble de normes communément acceptées comme justification à tout conflit militaire, à savoir que ces principes sont fondés sur l'histoire de la doctrine de la guerre juste. Avant le XXe siècle, ces principes n'étaient pas codifiés, répondant plutôt à un ensemble de coutumes et de normes établis sur les bases d'une entente mutuelle.[23] Par exemple, sauver un grand nombre de marins ennemis à l'issue d'une bataille navale était une action « digne d'un gentilhomme ». Sans être imposée par traité ou accord international, elle était héritée d'une pratique courante forgée au fil de siècles de guerre navale. Plus tard, cette pratique a été abandonnée avec la prolifération de la guerre sous-marine. Après la seconde guerre mondiale, dans le cadre des procès de Nuremberg, les alliés ont accusé l'amiral Donitz de crime contre l'humanité pour avoir employé la tactique nazie consistant à couler des navires ennemis sans remonter à la surface pour sauver les rescapés. Les poursuites judiciaires à son encontre ont toutefois échoué, car de par l'évolution de la guerre navale, il était devenu monnaie courante de ne pas assurer le sauvetage des rescapés de sous-marins coulés en raison de risques opérationnels extrêmes.

Le droit humanitaire international (DHI) tel qu'il s'applique dans le cadre des Conventions de Genève et de ses protocoles additionnels ne mentionne pas explicitement les SALA. Cela peut être un point positif dans l'élaboration de traités concernant ces systèmes d'armement, bien que le DHI interdise le recours à certains types d'armements. La Convention sur certaines armes classiques (CCAC) interdit l'utilisation de certaines formes d'armes frappant sans discrimination, ce qui confère un statut préférentiel aux armements guidés de précision dits armes « intelligentes » au détriment des armes aveugles dites « simples ». Afin de se conformer aux prescriptions du CCAC, il faudrait alors élaborer des SALA ne pouvant pas être employés

---

22. UNIDIR 2017, 31.
23. Bien que certains éléments de la loi internationale soient toujours fondés sur des normes et principes coutumiers, des réglementations sont désormais mises en place par traités, tels les Conventions de Genève (1949) et dans les statuts de la Cour pénale internationale. Avant la création de ces institutions par l'International Code Council (ICC), la plupart des états avaient pour seules garanties les principes de la guerre et des coopérations de défense bilatérales afin d'assurer le respect des normes et principes coutumiers, à noter que certaines nations, dont les Etats-Unis d'Amérique, ne font pas partie de l'ICC.

de manière « intrinsèquement aveugle ». Ce qui renvoie à la définition de l'arme ou du système d'armes simple : une mine antipersonnel ou un gaz toxique en sont des exemples type. Les deux catégories d'armes sont aveugles puisqu'à leur déploiement, elles sont dirigées indistinctement contre des cibles militaires légitimes et non légitimes. Une mine terrestre tuera ou mutilera tous ceux qui auront la malchance de marcher dessus, même des décennies après son déploiement. Toutefois, développer un SALA qui pourrait être dirigé contre des cibles précises est une tâche difficile, mais pas insurmontable.

2. Des Objections aux SALA: Arguments Pour L'interdiction

Depuis l'invention de l'arbalète au XIIIe siècle[24] des appels ont été lancés en faveur de la limitation des armes tolérées dans le conflit armé dit civilisé. D'autre part, des avancées technologiques, dont la mitrailleuse, la mine terrestre et le gaz toxique, ont aussi poussé les nations à se procurer des armes de pointe de plus en plus perfectionnées afin de pouvoir prendre l'avantage sur l'ennemi. Certaines de ces armes, telle la mitrailleuse, font encore partie du matériel militaire dont l'emploi est en vigueur. D'autres, comme les mines terrestres, ont été fortement réglementées et leur emploi est déconseillé à l'échelle internationale.[25] Quant au gaz toxique, son emploi a été expressément interdit en vertu d'un traité international.

Depuis 2013, les membres de la campagne contre les robots tueurs, *Campaign to Stop Killer Robots*, plaident en faveur d'une interdiction totale de la création et de la mise en service de systèmes d'armes létales autonomes.[26] Cette organisation non gouvernementale œuvre au niveau étatique et international en faveur d'une coalition comprenant états membres de l'ONU, organisations non gouvernementales, entreprises et citoyens dans le but exprès d'interdire les SALA. Les acteurs de cette campagne, de même que de nombreux universitaires, s'inquiètent de voir les SALA franchir un « seuil

---

24. Droit canonique issu du deuxième concile du Latran : « Nous interdisons sous peine d'anathème que l'art meurtrier des archers et des arbalétriers, que Dieu juge haineux, soit désormais utilisé contre les catholiques et les chrétiens. »

25. Les mines antipersonnel sont expressément interdites d'après le traité du Québec : les mines antichars ainsi que les mines antinavires restent tolérées. Les mines ayant une durée de vie raccourcie (devenues inertes un certain nombre d'heures après leur déploiement) sont également tolérées.

26. « *The Campaign to Stop Killer Robots* appelle à l'interdiction préventive et totale de la création, de la fabrication et de la mise en service des armements totalement autonomes, aussi connus sous la dénomination de systèmes d'armes létales autonomes ou robots-tueurs » (Campaign to Stop Killer Robots, https://www.stopkillerrobots.org/learn/).

moral » sacrifiant la dignité de la vie humaine en vertu de l'efficacité de la guerre automatisée. À noter que les arguments en faveur de l'interdiction des « robots-tueurs » peuvent être divisés en deux catégories : d'une part, l'argument dit « de la responsabilité » et, d'autre part, celui dit « de l'agent responsable ».

2.1 L'argument de la « responsabilité » ou qui tenir responsable

L'une des grandes préoccupations des militants contre l'utilisation des SALA est qu'il est envisageable de créer des robots pouvant cibler et tuer des humains sans qu'un agent moral puisse être tenu dûment responsable. Le problème qui persiste quant à l'attribution d'une juste part de responsabilité à un humain pour un élément de mission mené à bien par un SALA est souvent qualifié de « rejet de responsabilité ».[27] S'il est possible de retracer les actions d'un SALA pour les renvoyer directement à la personne qui a autorisé la mission (par exemple, un chef militaire voyou qui aurait programmé l'ordre de tuer des civils non armés et des soldats ennemis blessés), il est alors clair que les morts occasionnées engagent à juste titre la responsabilité du chef militaire ayant autorisé la mission. Cependant, la question se pose différemment lorsqu'il est impossible de faire porter sa juste part de responsabilité à la personne qui a autorisé l'emploi du SALA pour commettre un crime de guerre. Il s'agit alors d'un véritable « rejet de responsabilité ». Bonnie Docherty, militante en faveur de l'interdiction des SALA estime qu' « [il ne serait] ni juste ni juridiquement viable de…tenir un chef militaire ou un opérateur [humain] pour responsable. »[28] Elle n'est d'ailleurs pas seule à trouver problématique la question du déplacement de la responsabilité de l'humain vers l'agent, soit le SALA, qui a commis l'action moralement répréhensible ou illégale. Dans son plaidoyer en faveur de la non attribution de cette responsabilité, Robert Sparrow explore tout de même deux possibilités : faire porter la responsabilité aux humains (programmeur et chef militaire) des dégâts causés par le SALA ou considérer le SALA comme agent responsable.

En premier lieu Sparrow fait valoir que la responsabilité des dégâts causés par un SALA inopérant pourrait reposer, du moins en partie, sur le programmeur ou le concepteur de l'appareil : « ce ne serait juste que si

---

27. Scharre 2018, 261.
28. Ibid, 261.

la situation décrite s'est produite à la suite d'une négligence de la part de l'équipe de conception / programmation. »[29] Toutefois Sparrow rejette très vite l'idée d'attribuer la responsabilité au programmeur ou au concepteur dans les cas où il n'y a pas de démonstration de négligence. La première raison de ne pas mettre en cause le programmeur est que « la possibilité d'erreur de ciblage soit une limite connue du système. »[30] Si le fait que la machine frappe une cible non autorisée est un « effet secondaire » ou une « limite du système » et que le programmeur communique explicitement cette limite à tout utilisateur potentiel, il ne serait pas juste de tenir le programmeur responsable. Sparrow soutient que, dans ce cas, les chefs militaires qui déploient le système, avec ses limites connues ou effets secondaires possibles, doivent endosser la responsabilité de cette action. Il ajoute ensuite que « la possibilité qu'un système autonome fasse d'autres choix que ceux prédits et encouragés par ses programmeurs est intrinsèque à l'affirmation que le système est autonome ».[31] Ici Sparrow souligne qu'en raison de la conception opérationnelle d'un SALA et de la nature complexe des algorithmes et des réseaux neuronaux qui le composent, aucun humain ne sera en mesure de prédire les décisions du système d'armement de manière certaine. Si tel est en effet le cas, il est aussi injuste de blâmer le programmeur qui n'aura pas pu prévoir toutes les actions du SALA.

Sparrow soutient que s'il est impossible de demander des comptes au programmeur du SALA pour les réactions fautives du système, la responsabilité du chef militaire qui a ordonné son déploiement peut alors être engagée.[32] Il écrit : « Le risque que les actions du SALA puissent mal tourner est toléré lorsque la décision est prise d'enclencher la frappe. C'est d'ailleurs la logique guidant les forces militaires qui entendent déployer les SALA actuels. »[33] Sparrow soutient qu'en traitant les SALA de la même manière que les armes conventionnelles actuelles, simples ou intelligentes,

---

29. Sparrow 2007, 69.
30. Ibid, 69.
31. Ibid, 70.
32. Sparrow ne décrit pas à quel niveau de commandement un chef militaire pourrait être tenu responsable du fait. Si, par exemple, un commandant de division d'infanterie (un capitaine (O3) de l'armée de terre ou du Corps des Marines américains) prend la décision d'utiliser un SALA dans un village causant ainsi la mort d'un enfant, qui est responsable ? Le capitaine ? Son supérieur hiérarchique, à savoir un commandant de bataillon (lieutenant-colonel) ? Le commandant de brigade, le chef de division, le Corps, etc. ? S'agirait-il d'incriminer le tenant du grade le plus élevé pour avoir avalisé l'emploi généralisé du SALA dans sa division ?
33. Sparrow 2007, 70.

on peut simplement faire endosser la responsabilité de leur utilisation au chef militaire qui en a donné l'ordre. Toutefois, cette approche ne prend pas en compte tous les aspects qui font l'autonomie de l'arme. Sparrow fait valoir que la nature même de cette autonomie implique que les chefs militaires n'ont pas le contrôle du choix de cibles effectué par le SALA, et qu'ils ne devraient donc pas être tenus responsables des choix du système : « Si les machines choisissent véritablement leurs cibles, il est alors impossible d'incriminer le chef militaire pour les morts qui en découlent ». [34] Or, si programmeur et chef militaire en sont exempts, la responsabilité du SALA lui-même peut-elle alors être engagée ?

Sparrow ajoute que « l'autonomie et la responsabilité morale vont de pair. » [35] Si les SALA devenaient pleinement capables de prendre des décisions entraînant la mort de manière entièrement autonome (sans intervention humaine), le dispositif devrait alors porter la responsabilité morale de ses actions, ce qui est le cœur du problème. « Il est difficile de prendre au sérieux l'idée que la responsabilité d'une machine devrait ou pourrait être engagée par rapport aux conséquences de « ses actions. » [36] En partant du fait que tout engagement de responsabilité pour une action répréhensible implique une punition pour son auteur, Sparrow souligne « qu'une sanction pour être considérée comme telle doit provoquer un certain type de réponse. » [37] Quel est le type de réponse adaptée à la sanction selon Sparrow ? Selon lui, c'est la souffrance, et pour qu'un SALA puisse être puni, « il doit pouvoir souffrir ». [38] Or, la notion de souffrance complique la perception des fonctionnalités et autres capacités des SALA telles qu'on les interprète et les imagine actuellement. Il est peu probable qu'un programmeur puisse intégrer des réponses émotionnelles telles la souffrance ou la peur à la conception d'un SALA, car de telles émotions remettraient en question l'un des avantages potentiels que le SALA offre aux humains, à savoir de ne pas pouvoir provoquer des crimes de guerre motivés par la colère, la haine, la soif de vengeance, etc. [39] S'il est vrai qu'un SALA n'a pas la capacité de res-

---

34. Ibid, 71.
35. Ibid, 65.
36. Ibid, 71.
37. Sparrow 2007, 71.
38. Ibid, 72.
39. Ronald Arkin avance que le manque d'émotions spécifiques des SALA (peur, colère, tristesse, etc.) serait un des avantages potentiels de leur utilisation. Les SALA ne montrant pas les réponses émotionnelles caractéristiques des humains sur le champ de bataille seraient plus aptes à prendre des décisions justes selon l'éthique les gouvernant.

sentir de la douleur physique ou émotionnelle, il n'est probablement pas en mesure de souffrir et, selon Sparrow, ne pourrait donc pas être sanctionné.

En somme, Sparrow est d'avis que s'il n'est pas concevable de créer un SALA éthique qui puisse être « tenu responsable de ses actions à juste titre » [40], il est contraire à l'éthique de déployer ce type d'armement sur le champ de bataille. La décision de prendre une vie, selon lui, doit appartenir à un agent capable de responsabilité morale qui peut être puni en cas de non-respect du droit de la guerre.

2.2 L'argument dit « de l'agent responsable » : faut-il renoncer à engager la responsabilité humaine face à la mort ?

La décision de tuer un être humain est un élément intrinsèque aux conflits armés. Jusqu'à l'avènement de l'arme à feu, la plupart des morts était historiquement causée par des combats personnels entraînant une grande proximité physique. Les ennemis pouvaient se regarder dans les yeux, chacun luttant pour défendre sa vie. Dans son livre intitulé *On Killing,* le lieutenant-colonel Dave Grossman étudie les effets que la distance physique croissante par rapport à l'acte meurtrier peut avoir sur la capacité à ôter la vie. En étant face à face avec son ennemi, on se rend compte que celui-ci est humain et qu'il est possible de s'identifier à lui, même très partiellement. Dans ce cas, le meurtre est plus intime et plus brutal. Quand il s'agit de tuer à distance, l'ennemi paraît déshumanisé ce qui rend plus facile de trouver des raisons à l'acte de tuer. La distance la plus importante qu'il puisse y avoir entre le combattant et l'acte meurtrier réside dans le retrait pur et simple du pouvoir décisionnaire au combattant, la décision de tuer un agent humain revenant alors à un agent artificiel. Alex Leveringhaus soutient que « dans un conflit armé, le remplacement de l'agent humain responsable par l'agent artificiel que constitue la machine est tout à fait problématique. »[41] Le débat est critique quant à savoir s'il faut renoncer à la responsabilité humaine pour mettre en avant celle de l'armement.

Leveringhaus prétend que le problème majeur posé par l'abandon de l'hégémonie de l'agent humain sur la décision de tuer pourrait causer une perte d'« équivalence morale des soldats ». Formulé par Michael Walzer, le principe d'équivalence morale stipule que les soldats de chaque côté du conflit, dont parmi eux, attaquants et défenseurs, ont tous la même valeur

---

40. Sparrow 2007, 66.
41. 40 Leveringhaus 2016, 2.

morale du point de vue des lois de la guerre, ce qui confère à chacun un droit équivalent de recourir à la force pour tuer l'ennemi et se défendre. [42] Selon Walzer, cette équivalence morale existe indépendamment de la juste raison du conflit en cours : chacun doit conserver le droit moral de se battre. Toutefois, lorsqu'une des deux parties présidant au conflit est remplacée par un SALA, la notion d'équivalence morale disparaît. En effet, le SALA n'a pas de prétention morale à la légitime défense et, à ce titre, ne saurait être sur un pied d'égalité avec l'humain.

Leveringhaus aborde un deuxième problème, à savoir l'incapacité d'un SALA à exercer un « jugement moral ». Cette incapacité est particulièrement notable lorsque le système d'armement détermine le niveau de force à employer parce que «...l'application du critère de proportionnalité [dans le DHI] implique d'avoir à faire des jugements moraux. » [43] Comme un SALA n'est pas en mesure de porter un jugement moral sur la proportionnalité des moyens adaptée à une situation donnée, devrait-il pouvoir prendre la plus finale des décisions morales, en l'occurrence celle d'ôter la vie ? Leveringhaus déclare que non en soulignant que la capacité de tuer sans pouvoir mettre en balance les conséquences morales de cette action est, en substance, un manque de respect aux droits de l'homme et à la dignité de l'individu visé.

Le nœud de l'argument défendu par Leveringhaus repose sur l'affirmation qu'en employant un SALA pour tuer un être humain, toute possibilité de pitié dans la chaîne de mise à mort est purement annihilée. Selon lui, cela donne lieu à la mise à distance morale d'un meurtre qui constitue un manque de respect à la dignité et aux droits humains des personnes décédées. La notion de pitié dans la chaîne de mise à mort signifie qu'à tout moment un soldat peut choisir de ne pas appuyer sur la détente. À ce sujet, Leveringhaus écrit : « Il manque aux robots tueurs en tant qu'agents artificiels une composante centrale caractéristique de l'agent humain, à savoir la capacité de prendre une autre décision : celle de ne pas tirer sur la cible choisie. » [44] Cette incapacité des robots à épargner un combattant ciblé manque de respect à la dignité inhérente à chaque être humain. « L'ennemi, en tant que cible légitime, ne prétend pas demander sa grâce aux soldats attaquants. Toutefois, la capacité

---

42. Walzer 2015, 34.
43. Leveringhaus 2016, 2.
44. Leveringhaus 2016, 9. Leveringhaus emploie délibérément l'expression robots-tueurs au lieu de faire référence à des systèmes d'armes létales autonomes. C'est une subjectivisation émotive qui vise à convaincre le lecteur du dilemme moral que présentent ces dispositifs. Je suis d'avis qu'il s'agit d'un moyen de s'éloigner de la nature intrinsèquement objective de ce débat, et qui contribue à sa dilution.

humaine de gracier, la capacité à éprouver de la pitié ou à compatir avec les autres humains, même s'ils appartiennent au camp opposé, est sans nul doute moralement pertinente et mérite d'être défendue. » [45] Leveringhaus soulève un problème au sujet des SALA opérant une action mortelle sur un être humain : il manque fondamentalement au robot une capacité intrinsèque à la compassion et à la conscience du prix de la vie humaine. Ainsi, il écrit : « Je pense qu'il est essentiel de conserver le libre arbitre humain au point d'engagement de la force, protégeant ainsi la liberté de ne pas appuyer sur la détente, actionner un bouton ou lancer une grenade, ceci dans le but de préserver notre humanité au cœur de la situation où elle est le plus facilement mise à l'épreuve : la guerre. » [46] Si un SALA n'est pas en capacité de choix d'épargner un ennemi, c'est qu'il n'a pas la capacité de faire preuve de compassion ou de miséricorde, et c'est bien cette capacité-là qui est nécessaire au respect de la dignité humaine. Leveringhaus conclut son argument d'un message dérangeant qui s'inscrit contre l'optimisme de certains créateurs et chercheurs en technologie des armements de pointe : « Les robots-tueurs ne nous sauveront pas des affres de la condition humaine. » [47]

3. Rejet des Arguments Précédents

Comme le souligne J. Glenn Gray, il existe une relation nécessaire entre la mort et la guerre : « la mort en temps de guerre est communément causée par des membres de mon espèce qui veulent activement ma fin, en dépit du fait qu'ils n'ont peut-être jamais eu de contact avec moi et n'ont aucune raison personnelle à une inimitié causant la mort. » [48] Cet état de fait incite à se demander comment il est alors possible de réduire la souffrance de ceux qui sont activement engagés dans un conflit armé et des civils innocents pris dans la fureur de la guerre. Un élément de réponse pourrait se trouver dans l'implémentation de l'intelligence artificielle et de systèmes d'armes autonomes sur le champ de bataille de demain. Dans la suite de ce mémoire, et comme beaucoup l'ont déjà fait dans les secteurs de la sécurité nationale et de la défense [49], je soutiens l'idée que l'avenir verra probablement les SALA opérer en tandem avec les soldats. S'il est vrai

---

45. Ibid, 10.
46. Ibid, 10.
47. Ibid, 15.
48. Gray 1959, 100.
49. Voir livre blanc General Mick Ryan's (armée australienne) "Human-Machine Teaming for Future Ground Forces" https://csbaonline.org/uploads/documents/Human_Machine_Teaming_FinalFormat.pdf.

qu'il existe au sein de l'armée de nombreux éléments de mission pouvant facilement être confiés à un système autonome (telles que la conduite de convois logistiques le long d'itinéraires dangereux ou le traitement des formalités administratives des ressources humaines), certains éléments ne seront probablement jamais automatisés dans leur intégralité. En revanche, il est probable qu'une association d'humains et de machines complémentaires pourrait optimiser l'intelligence, l'endurance, la force et la puissance de feu du soldat humain. Je soutiens que les arguments qui ont été présentés jusqu'à présent en faveur d'une interdiction de l'emploi des SALA ne donnent pas de raison convaincante à la mise en œuvre d'une telle interdiction. Tout au contraire, ces arguments peuvent logiquement défendre la mise en place d'un système de réglementation par lequel les nations pourront suivre et encadrer le développement de ces systèmes autonomes de manière à ce que leurs attributions soient compatibles avec le DHI et acceptables d'un point de vue moral.

3.1 Contre-réponse à l'argument dit « de la responsabilité »

Bien que l'argumentation de Sparrow soit convaincante à première vue, elle est en fait nourrie de suppositions précaires et ignore les chaînes causales de responsabilité telles qu'elles s'entendent actuellement dans l'armée. Tout d'abord, nous nous pencherons sur la perspective de Sparrow quant à la possibilité de blâmer le programmeur du SALA et le chef militaire qui déploie le système, puis nous évoquerons son idée selon laquelle il serait impossible de sanctionner un SALA.

Sparrow est du côté de la raison quand il hésite à attribuer au programmeur du SALA une responsabilité morale équivalant plus ou moins à tenir le fabricant d'un fusil moralement responsable de l'emploi qui en est fait lors d'une fusillade dans un établissement scolaire. Si faire porter cette responsabilité à un fabricant d'arme peut apaiser les sentiments liés à cet emploi fautif de l'arme, cela ne résout pas la question de la responsabilité morale. Certes, Sparrow établit qu'il est possible de tenir le programmeur responsable si un dysfonctionnement grave était dû à une négligence de programmation, de la même façon qu'un fabricant est aujourd'hui tenu responsable des défauts d'un produit ayant causé des dommages ou la mort de son utilisateur. Il faut toutefois éviter qu'un programmeur soit incriminé parce que l'utilisation de son produit peut être jugée moralement répugnante. En ce qui concerne la responsabilité du programmeur, on peut accorder à Sparrow que celui-ci n'est responsable qu'en cas d'erreur par négligence.

Sparrow poursuit son argumentation en disant que les chefs militaires n'ont pas à endosser la responsabilité des actions d'un SALA survenues sous leur commandement, car ce système d'armes est entièrement autonome et, qu'en tant que tel, ses actions ou motivations peuvent être obscures. Pourtant, cette affirmation fait fi de certains principes fondamentaux de leadership et de responsabilité qui sont à la base de la culture militaire américaine actuelle.

Par exemple, le concept de responsabilité est un principe fondamental de la culture au sein des forces armées. Tout militaire est imprégné d'un certain niveau de responsabilité proportionnel à son grade et à son poste. Chacun a la responsabilité majeure de conformer sa conduite à la loi, aux règlements militaires et à la tradition. Au fur et à mesure que l'on gravit les échelons hiérarchiques d'une armée, on acquiert des niveaux de responsabilité croissants, à la fois envers le personnel et les ressources matérielles à disposition. Le sommet de la responsabilité militaire consiste à atteindre le grade de commandant. D'une armée à l'autre, un commandant est responsable du personnel et du matériel à différents niveaux, en fonction de la taille de l'unité, mais les principes de base restent les mêmes entre toutes les armées. Le manuel de leadership des forces armées américaines [50] précise que « le commandement inclut l'autorité et la responsabilité d'utiliser efficacement les ressources disponibles, et donc de planifier l'emploi, l'organisation, la direction, la coordination et le contrôle des forces militaires engagées pour mener à bien les missions assignées à l'armée. » [51] Ce qui nous intéresse ici est la définition des responsabilités du commandant. Celui-ci est responsable en tout temps de chaque action entreprise ou omise par ses soldats. De par leur poste d'autorité supérieur, les commandants de l'armée américaine assument la lourde responsabilité des actions de leurs subordonnés. En cela, les commandants pourraient être au moins partiellement responsables des ratés et des dysfonctionnements des SALA même si un incident se produit sans contrôle humain direct.

La norme Yamashita a été établie comme précédent juridique à la suite de la Seconde Guerre mondiale. Lors des procès militaires qui ont suivi la guerre du Pacifique, le général Tomoyuki Yamashita a été jugé pour les crimes contre l'humanité perpétrés par les troupes placées sous son commandement. Le général Yamashita a fait valoir qu'il ne pouvait ni connaître l'étendue des atrocités qui avaient été commises, ni exercer un contrôle

---

50. Army Doctrine Reference Publication 6-22 Army Leadership.
51. ADRP 6-22 2012, 1-3

direct sur des troupes déployées dans une zone géographique très large afin de pouvoir empêcher de tels actes. Le tribunal trouvant cet argument peu convaincant a déclaré :

> Le droit de la guerre impose au commandant d'une armée le devoir de prendre les mesures adaptées en son pouvoir afin de contrôler les troupes placées sous son commandement et prévenir les actes allant à l'encontre du droit de la guerre et susceptibles de participer à l'occupation de territoires hostiles par une soldatesque incontrôlée, et par là même, sa responsabilité personnelle peut être engagée pour avoir omis de prendre de telles mesures en cas d'infraction au droit de la guerre. [52]

Le verdict rendu dans l'affaire Yamashita établit catégoriquement que les chefs militaires, à tous les niveaux, ont le devoir d'empêcher que des atrocités ne se produisent dans les unités placées sous leur commandement. Il existe cependant un possible contrepoint à ce verdict, à savoir qu'un chef militaire est globalement responsable des actions de ses troupes, mais ne pourrait être raisonnablement tenu responsable des actions d'un SALA « conçu sans négligence » et dont le processus décisionnel est essentiellement inconnu. J'ajouterai que non seulement les chefs militaires sont tenus au moins partiellement responsables des actions de leurs subordonnés (quel que soit le processus décisionnel du subordonné), mais qu'ils sont également responsables de promouvoir un environnement dans lequel les choix du subordonné pourront être considérés comme légitimes. Premièrement, l'armée considère un commandant comme responsable des actions de tous ses subordonnés dans la hiérarchie militaire, qu'il puisse ou non exercer un contrôle direct sur eux. Prenons, par exemple, la récente vague d'importants accidents navals survenus dans la 7e flotte de la marine américaine stationnée au Japon. Les commandants des deux vaisseaux ont été jugés coupables (l'un d'entre eux a même été renvoyé aux assises pour homicide involontaire), en dépit du fait qu'ils n'étaient pas physiquement à la barre, ni même sur le pont au moment de l'incident. [53] La Marine a conclu avoir fait preuve de négligence quant à son devoir d'assurer le bon fonctionnement de ses équipements. On a aussi pu déterminer qu'à bord de ces navires, et au niveau du commandement de la flotte (quartier

---

52. In re Yamashita.
53. Il est important de noter que des chefs militaires de rang supérieur, comme le commandant de la 7e division, ont été forcés de présenter leur démission en conséquence de ces incidents.

général), les hauts gradés encourageaient un environnement où des normes laxistes et le recours à des expédients étaient considérés comme acceptables. [54] Pour revenir aux SALA, selon la structure juridique militaire actuelle, il est raisonnable de supposer que si un système était autorisé à commettre un crime de guerre ou n'en était pas empêché, le commandant pourrait être à la fois juridiquement et moralement responsable.

Si l'on est collectivement disposé à rendre un commandant partiellement responsable du comportement de ses soldats (qui sont eux-mêmes des agents autonomes), il n'y a aucune raison légale ou morale de ne pas tenir les troupes au même niveau de responsabilité pour les actions ou l'inertie d'un SALA. Sparrow est d'avis qu'il serait injuste de faire porter la responsabilité du fonctionnement d'un SALA à un chef militaire, car ce dernier ne peut en aucun cas prédire le comportement de la machine. Toutefois, cela soulève un dilemme, à savoir si le chef militaire peut également prédire le comportement de ses troupes au combat. Les chefs militaires entraînent leurs soldats de manière aussi régulière que rigoureuse afin que leurs réactions soient prévisibles dans une situation tendue, mais cela n'exclut pas la possibilité qu'un soldat puisse franchir un seuil moral en commettant un crime de guerre. Le roboticien Ronald Arkin écrit : « Personnellement, je n'ai pas confiance en l'exemption du droit [de la guerre (DG) ou les règles d'engagement (RE)] opérée par un agent autonome [le SALA], car cela soulève la question de la responsabilité du fait. En revanche, il n'est pas impossible qu'un humain assume la responsabilité d'une telle entorse au droit, si c'est pertinent. » [55] Arkin soutient ici que ni à la conception, ni à la construction d'un SALA, on ne doit conférer à la machine la capacité de prendre la décision autonome de mettre de côté le DG ou le RE (ce qui ferait partie de sa programmation de base) et que cette responsabilité doit demeurer exclusivement aux mains d'un humain. La responsabilité du SALA allant à l'encontre du DG ou du RE s'en verrait transférée à un décideur humain (à savoir un chef militaire à un niveau donné). [56] Si un chef

---

54. Voir les comptes rendus de la Marine américaine au sujet des incidents du USS Fitzgerald et du USS John S McCain : https://www.secnav.navy.mil/foia/readingroom/ HotTopics/CNO%20USS%20Fitzgerald%20and%20USS%20John%20S%20McCain%20 Response/CNO%20USS%20Fitzgerald%20and%20USS%20John%20S%20McCain%20 Response.pdf.

55. Arkin 2009, 40.

56. Selon moi, cela s'apparente à l'emploi des services d'un officier en charge du ciblage dans les conflits actuels qui engagent les Etats-Unis. Dans ce type de situation, lorsqu'une cible est désignée, on demandera à un officier supérieur, le plus souvent à un général, de valider la cible et d'autoriser l'engagement de la force. L'officier agira en présence d'un

militaire, aussi éloigné qu'il puisse être de la décision finale de la frappe, décide d'avoir recours à un SALA dans une situation où de trop grands dommages collatéraux sont possibles, il ne semble y avoir aucun tort moral à incriminer ce chef militaire en cas d'incident.

On pourrait douter que suffisamment d'éléments probants ont été évoqués jusqu'ici dans le but d'affirmer que la norme Yamashita justifie moralement une responsabilité attribuée au chef militaire. Je soutiens qu'au lieu de chercher des justifications, il serait préférable d'appréhender ce débat par l'affirmation que la norme Yamashita fournit une raison moralement justifiable de tenir un commandant responsable (même si son rôle est de superviser l'emploi d'un SALA). Pourquoi cette doctrine de la responsabilité peut-elle être moralement justifiable ? Parce qu'elle procède d'un désir de contraindre les commandants de théâtre en temps de guerre à prendre toutes les précautions nécessaires pour créer un environnement respectueux du droit de la guerre, du droit international humanitaire et des règles d'engagement applicables à la zone d'opérations donnée. La norme Yamashita (ou *Medina standard*, dans sa dernière mise à jour) propose une voie moralement acceptable dans ce but donné et rappelle aux chefs militaires tout au long de la chaîne de commandement qu'ils sont personnellement responsables des actions de leurs subordonnés. Cela ne signifie pas pour autant qu'ils aient à endosser l'entière responsabilité des actions ou des manques de leurs subordonnés, mais qu'ils doivent prendre leur juste part de responsabilité. [57]

Le point d'achoppement de l'argument présenté par Sparrow tient à sa réticence à tenir les SALA responsables de leurs exactions en tant qu'agents moraux. Sparrow soutient qu'il est impossible de sanctionner un SALA qui ne peut ressentir de souffrance, ajoutant que de ce fait le système ne peut encourir de sanction. Cet argument semble tenir à l'idée d'une justice rétributive, le problème résidant dans l'affirmation de Sparrow que la justice rétributive est nécessairement la voie à suivre (explicitement pour les SALA et implicitement pour les humains). À ce sujet, il dit : « de façon à ce que ces actes de sanction servent de punition, ils doivent susciter une réponse de la part de leur objet…pour être en mesure de recevoir une punition, l'agent

avocat proposant un conseil juridique adapté à la situation, bien que la responsabilité incombe au décideur. Il pourrait en être de même pour autoriser l'emploi d'un SALA déviant des normes de sa pré-programmation en termes de DG et de RE, si un chef militaire en décidait ; dans ce cas, celui-ci serait tenu d'accepter la pleine et entière responsabilité de cette action.

57. Je crois que le débat concernant « la juste part de responsabilité » est important et nécessaire, mais qu'il échappe à la portée voulue pour ce mémoire.

[artificiel ou humain] doit être jugé capable de souffrance. »[58] Néanmoins, il est possible de rejeter la souffrance, en tant que condition à la possibilité de la punition, par l'adoption d'idées morales prospectives qui font l'objet d'une littérature établie. Par exemple, il pourrait être envisagé d'adopter un type de sanction participatif visant à généraliser à tous les SALA la programmation d'actes jugés inacceptables. On pourrait également souhaiter une approche fondée sur la réadaptation de la sanction selon laquelle le SALA ferait l'objet d'une nouvelle programmation ou d'un paramétrage afin d'exclure toute action jugée indésirable sur la base de faits passés. En revanche, si on se focalise sur la punition par rétribution comme le préconise Sparrow, la sanction d'un SALA donc rendue impossible validerait son argument. Cependant, il n'y a que peu de raisons de penser que Sparrow ne fait pas fausse route.

Quant à la responsabilité morale liée à la mort d'un ennemi combattant, Sparrow dit ceci : « la moindre des choses que l'on doive à nos ennemis est de donner suffisamment de valeur à leur vie pour accepter la responsabilité de leur mort. »[59] Sparrow exige que le SALA soit tenu responsable alors qu'il est apparent que le chef militaire ayant décidé de déployer le système d'armes ou le politicien ayant engagé le conflit armé devraient être au centre du débat. Si le SALA est employé en toute légitimité, il ne devrait y avoir aucune obligation de tenir individus ou systèmes d'armement responsables de pertes humaines en temps de guerre.[60]

En revanche, concernant la question de la prise de responsabilité pour un SALA dont le déploiement a causé un crime de guerre, je soutiens qu'au lieu de sanctionner l'emploi du système, il est plus judicieux de se pencher sur les circonstances spécifiques à chaque incident. En effet, vues les spécificités de chacun, il ne convient pas de faire des généralisations ou de dégager des principes universels pour engager la responsabilité d'un agent. Il vaut mieux étudier les mécanismes de la décision ayant conduit à l'emploi de l'arme (par rapport à des probabilités accrues de nombreux dommages collatéraux) ainsi que les autres décisions prises par le chef militaire détenteur des renseignements utiles au moment de l'attaque avant de faire porter le

---

58. Sparrow 2007, 72.
59. Sparrow 2007, 67
60. Il est évident que McMahan, pour ne citer que lui, serait en désaccord avec cette assertion, préférant dire que ces soldats ou le SALA qui prennent part à une guerre injuste sont individuellement responsables de la mort d'un ennemi combattant parce que le soldat présumé avoir des intentions justes ne peut pas constituer une cible légitime. (McMahan 2011, 14)

blâme à un agent en particulier. En somme, s'il peut être démontré qu'un chef militaire ou un SALA ont pris toutes les précautions nécessaires pour éviter un incident grave, mais que des atrocités sont survenues (dues, par exemple, à une bombe perdue), on ne devrait tenir aucune des deux entités responsable (en appliquant possiblement la doctrine de la double finalité).

Sparrow répond que suivre cette voie donne cours à un déficit de responsabilité, le seul remède adapté à la situation étant de ne pas avoir recours aux SALA. En réponse à cette opinion, je maintiens que Sparrow fait erreur. Comme je l'ai mentionné auparavant, si la norme Yamashita (ou *Medina standard*) est mise en pratique, il sera alors possible d'établir un lien de responsabilité morale avec le chef militaire dans les cas où il est impossible de démontrer clairement que le SALA est à l'origine d'une action illégale ou immorale. Dans ce cas, on est confronté à deux options, soit a) « punir » le SALA en se fondant sur une base morale adaptée (impliquant communication, réadaptation, etc.) ou b) sanctionner le chef militaire, quel que soit son rang (mais qui pourrait ne pas correspondre au plus bas niveau de commandement) en appliquant la norme Yamashita / *Medina standard*.

Comme nous l'avons démontré sur la base de précédents dans le droit international actuel, par l'étude des normes de leadership militaire américain et en évoquant une possible refonte de l'idée de punition, l'argument de la responsabilité s'avère peu concluant. Au lieu de fournir des preuves convaincantes que la communauté internationale aurait tout intérêt à interdire purement et simplement le développement et l'utilisation des SALA, cet argument constitue, à l'inverse, une forte incitation à la réglementation du développement et de l'utilisation de ces systèmes d'armement.

3.2 Contre-réponse à l'argument dit « de l'agent responsable »

L'argument le plus convaincant qui ait été soutenu jusqu'à présent dans cette étude soutient qu'il est inenvisageable de céder le contrôle de la décision de tuer à un agent artificiel. D'une part, celui-ci est incapable de faire preuve de clémence au moment même d'une action létale, contrairement à un être humain ; d'autre part, qu'une personne perde la vie par décision d'un robot autonome est fondamentalement irrespectueux de la dignité humaine. Cependant, les deux côtés de cet argument sont intrinsèquement biaisés.

Leveringhaus veut rendre possible le choix de ne pas suivre un ordre légitime de tuer l'ennemi sur le champ de bataille, et en l'occurrence, le choix de ne pas tirer sur un combattant légitime, afin de laisser s'exprimer des sentiments humains dont la pitié. Il dit : « ce qui rend précieux l'agent humain, comparé à l'agent artificiel, dans la guerre et dans la vie courante, est la possibilité de s'engager à tout moment dans un autre plan d'action. » [61] Leveringhaus croit sincèrement que sur le champ de bataille, il faut être capable de ne pas tuer en dépit de l'aval qui enjoint à exercer une force meurtrière. Il suppose que si un SALA est préprogrammé pour certains ordres et paramètres de mission au vu du droit de la guerre et des règles d'engagement, il lancera l'attaque contre tous les ennemis rencontrés sur son passage. Je suis d'avis que cette supposition n'est pas nécessairement vraie. En suivant les conseils d'Arkin au sujet des algorithmes pour robots militaires, également connus sous le nom de « gouverneur éthique », la conception adéquate d'un SALA lui fera prendre par défaut des mesures non létales pour échapper à l'ennemi ou le maîtriser. Il lui serait donc impossible de passer immédiatement à une action létale. Grâce à la présence d'un algorithme construit sur le modèle de ce système d'armement, les attaques mortelles ne se produiraient que si elles étaient inévitables. À supposer qu'un SALA soit en patrouille avec une brigade de soldats de l'infanterie américaine, l'un des RE pourrait être défini comme suit : « Si un membre de la brigade est en danger imminent d'être capturé, il y a obligation de faire usage de moyens proportionnels adaptés à la situation afin d'empêcher la capture. » Ce qui implique que si aucun membre de la patrouille n'est en danger imminent d'être capturé, le SALA doit choisir par défaut une action non létale, à moins que le système n'ait à répondre à d'autres exigences prédéfinies.

Le système d'armement létal autonome en tant qu'outil doit être contraint [62] de *suivre* des ordres légitimes et légaux et d'*ignorer* des ordres illégitimes et illégaux. Le dernier point est tout aussi important que le premier en vertu de la prévention des crimes de guerre sur le champ de bataille. Il s'agirait d'une sorte de « contrôle du comportement éthique » [63] selon Arkin. Sur ce point, il écrit : « pour ce qui est du cas particulier des robots de terrain (mais aussi pour le soldat), l'agent responsable ne doit pas pouvoir se faire sa propre idée des implications morales inhérentes à l'utilisation de la force létale ; en revanche, on attend de lui qu'il mette en pratique les croyances

---

61. Leveringhaus 2016, 9
62. On pourrait ici définir les obligations d'un SALA par rapport aux caractéristiques de sa programmation le contraignant à suivre des règles prédéterminées, mais cette définition pourrait s'étendre à une vision plus extensive de ses obligations morales, le cas échéant.
63. Arkin 2009, 66-67.

et les règles ayant été précédemment déduites par la communauté humaine et dont le DG et le RE sont le reflet. » [64]

Leveringhaus en déduit que l'une des caractéristiques distinguant les agents humains des agents artificiels est la capacité humaine à prendre ses ennemis en pitié. Selon lui, « la capacité humaine de gracier, la capacité à se sentir pris de pitié ou à compatir avec autrui, même dans le camp opposé, est sans nul doute moralement pertinente et mérite d'être défendue. » [65] De quoi est faite la pitié, si ce n'est de la capacité à penser et à agir autrement ? Il semble que le point central de réponse pour Leveringhaus réside dans le fait de pouvoir s'identifier à l'ennemi, de pouvoir reconnaître son humanité et ainsi de s'abstenir de lui faire du mal lorsque c'est possible ou indiqué. « Ces soldats qui n'ont pas tué ont pu s'en dispenser en reconnaissant l'humanité de l'ennemi et en réalisant la gravité de la décision qui consiste à appuyer sur la détente. » [66] Est-il possible de se méprendre quant à la véritable nature de la compassion sur le champ de bataille ? La décision de ne pas tuer un ennemi pour le laisser vivre un jour de plus, bien qu'il soit potentiellement en captivité, n'est-elle pas en soi une reconnaissance de son humanité ? Je dirais qu'épargner une vie par décision fondée sur l'absence de nécessité militaire à causer la mort est une forme adéquate de compassion et de pitié qui pourrait tout à fait être mise en œuvre sur le champ de bataille de demain. Ce type de décision permettrait de réduire le nombre de massacres survenus sur le champ de bataille et de limiter le nombre de morts soit à la plus stricte nécessité en vertu d'un objectif militaire, soit à ces décès imprévisibles et regrettables survenus en conséquence d'une autre action sans lien. Il faut également reconnaître qu'à l'heure actuelle le bilan à grande échelle des actes de compassion n'est pas très satisfaisant, même au niveau individuel, durant les conflits armés. Bien souvent, la machine de propagande en vigueur dans un pays présente l'ennemi comme un intrus ou comme un être tout « autre » que l'on privera de son humanité en le traitant de « Teuton » ou de « Viêt-Cong » (en cela, on repense respectivement aux Allemands de la Première Guerre mondiale et aux Vietnamiens durant la guerre du Vietnam), cela rendant sa mort plus facile, car plus acceptable. S'il était envisageable, dans le cadre d'une réglementation internationale stricte, de créer un SALA ayant pour fondement le respect des règles du droit international et de la vie humaine (pour restreindre les morts à des

---

64. Ibid, 117.
65. Leveringhaus 2016, 9–10.
66. Ibid, 10.

cibles légales conformément aux nécessités militaires), il serait plus facile de faire preuve de clémence sur le champ de bataille que ce qu'il a été rendu possible jusqu'ici.

Cette objection pourrait se voir opposer l'argument de la faisabilité. Est-il raisonnable d'espérer pourvoir un SALA d'un logiciel incluant, autant que possible, une forme de capacité à la clémence envers les combattants du camp adverse ? Voilà une ambition solide qu'il faudra continuer à défendre durant le développement futur de ces systèmes. On pourrait mettre en avant la possibilité de « tout simplement » [67] inclure dans l'algorithme directeur du SALA qu'« à chaque rencontre avec un soldat ennemi ne présentant pas de menace directe pour soi ou pour tout autre soldat humain dans les environs, il faudra faire preuve de clémence en réfrénant toute tentative d'action mortelle visant à le neutraliser. » Ce n'est là qu'un exemple de technique possible, mais qu'il serait bon de prendre en considération. Pour revenir à Ronald Arkin et à ses travaux théoriques au sujet de la construction d'un algorithme régissant les choix d'une semblable machine, il semble que la clémence serait inhérente à une option non létale sélectionnée par défaut comme plan d'action initial. À la place d'un soldat humain faisant le choix d'épargner l'ennemi (probablement en utilisant des mesures non létales pour le capturer et pas seulement en le laissant partir), il y aurait un SALA dont la programmation par défaut présiderait à la capture de l'ennemi en utilisant des tactiques non létales et humaines. [68]

Le dernier argument de Leveringhaus détaille un impératif, celui de préserver la dignité humaine dans la décision d'ôter la vie. Leveringhaus soutient que cette dignité ne peut être préservée qu'à la seule condition qu'un agent humain prenne la décision ultime au moment même de la mort. Cela soulève la question de savoir si la présence d'un agent humain responsable de tuer est nécessaire pour préserver cette dignité. Je dirais que non. Paul Scharre fait valoir un argument fort en écrivant ce qui suit :

> Du point de vue du soldat tué sur le champ de bataille, cette
> [mort digne] est une critique inhabituelle, presque étrange, des
> armes autonomes. Il n'y a pas de tradition juridique, éthique
> ou historique selon laquelle les combattants accordent à leurs

---

67. J'ai tout à fait conscience du fait que ce ne serait pas tâche facile.

68. L'emploi de tactiques non létales mais inhumaines nierait les bases du projet. De telles tactiques, consistant éventuellement à étourdir l'ennemi, sont aussi suspectes d'un point de vue moral que l'idée de faire feu sur tout individu dont la présence ne constituerait pas une grave menace.

ennemis le droit de mourir dignement dans un conflit armé. Il n'y a d'ailleurs rien de digne à être fauché par une mitrailleuse, réduit en pièces par une bombe, brûlé vif dans une explosion, noyé dans un navire en perdition, lentement suffoqué par une lésion thoracique aspirante, ou de même à toute autre mort effroyable en temps de guerre. [69]

Le souhait que seules des morts dignes puissent se produire pendant la guerre s'assimile à une tentative futile d'aseptiser le combat en déclarant qu'« au moins l'ennemi est mort dans la dignité ». Bien que l'idée soit gênante pour la plupart des gens, il faut bien reconnaître que la guerre, dans son fondement même, se définit par la mort et la destruction. Réduire la fréquence des massacres et limiter les souffrances infligées aux gens, combattants et civils, est un but à poursuivre, mais exiger que « la mort dans la dignité » devienne un impératif est une tentative futile d'ignorer la cruauté intrinsèque de la guerre. Il est tout à fait acceptable d'exiger que les nations n'entrent en conflit que lorsque c'est moralement justifié, ou justifiable tout du moins. Cependant, imposer de tuer seulement dans la dignité est à la fois trop naïf et éloigné de la réalité la plus brutale des relations humaines.

La mort la plus digne à laquelle on puisse prétendre [70] lors une guerre est celle qui cause le moins de souffrances possible. Une mort « propre », pour ainsi dire, qui ôte rapidement et efficacement la vie à un combattant, sans causer ni douleur, ni longues souffrances, serait vraisemblablement la plus enviable des morts. Ce n'est pas là une tentative de minimisation de l'importance de la mort sur le champ de bataille, comme s'il était question de laisser opérer un système de tuerie de masse brutalement efficace et semblable à un abattoir ; il s'agirait plutôt d'un désir de mettre fin aux hostilités le plus rapidement possible sans douleur ni souffrances inutiles. Comme l'a écrit Paul Scharre sur la base de ses expériences personnelles de la guerre, il semble ridicule d'insister sur le fait que la mort laissée aux « mains » d'une machine serait en quelque sorte moins digne que les autres manières dont on peut trouver la mort dans la guerre moderne.

Au lieu de se préoccuper d'une éventuelle « dignité trouvée dans la mort » (étant donné qu'on ne peut jamais être sûr de mourir dignement), il est nécessaire de se pencher sur une réduction des souffrances causées par la guerre. En cela, les systèmes d'armes autonomes représentent une

---

69. Scharre 2018, 288.
70. Si tant est qu'il soit possible de formuler une telle espérance dans le combat.

solution possible. Comme j'en ferai état dans la partie suivante de ce travail, l'objectif premier dans la guerre devrait consister à réduire douleurs et souffrances inutiles. Il faudrait concevoir des SALA programmés à cet effet. En acceptant cet état de fait, on ne peut que rejeter la revendication de Leveringhaus selon laquelle la mort par l'intervention d'un SALA est intrinsèquement indigne.

4. Le SALA, Choix Rationnel dans L'évolution de la Guerre Moderne

Limiter le nombre de morts de non-combattants et de civils sur le champ de bataille devrait être l'objectif de toute force morale intègre. Le DHI exige des armées de tous les états souverains, qu'ils aient ou non ratifié les conventions de Genève, de prendre tout le soin et les précautions nécessaires pour ne pas tuer ou blesser des catégories de personnes protégées par les dispositions générales du droit humanitaire, ni endommager ou détruire inutilement des biens meubles et immeubles (en particulier des catégories de biens protégés par convention). C'est dans ce but donné que les forces militaires du monde entier ont voulu concevoir des « armes intelligentes ». Et il faut considérer les systèmes d'armes autonomes comme la prochaine étape logique de ces armes intelligentes, car ils ont au moins un double avantage par rapport aux « armes aveugles » : 1) ils peuvent être dirigés vers une cible spécifique (souvent avec des marges d'erreur de quelques mètres seulement) et 2) leur emploi est relativement économique. Or, ces deux avantages participent d'une volonté de limiter au maximum les dommages collatéraux inutiles. En ciblant une zone avec une marge d'erreur minimale, il est possible d'employer un nombre limité d'armes pour neutraliser une menace, ce qui limite l'exposition au danger des civils et des infrastructures. Ce calcul s'aligne sur l'architecture fondamentale du logiciel qu'Arkin exhorte les chercheurs et développeurs à inclure dans leur conception des SALA modernes. [71] Cette nouvelle programmation réduirait au strict minimum les « massacres sur le champ de bataille » et les dégâts collatéraux. D'autre part, l'emploi des armes intelligentes est avantageux économiquement parlant par rapport à l'emploi des armes simples. Cela peut sembler contraire au bon sens, car les armes intelligentes coûtent souvent des centaines de milliers, voire des millions de dollars.

---

71. A+B+C+D= massacre sur le champ de bataille. A= combattants supposés, B = Forces amies non escomptées, C= Non-combattants supposés, et D= Non-combattants non escomptés. Le but consiste à optimiser le groupe A, à éliminer les groupes B & C, à s'assurer que le groupe D compte aussi peu d'effectifs que possible (Arkin 2009, 128)

Le raisonnement qui préside à cette logique est le suivant : s'il est possible d'accomplir une mission avec peu d'armes (quoique leur coût individuel puisse être supérieur) qu'avec de nombreuses munitions « classiques » relativement bon marché (mais qui dans l'ensemble peuvent coûter plus cher qu'une arme intelligente), il est logiquement plus avantageux d'avoir recours à une arme intelligente. S'il est possible de ne déployer qu'un seul missile guidé dans le but d'éliminer un bunker très surveillé à un endroit stratégique, action qui aurait auparavant nécessité l'emploi de deux cents bombes aveugles, il est clair qu'il faudra privilégier l'emploi d'un seul missile guidé intelligent. S'il était question d'employer des missiles et des bombes larguées, on pourrait alors considérer que si un SALA peut faire le travail de dix soldats humains, il est économiquement plus viable d'utiliser uniquement ce système d'armes. Si grâce aux SALA les armées peuvent maîtriser leurs coûts tout en limitant les souffrances des non-combattants, il y a de bonnes raisons de croire que la voie à suivre dans la guerre moderne passera par le développement et l'utilisation de ces systèmes.

Arkin, parmi tant d'autres, croit que l'utilisation des SALA (et plus généralement de l'AI) sur le champ de bataille pourrait être la voie morale à suivre en raison d'un ensemble de caractéristiques inhérentes à leur nature. Premièrement, un SALA peut aussi être employé de manière convention-nelle. [72] La machine doit alors être programmée par défaut pour mener une action non létale, car contrairement aux humains, elle n'a aucun instinct de conservation. [73] N'étant caractérisé par aucun des instincts humains de survie et de protection, un SALA peut prendre des mesures non létales audacieuses (comme sortir de la zone dangereuse dont un humain ne pourrait pas s'échapper) ou se sacrifier en vertu du succès sa mission en créant une diversion pour sauver son unité. Un SALA sera également à l'abri d'illusions de la perception (brouillard émotionnel et prophéties auto-réalisatrices) pouvant occasionner des troubles du jugement chez les agents humains. [74] Il arrive souvent que des crimes de guerre soient commis dans le feu de l'action alors que les émotions sont vives et que le jugement est assombri par la peur ou la colère. Selon les termes de J Glenn Gray, un soldat « devi-ent un combattant, un homme devient enragé » [75]. Un SALA dépourvu d'émotions fortes, selon une conception logicielle morale et logique, ne

---

72. Arkin 2009, 29
73. Ibid, 29
74. Arkin 2009, 30.
75. Gray 1959, 27.

serait pas esclave de la peur ou de la colère, ni ne répondrait par l'agression à la destruction d'un autre SALA ou à la mort d'un membre de son unité. Il pourrait en soi faire un meilleur agent éthique et moral que les humains dans la bataille. Dans la même veine, Arkin écrit : « Je ne crois pas qu'un système autonome sans pilote puisse agir de manière parfaitement éthique sur le champ de bataille, mais je suis convaincu qu'il se comportera de façon plus éthique que les soldats humains n'en sont capables. »[76]

Si, comme le soutient Arkin, il est possible d'inclure à la conception d'un SALA la capacité d'agir à la fois de façon éthique et morale, au moins à égalité avec les soldats humains, il est alors évident que la création d'un tel système est un choix rationnel. De même, s'il est prouvé qu'un SALA peut avoir des réactions au moins aussi justes, éthiquement et moralement, que les meilleurs soldats dans la bataille, il est alors certain qu'il y a une obligation morale à la conception d'un système d'arme de ce type. Cet équipement limiterait en grande partie le nombre de soldats exposés au danger, même s'il faut reconnaître que des systèmes d'armement ne peuvent pas remplacer tous les humains. Si un système autonome est capable d'emprunter un itinéraire semé d'engins explosifs improvisés afin de livrer une cargaison importante, et ceci sans risquer la vie des chauffeurs, on est moralement obligé de recourir à ce système. En choisissant de ne pas privilégier cette solution alors que la technologie nécessaire est à disposition, on agit en fait de manière immorale. De plus, si un SALA peut prendre des décisions plus justes, d'un point de vue éthique et moral, que les humains sur le champ de bataille, on est alors contraint de déployer ce type de système. Enfin, si un système regroupant toutes ces caractéristiques (prise de décisions moralement et éthiquement plus justes que celles des agents humains, reconnaissance précise des cibles, frappes chirurgicales pour empêcher la destruction totale des cibles, réduction des dégâts collatéraux) peut être conçu et mis à disposition, on est moralement obligé en tant que chef militaire de déployer ce type de dispositif. Toutefois, son déploiement ne saurait exempter les chefs militaires (de rang probablement plus élevé que les commandants de compagnie et de bataillon[77]) du poids moral lié au fait d'ôter la vie, ni ne

---

76. Arkin 2009, 31.
77. Au sein de l'armée américaine, la compagnie est la plus petite unité ayant un chef désigné (bien qu'il existe de plus petites unités appelées détachements, mais il y a des exceptions à la règle). L'effectif d'une compagnie peut aller de 50 à 300 soldats. La compagnie est le niveau de base de l'action de terrain que l'on investit d'un leadership et de responsabilités. Une compagnie est commandée par un Capitaine (O-3) qui, s'il ne jouit d'aucune expérience préalable en tant que soldat, a en général de 4 à 6 ans de service.

pourrait les exonérer de la responsabilité des dégâts collatéraux excessifs en découlant. [78] De fait, comme l'a mentionné Arkin, il est peu probable qu'en pratique, même avec le concours de la technologie de pointe, il soit possible d'éviter totalement les dégâts collatéraux. Pourtant, en tant que chef militaire, on reste moralement obligé de déployer un SALA qui pourrait prendre des décisions moralement plus justes que celles des humains qui, autrement, feraient usage de la force létale.

Telle est la ligne de conduite la plus rationnelle en vertu du développement et du déploiement d'un système d'armes qui limite les massacres sur le champ de bataille. Ce point de vue n'assainit en rien la guerre, car il y aura toujours des combattants légitimes qui trouveront la mort et, comme le dit Leveringhaus, « l'ennemi, en tant que cible légitime, ne prétend pas demander sa grâce aux soldats attaquants. [79]

5. Proposition d'un Schéma de Réglementation des SALA

Au cours de ce mémoire, on a présenté en premier lieu les arguments les plus convaincants contre l'utilisation des SALA sur le champ de bataille de demain. Ensuite, on a évoqué les sources de l'obligation morale liée au déploiement de ce type d'armement. À ce point de notre travail, ces réflexions font ressortir la nécessité d'envisager l'élaboration d'un cadre théorique de gouvernance destiné à réglementer la conception et le déploiement de ces systèmes d'armement au niveau international. Comme on l'a évoqué précédemment, il n'existe aucune loi inscrite dans le DHI actuel dont le but spécifique serait d'encadrer la conception et le déploiement des SALA. La dernière partie de ce travail se veut comme un point de départ aux débats concernant un potentiel cadre juridique, trois grands sujets de préoccupation s'y rattachant. Ces trois domaines d'intérêt recouvrent les inquiétudes les plus prégnantes et les plus communes concernant ces systèmes d'armement. Sans prétendre couvrir toutes les potentialités d'utilisation des systèmes d'armes, cet exposé donne un cadre théorique suffisamment

---

Un bataillon standard comprend de 5 à 7 compagnies, ce qui constitue un regroupement comptant de 700 à 1500 soldats selon la composition et la mission de l'unité. Le bataillon fait partie de l'armée de terrain. Il est commandé par un Lieutenant-Colonel (O-5) qui a généralement de 17 à 19 ans de service.

78. Il y a une impossibilité physique à la limitation de tous les dégâts collatéraux quand des conflits armés ont lieu en zone habitée. C'est un fait admis. On a pour but de réduire ou de limiter les dommages collatéraux. Ainsi, les dégâts excessifs peuvent être classés comme crime de guerre contrairement aux dommages accessoires.

79. Leveringhaus 2016, 10.

large pour orienter l'élaboration du droit international concernant leur emploi. Les trois domaines en question dans ce schéma théorique sont 1) les circonstances possibles de déploiement des SALA, 2) le respect du DHI actuel et futur, et 3) la mise en place d'une chaîne de responsabilité.

Tout d'abord, la question majeure est d'identifier les circonstances possibles dans lesquelles déployer ces systèmes d'armement. À ce sujet, le DHI devrait adopter une législation stipulant qu'aucun SALA ne peut être déployé par une armée ou une nation sans que des experts techniques aient pu en homologuer la programmation de fonctionnement et s'assurer que cette dernière est en conformité avec le DHI. De plus, tout chef militaire déployant un système d'armement non homologué devrait être passible de sanctions, que le système ait ou non causé des crimes de guerre. Une telle exigence ne saurait être étrangère aux armées tenues de suivre le même type de processus de certification pour s'assurer que les systèmes d'armes standard ou conventionnels (un char, par exemple) sont conçus et fonctionnent dans le respect de la législation les gouvernant. Une fois la certification obtenue, l'armée ou la nation en question pourrait mettre en place un protocole comprenant deux parties distinctes et également importantes afin de décider des circonstances 1) de l'utilisation de la force non létale vs. la force létale (déploiement tactique vs. déploiement opérationnel) et 2) du déploiement un SALA (déploiement stratégique). Les deux composantes de ce protocole seront évoquées ci-après.

La décision d'avoir recours à un SALA dans une situation tactique signifie simplement que le chef militaire choisit de déployer un système d'arme dans le cadre d'une mission donnée. Ces commandants mènent des opérations de « niveau tactique », c'est-à-dire qu'ils ont la liberté de décider sur le terrain de l'emploi direct des troupes et des armes nécessaires pour accomplir une mission ou suivre une directive donnée. Ainsi, un commandant est investi de l'autorité légitime « appropriée » pour avaliser la décision d'employer un véhicule aérien sans pilote appartenant à sa compagnie afin d'élargir son espace visuel. En revanche, il n'aura pas le pouvoir de disposer de matériel de niveau stratégique (tel un satellite) afin d'accomplir sa mission. Pour en revenir au SALA, l'autorité décisionnaire et la responsabilité liées à l'emploi de ces systèmes devrait être confiée à un chef militaire de niveau tactique (c'est-à-dire jusqu'au rang de commandant de brigade, qui est à la tête d'environ 5000 soldats). Par exemple, si un commandant de compagnie est chargé de sécuriser un village, sa décision, prise en consultation avec des ordres de gradés supérieurs, doit être immédiate quant à l'emploi d'une arme ou d'une tactique spécifique. Il en va de même pour l'emploi d'un

SALA. De manière à contrôler efficacement l'emploi mesuré de la force, le droit humanitaire international doit spécifier que l'utilisation tactique d'un SALA sera assortie de garanties visant à limiter les dégâts collatéraux potentiels causés par leur utilisation.

Le deuxième défi concernant l'utilisation d'un SALA concerne son déploiement stratégique. Par emploi stratégique d'un SALA, on entend l'autorisation morale ou légale d'utiliser ce type d'arme dans une guerre ou un conflit donné, selon ses spécificités. Afin de répondre à cette préoccupation, il semble assez simple de légiférer pour rendre l'utilisation d'un SALA concordante avec les principes spécifiques du JWT (JSON Web Tokens, protocole d'échange numérique sécurisé de renseignements) et du DHI, en se posant la question de savoir si le déploiement d'un SALA pourrait être plus susceptible de causer des dégâts collatéraux excessifs lors d'un déploiement dans un théâtre d'opération X plutôt que dans un théâtre d'opération Y. Par exemple, selon le niveau de perfectionnement technologique au moment de la frappe, il peut être contraire à l'éthique de déployer un SALA dans une zone de combat fortement urbanisée (par exemple, Singapour) par rapport à une zone de combat plus éloignée ou rurale (par exemple, la steppe russe). Cette législation devrait mentionner une interdiction applicable à toute nation ou armée de déployer un SALA dans une zone de combat où la probabilité de dommages collatéraux excessifs résultant de son utilisation est plus élevée que celle concernant les dégâts provoqués par l'envoi de troupes. Par exemple, si l'emploi même d'un SALA dans une zone donnée était susceptible d'entraîner un recours aveugle à la force, la machine (ou un humain) ayant eu des difficultés à distinguer les combattants des non-combattants, l'emploi du SALA constituerait alors un crime de guerre, en marge de toute erreur de reconnaissance des combattants légitimes par le système. Il n'y a aucune raison de penser qu'il ne pourrait y avoir d'examen de responsabilité lorsqu'un SALA est à l'origine d'une erreur, bien que persistent des doutes possibles quant à l'agent coupable de l'incident. En effet, si un soldat est à l'origine d'une erreur (entraînant potentiellement un crime de guerre), il doit pouvoir être tenu responsable des conséquences de même que sa chaîne de commandement.[80]

Par conséquent, le deuxième grand domaine de réglementation devrait interdire l'emploi d'un SALA qui, de par sa conception même, serait inca-

---

80. Ce serait présumer d'une erreur délibérée ou provoquée par négligence, détail qui a peu d'importance à ce point donné de notre argumentation puisqu'il ne défie pas sa logique.

pable d'adhérer aux principes de base du JWT ainsi que du DHI dans ses évolutions actuelles ou futures. Comme cela a été dit précédemment, il serait fondamentalement erroné, tant du point de vue moral que juridique d'employer un système ne pouvant être tenu pour responsable de ses actions de par la nature de sa programmation. Il est peu probable de toute manière qu'un système d'armes d'ancienne génération dispose d'un fichier mémoire pouvant faire l'objet d'une vérification de toutes les actions du SALA ; selon toute probabilité, la réponse initiale par défaut d'un système de ce type consisterait en une action létale. Bien qu'il ne soit pas du ressort du DHI de choisir les technologies pouvant ou non être employées dans la guerre, un SALA muni d'un gouverneur éthique, dans la veine de celui que décrit Arkin, serait un excellent exemple de modèle en mesure de se conformer à cette réglementation théorique. Tout système de ce type pouvant adhérer à l'esprit de la réglementation, et donc au JWT et au DHI, devrait être autorisé.

Le dernier domaine d'intérêt lié à cette future modification du DHI est la nécessité de créer une chaîne de responsabilité bien établie. Dans ce but, le DHI devrait prévoir qu'un chef militaire ou un leader politique assume la responsabilité morale et juridique de la décision stratégique de déploiement d'un SALA. La loi devrait également stipuler qu'au niveau tactique un chef militaire ayant recours à ce type d'arme est à la fois moralement et légalement responsable des actions opérées ou non par le système. Certains opposants à ces réglementations dénonceront la contrainte qu'elles posent aux chefs militaires. Je réponds à cela que ces lois sont un poids nécessaire afin d'empêcher la libre utilisation des systèmes d'arme dans des situations susceptibles d'aller à l'encontre du JWT, du DHI ou d'augmenter considérablement les dommages collatéraux. Une telle réglementation aurait pour effet positif de réserver l'utilisation des SALA uniquement aux situations dans lesquelles les résultats sont raisonnablement bien contrôlés ou aux situations dans lesquelles la probabilité de dommages collatéraux est faible. (Par exemple, la réglementation peut décourager l'utilisation des SALA dans des lieux urbains densément peuplés, mais peut encourager son utilisation dans des zones peu densément peuplées telles que la haute mer).

Il y a un avantage évident à l'élaboration d'un droit international encadrant la moralisation de la conception et de l'usage des SALA, mais ce dispositif législatif doit aussi inclure un mécanisme pour assurer la conformité à ses réglementations. Ce mécanisme pourrait être semblable à la CPI déjà existante ou prendre une autre forme de mise en application internationale. Les réglementations légales envisagées plus haut ne dépendent d'aucune méthode spécifique d'application et sont compatibles avec un mécanisme visant à inciter les nations à concevoir leurs SALA en conformité avec la loi. Il ne m'appartient pas de décider du mode de fonctionnement de ce mécanisme, mais seulement de présenter un plaidoyer en faveur d'un système capable de limiter les crimes de guerre envisagés avant qu'ils ne soient commis.

6. Conclusion

Le progrès humain est analogue à une machine à mouvement perpétuel. Sans commencement définitif et sans fin apparente, la marche vers le progrès est inexorable. Il en est de même pour le développement de moyens plus efficaces de s'entretuer. Dès les premiers temps de l'existence humaine, depuis le moment où l'homme s'est rendu compte que l'atlatl, ingénieux propulseur à crochet, lui permettait de propulser sa lance plus loin que son adversaire, jusqu'à nos jours où les avancées modernes dans le domaine de l'intelligence artificielle vont toujours plus loin, l'humanité fait preuve du désir irrépressible de trouver des armes sans cesse plus performantes. Le moment historique est maintenant venu d'adopter un cadre réglementaire qui façonnera la manière dont les humains, en tant qu'espèce, entendent concevoir et déployer la future génération des systèmes d'armes.

Dans ce mémoire ont été présentés deux des arguments les plus convaincants contre l'utilisation des systèmes d'armes autonomes sous la forme des arguments dits « de la responsabilité » et « de l'agent responsable ». Bien qu'ils soient convaincants, du moins en partie, aucun de ces deux arguments ne fournit de motifs suffisants individuellement ou collectivement pour faire pencher la balance vers une interdiction pure et simple de l'utilisation de cette technologie émergente. Au contraire, ces arguments parmi d'autres fournissent une motivation pour exiger une réglementation internationale en vertu d'une conception et d'un déploiement moralement viables de ces systèmes. Au cours de ce travail, j'ai également soutenu que la conception et le déploiement encadrés d'un système d'armes autonome est un choix rationnel, si tant est que le fonctionnement des SALA peut répondre à des normes morales strictes. Le but en est d'imposer des limites à l'horreur du champ de bataille. Comme l'a dit un jour le général Sherman « la guerre est un enfer », mais il faut faire au mieux pour rendre cet enfer aussi tolérable que possible.

Un des instincts primaires des humains est la peur de l'inconnu. Les films de science-fiction n'ont pas peu fait pour attiser les angoisses selon lesquelles, en continuant sur la voie des améliorations technologiques, les robots se libèreront du joug de leur oppression et se retourneront contre leurs maîtres. Cette crainte, bien qu'elle soit très répandue, ne peut s'imposer comme base solide à des décisions morales ou juridiques.

Remerciements

Je tiens à rendre hommage au corps enseignant et au personnel du département de Philosophie, en particulier au Dr. Andrew Altman et au Dr. Andrew I. Cohen ; sans votre présence, je ne serais pas venu à bout de ce travail. Je voudrais également remercier les professeurs avec qui j'ai eu l'honneur de suivre des cours ; merci de m'avoir épaulé. Je veux aussi remercier ceux qui, au sein de l'armée américaine, ont su déceler mon potentiel et m'ont ainsi accordé leur confiance. Merci à tous.

Références

Arkin, Ronald. *Governing Lethal Behavior in Autonomous Systems.* Boca Raton: Chapman and Hall Imprint (Taylor and Francis Group), 2009.

Army Doctrine Reference Publication. "6-22 Army Leadership." *Army Doctrine Reference Publications* (2012). https://usacac.army.mil/sites/default/files/misc/doctrine/cdg/cdg_resources/manuals/adrp/adrp6_22_new.pdf.

Boyd, John. *A Discourse on Winning and Losing.* Maxwell Air Force Base: Air University Press, 2018.

Campaign to Stop Killer Robots. "About Us." Accessed 25 July 2018. https://www.stopkillerrobots.org/about/.

Department of Defense. "Directive 3000.09-Autonomy in Weapon Systems." *Office of the Deputy Secretary of Defense* (November 2012). http://www.esd.whs.mil/Portals/54/Documents/DD/issuances/dodd/300009p.pdf.

In re Yamashita 327 U.S. 1 [1946] 61 (United States Supreme Court). https://supreme.justia.com/cases/federal/us/327/1/.

Government of China. "Group of Governmental Experts of the High Contracting Parties to the Convention on Prohibitions or Restrictions of the Use of Certain Conventional Weapons which may be Deemed to be Excessively Injurious or to have Indiscriminate Effects." *Convention on Certain Conventional Weapons—Position Paper* (April 2018). https://www.unog.ch/80256EDD006B8954/(httpAssets)/DD1551E60648CEBBC125808A005954FA/$file/China's+Position+Paper.pdf.

Gray, J. Glenn. *Warriors: Reflections of Men in Battle.* New York: Harcourt, Brace and Company, 1959.

International Criminal Court. "Rome Statute." Article 8(2)(b)(xx) (1998). https://www.icc-cpi.int/nr/rdonlyres/ea9aeff7-5752-4f84-be94-0a655eb30e16/0/rome_statute_english.pdf.

Leveringhaus, Alex. "What's so Bad about Killer Robots." *Journal of Applied Philosophy*, (March 2016). DOI: 10.1111/japp.12200.

McMahan, Jeff. *Killing in War.* Oxford: Oxford University Press, 2011.

Military Leadership Diversity Commission. "Outreach & Recruiting." *United States Department of Defense*. November 2009. https://diversity.defense.gov/Portals/51/ Documents/Resources/Commission/docs/Issue%20Papers/Paper%2002%20 -%20Requirements%20and%20Demographic%20Profile%20of%20Eligible%20 Population.pdf.

Papal Encyclicals Online. "The Second Council of the Lateran- 1139 A.D." Accessed 18 January 2019. http://www.papalencyclicals.net/councils/ecum10.htm.

Program Executive Office- Missiles & Space. "Counter-Rocket, Artillery, Mortar (C-RAM)." Accessed September 1. 2018. https://missiledefenseadvocacy.org/ defense-systems/counter-rocket-artillery-mortar-c-ram/.

Raytheon. "Phalanx Close-In Weapon System." Accessed 15 August 2018. https:// www.raytheon.com/capabilities/products/phalanx.

Scharre, Paul. *Army of None: Autonomous Weapons and the Future of War*. New York: W. W. Norton & Company, 2018.

Sparrow, Robert. "Killer Robots." *Journal of Applied Philosophy*, vol. 24, no. 1 (2007):62–71. DOI: 10.1111/j.1468-5930.2007.00346.x.

United Nations Institute for Disarmament Research. "The Weaponization of Increasingly Autonomous Technologies: Concerns, Characteristics and Definitional Approaches." *UNIDIR Resources*, no. 6 (2017): 1–33. http://www.unidir.org/files/ publications/pdfs/the-weaponization-of-increasingly-autonomous-technologies-concerns-characteristics-and-definitional-approaches-en-689.pdf.

United Nations Office for Disarmament Affairs. "Perspectives on Lethal Autonomous Weapon Systems." *UNODA Occasional Papers*, no. 30 (November 2017): 1–61. www.un.org/disarmament.

US Army Acquisition Support Center. "Excalibur Precision 155MM Projectiles." Accessed 25 July 2018. https://asc.army.mil/web/portfolio-item/ammo-excal-ibur-xm982-m982-and-m982a1-precision-guided-extended-range-projectile/.

Empathy and *Jus in bello*

Kevin Cutright
Lieutenant Colonel, US Army

I. The Neglect of Right Intention

The principle of right intention is "the appropriate disposition of those [individuals] fighting wars" toward a just and lasting peace.[1] Early just war theorists emphasized right intention as essential to the moral warrant for war and to soldiers' conduct in it.[2] The principle is meant to serve as a correction for statesmen or soldiers who may have a justified cause for war, but use that cause merely as a screen for other purposes. As modern thinkers drew brighter lines between jus ad bellum and jus in bello (and eventually jus post bellum), right intention only appeared in the ad bellum category. Presumably, it could still influence in bello considerations by its presence in the deliberations precipitating war. However, right intention received circumspect attention in modern discussions of jus ad bellum.[3] Some scholars have since suggested that right intention is redundant or impossible to corroborate and should be subsumed under the principle of just cause.[4]

Others have focused on laws and rules to externally restrain politicians and soldiers, shifting away from intentions and virtues that might internally restrain them.[5] A. J. Coates contrasts this trend toward a "rule-based

---

1. Joseph Capizzi, *Politics, Justice, and War: Christian Governance and the Ethics of Warfare* (Oxford: Oxford University Press, 2015), 108–109.
2. Augustine was the first advocate for right intention; see *The City of God*, trans. R. Ryson (Cambridge: Cambridge University Press, 1998). Aquinas lists right intention as one of his three principles governing war; see *Summa theologiae* II–II q. 40 art. 1 and q. 64 art. 3.
3. Daniel Bell marks the beginning of this dim view with Hugo Grotius; see Just War as Christian Discipleship: Recentering the Tradition in the Church Rather Than the State (Grand Rapids, MI: Brazos Press, 2009), 56–58.
4. As one prominent example, see Jeff McMahan, "Just Cause for War," Ethics and International Affairs 9:3, 1–21. For arguments against the dismissal of right intention, see Capizzi 2015, 71–126; Todd Burkhardt, Just War and Human Rights: Fighting with Right Intention (Albany, NY: SUNY Press, 2017); and Bell 2009, 153–158.
5. For a summary of this trend, see Brian Orend, *The Morality of War* (Toronto: Broadview Press, 2006), 17–23.

approach" with a more traditional "character-based approach."[6] While he recognizes merits in both, he finds in the rule-based approach an antagonism toward the character-based approach. The rule-based approach prioritizes deliberative reflection about moral demands at the exclusion of dispositional considerations:

> 'Reflective' morality is not just neglectful of, or indifferent towards, the idea of a moral life centred on moral dispositions, it is opposed to it on principle, since 'the mind *without disposition* is alone the spring of "rational" judgement and "rational" conduct.' Moral conduct is 'rational' in the narrowly conceived sense of 'conduct springing from an antecedent process of "reasoning,"' excluding conduct which has its source in 'the unexamined authority of a tradition, a custom or a habit of behavior.' From a reflective standpoint, the communal and habitual aspects of traditional morality are seen less as sources of moral empower-ment than as fundamental obstacles to the achievement of moral autonomy. Moral progress is dependent upon the emancipation of the rational individual from the heteronomous influences of traditional morality.[7]

The premodern principle of right intention has largely been set aside as one of these questionable dispositions of traditional morality, or as irrelevant to morality (as are all intentions in consequentialist ethics), or has been redefined in terms of a rule (as in deontological ethics). As a result, right intention, understood as a disposition of character, is virtually absent in contemporary scholarship on *jus in bello*.

The Impact of this Neglect

A rule-based approach to morality has made valuable contributions to better meeting moral demands, such as the codification of moral prin-ciples in international law.[8] Also, the reflection entailed by a rule-based approach is vital to a person's moral well-being, arguably demonstrated by the lack of reflection involved in some cases of moral injury among

---

6. A. J. Coates, *The Ethics of War*, 2nd ed. (Manchester, UK: Manchester University Press, 2016), 1–18.
7. Coates 2016, 12. He quotes Michael Oakeshott, *Rationalism in Politics* (London: Methuen, 1962) 87, 84–85.
8. Brian Orend, *The Morality of War* (Toronto: Broadview Press, 2006), 20–23.

soldiers.[9] However, the rise of a rule-based framework at the exclusion of a character-based approach has resulted in three shortcomings. First, it fosters a hollow "checklist" technique in military ethics.[10]

A checklist of moral rules can never accommodate the unanticipated and fast-developing circumstances that soldiers face, nor provide the forward-looking intention that soldiers require to navigate those circumstances.[11] As Coates observes, the "ubiquity of the unforeseen or unforeseeable [in war] impedes reflection and strengthens the claims of traditional morality."[12] Soldiers require a disposition toward a just and lasting peace (which, undoubtedly, implies a complementary, reflective understanding of that peace) to properly fulfill their duties. Extrinsic restraint cannot effectively replace intrinsic restraint.[13]

Secondly, an exclusive focus on rules produces an overly bureaucratic mindset among soldiers. They come to resemble Alasdair MacIntyre's bureaucratic manager, who "treats ends as given, as outside his scope..."[14] Instead of an ends-oriented rationality, this manager applies a bureaucratic "rationality of matching means to ends economically and efficiently," considering the ends themselves to be "predetermined."[15] There is little emphasis in military doctrine, training, or professional education for a genuine understanding of what killing in war is meant to promote. The emphasis is on rules that ought to be followed.[16] The division between *jus*

---

9. David Wood observes: "The US military has spent years and fortunes perfecting the most realistic and thorough combat training in the world. But in preparing young Americans for war, it has failed in one glaring aspect. Those we send to war are never trained to anticipate the moral quandaries of killing that they will face; they are given no opportunity or encouragement to think about or to discuss what makes some killings moral and others a sin or even illegal" (*What Have We Done: The Moral Injury of our Longest Wars,* [New York: Hachette Book Group 2016], ch. 11 [digital edition]).

10. Orend 2006, 105; Bell 2009, 8.

11. Bell 2009, 73–88.

12. Coates 2016, 14.

13. In this regard, the modern rule-based approach to morality shares the deficiency many have leveled at the Catholic manualist tradition in its attempt to codify morality. My thanks to Luis Pinto de Sa for this connection.

14. Alasdair MacIntyre, *After Virtue: A Study in Moral Theory,* 3rd ed. (Notre Dame: University of Notre Dame Press, 2007), 30.

15. Ibid., 25.

16. There are some exceptions to this general criticism: the service academies all mandate a core course in ethics, which includes several lessons devoted to the just war tradition. The Reserve Officer Training Corps (ROTC) program at college campuses, which provide the majority of commissioned officers, requires a few hours of instruction in military ethics that also move beyond the topic of rules to follow (barely). These commissioned officers are a small, though authoritative, minority within the larger military population. The

ad bellum and *jus in bello* (war's ends and war's means) can further reinforce this bureaucratic rationality, since the *ad bellum* issues are ultimately the responsibility of political leaders. Add in the US military's deference to civilian authority (appropriate as it is), and the analytical division of moral categories can deepen to a disturbing compartmentalization that seemingly absolves soldiers of an obligation to understand the moral underpinnings of their service. Soldiers are commonly seen, by themselves as well as others, as virtually automatons instead of moral agents.

Thirdly, a strictly rule-based moral framework is deficient because reasoning alone does not prompt action but requires a corresponding affective commitment to principles or values that lead to right action. "Reflective morality puts its faith in the rule. It neglects the fundamental issue of will and motivation by assuming (wrongly) the self-motivating power of reason."[17] This fact is especially pertinent given the contrary affective reactions that persons have in stressful situations like war. Traditional morality, with its focus on character traits instead of solely intellectual reflection, "acknowledges that, to be effective, moral judgements require the support of moral dispositions, feelings and inclinations."[18] It is, in this regard, more apt for the challenges of war. The principle of right intention emphasizes the *character* required for the pursuit of justice, not the *state of affairs* required to realize justice (as does the principle of just cause). Thus, right intention is an indispensable component of *jus in bello*.

A Worse Intention

The checklist, the bureaucratic mindset, and the myth of reason alone prompting action all set the conditions for a thoroughgoing disposition to develop among many soldiers (and, indirectly, many civilians) that their essential purpose is to kill—killing is their raison d'etre. The lethal act is not considered a regrettable, though necessary, task that is subordinate to the goal of a just and lasting peace. Instead, the act fills the void in military culture left by the absence of right intention as a guiding principle. It is a confusion of task and purpose. If there is no cultivation of a disposition toward a just peace, then there will be a disposition toward something else;

---

enlisted majority of service members receive the least instruction in military ethics. I draw these facts from my own experience, but they are also corroborated by Burkhardt 2017, 37–38.

17. Coates 2016, 15.

18. Ibid.

a disposition-less soldier is an impossibility. In the worst case, a disposition forms toward killing for its own sake, involving a kind of dark-hearted relish for it. More often, and only marginally better, is a disposition toward a "negative peace," the kind established by eliminating the enemy.[19] This is the aim that the ancient historian Tacitus had in mind when he noted "where [empires] make a desert, they call it peace."[20]

This negative peace may be legitimate in extreme cases of aggressors who are fanatically committed to the elimination of others. However, soldiers (and, again, civilians) should not be *disposed* to this peace, but only settle for it when these circumstances arise. Their disposition should remain toward a peace involving a reconciliatory coexistence within an international community, a harmony between political bodies based on justice, instead of toward an absence of conflict because only one political body remains standing. Even a softer version of this negative peace, in which adversaries are subjugated instead of outright killed, rarely meets the standards of justice and should, therefore, rarely be taken up as the peace to aim for. Besides being unjust, such a peace will rarely last: "The peace of subdued men is not genuine peace, but a peace marked by profound instability..."[21]

When soldiers understand peace only negatively, they elevate killing too prominently. Killing is treated casually and more efficaciously than it really is, especially when professional norms promote an application of moral principles with the insufficient depth of a legalistic checklist, the mechanical efficiency of a bureaucracy, and the detached indifference of an automaton. A sobering example is the Vietnam War, with political and military leaders emphasizing quantifiable metrics of progress, chiefly the notorious body count.[22] More recently, in a presidential election debate of 2015, candidate Mike Huckabee commented, "The purpose of the military is to kill people and break things."[23] While possibly said more for rhetorical

---

19. Coates 2016, 293; Capizzi 2015, 7.
20. Publius Cornelius Tacitus, *The Works of Tacitus: The Oxford Translation, Revised with Notes*, Vol. 2 (London: Bell and Daldy, 1872), 372.
21. Capizzi 2015, 9.
22. Robert McNamara transferred his highly quantitative approach from the car industry to his new role as Secretary of Defense (serving 1961–1968). However, a few years into the Vietnam conflict, he privately expressed doubts to President Johnson about its suitability. It is an insider's critique that historians have revealed relatively recently, due in part to the recent declassification of material. See Ken Burns and Lynne Novick, "The Vietnam War," Florentine Films and WETA (2017), episode 6; and Errol Morris, "The Fog of War: Eleven Lessons from the Life of Robert S. McNamara," Sony Pictures Classics (2003).
23. Janell Ross, "Mike Huckabee Says the Military's Job Is to 'Kill People and Break

effect than plain truth, the sound bite still sparked a public discussion that reveals the disposition of many soldiers toward merely a negative peace and the killing entailed by it.[24] Another example: Admiral Michael Mullen, as chairman of the Joint Chiefs of Staff in 2008, advised members of Congress that "We can't kill our way to victory" in Afghanistan.[25] Two retired military officers argued that Mullen was wrong, that soldiers needed to be free of the "timidity" behind Mullen's comment in order to "act with the necessary savagery and purposefulness to destroy…Islamic terrorists worldwide."[26] In the retired officers' review of military history to support their point, making a desert and calling it peace appears to be the only state of affairs to seek with military forces. It is noteworthy that these two officers served as military lawyers in Iraq and Afghanistan, advising field commanders on rules of engagement and obligations under international law (which, they state, should be bent in favor of one's own forces).[27]

A charitable reading of their argument requires distinguishing between two notions of victory. Presumably, Mullen refers to victory in the overall effort at establishing a stable Afghan regime that can resist the unrest of violent extremist groups and provide for its citizens, such that the extremists find no safe haven or support. The two officers, however, are focused on tactical victory in combat. What is more, they seem to define victory at any scale in terms of tactical conflict. The stance of these officers reveals an underlying assumption that international relations, generally, and the wars those relations sometimes generate, are always zero-sum games. While moments of actual combat qualify, it is important to never lose sight of the context outside of those violent clashes, where another's gain is not necessarily one's own loss, and where something better than a negative peace is possible. Where this better peace is an option, we are morally and prudentially obliged to pursue it. This obligation is what is meant by right

Things.' Well, Not Quite," *The Washington Post*, 7 August 2015.

24. For a sample of the debate, see Matt Cavanaugh, "The Military's Purpose is Not to Kill People and Break Things," War on the Rocks, 26 August 2015; Jim Gourley, "The military's purpose isn't to break things and kill people, but it should be," *Foreign Policy* (24 September 2015).

25. CNN Politics, "Troops alone will not yield victory in Afghanistan," CNN.com, 10 September 2008.

26. David Bolgiano, John Taylor, "Can't Kill Enough to Win? Think Again," *Proceedings Magazine*, Vol. 143/12/1,378 (US Naval Institute, December 2017). For one dissenting opinion, see Adam Weinstein, "No, We Can't Kill Our Way to Victory Despite What 2 Misguided Lieutenant Colonels Might Think," *Task and Purpose* (8 December 2017).

27. Bolgiano, Taylor 2017.

intention. It is a disposition toward a positive peace, an insistence on keeping an eye on its possibility, even in the midst of concessions otherwise.[28]

A disposition toward a negative peace and its corresponding fixation
on killing is easier to maintain if enemies are considered less than human.
Subhuman adversaries, animals or insects, arguably do not warrant the
kind of restraint one grants to fellow humans, nor the same commitment
to a shared future. Besides the social influences of nationalism, racism, or
negative cultural stereotypes, the ostensible justice of one's war can prevent
one from seeing the enemy "as anything other than a criminal, and as such
subject to anything he has coming to him."[29] This crusading mentality is
one more pressure to dehumanize enemies, as well as the noncombatants
associated with them. Instead of a subhuman status of an insect, however,
the crusading mentality casts enemies as morally evil monsters.[30] Killing
becomes a central moral obligation, whatever peace it produces.

In addition, a killing intention is easier to maintain with a militaristic
view of war. If war is considered to have intrinsic value, a nobility with
no recognition of its tragedy, then the killing it entails is not regretted, but
embraced. This militaristic stance is often a coping mechanism for soldiers
confronted with the tension between the *prima facie* immorality of killing and
yet the *prima facie* duty to kill. Instead of working through this tension (which
might propel him to the principle of right intention), the soldier may dismiss
the former and settle on the latter, usually with the help of others in a similar
predicament and due to cultural forces at large. As one veteran describes it,
"Once you learn to push past immoral behavior, it becomes easier."[31]

A killing intention, dehumanization, and militarism all reinforce each
other in a military culture unanchored by a disposition to a just and lasting
peace. An analogy with surgery can help illustrate the danger of distorting

---

28. The degree and extent of this obligation varies with one's position and duties. Soldiers
in the heat of combat should not be focused on what peace terms the opposing political leaders might accommodate. They should, however, remain attentive to the possibility
of their enemy counterparts surrendering. The degree of obligation increases for those
soldiers involved not in the heat of combat, but in the cooler endeavors of determining
strategic objectives, planning the campaigns to secure those objectives, and assessing the
war's progress.
29. Capizzi 2015, 121.
30. I take these two subhuman categories, "base, as an animal or insect, or evil, as a
monster or demon," from Michael Brough, "Dehumanization of the Enemy and the Moral
Equality of Soldiers," in *Rethinking the Just War Tradition*, eds. Michael Brough, John Lango,
Harry van der Linden (Albany, NY: State University of New York Press, 2007), 160.
31. Wood 2016, ch. 1.

the soldier's overarching purpose.[32] No one wants to be the patient of a surgeon obsessed with surgery, ignoring what would actually contribute to full health. As much as the surgeon's skill with a scalpel matters, her essential purpose remains the promotion of physical well-being. She should not attempt surgery just because she has the authority and the skill to do it. She should fully understand when, and in what way, wielding her scalpel will best contribute to that health. She also must be able to adjust to unforeseen details or complications during the surgery. In the same way, soldiers must expertly wield lethal force, but must also understand the just peace that the killing act is supposed to promote, understand when lethal force may undermine it, and adjust their actions in unexpected circumstances to still bring it about. As the American general John Schofield noted in 1881, "the object and end in war is *not* 'to kill.' This is but one of the *means* necessary to that end....The object of war is to conquer an honorable, advantageous, and lasting peace."[33] When soldiers have no appreciation of this peace nor a commitment to it, as entailed by the principle of right intention, they are dangerously ill- equipped to wield lethal force wisely.

II. Reviving Right Intention

So far, I have highlighted the neglect of right intention as a principle of *jus in bello*, the resulting void that enables a killing intention to grow in its place, and the dehumanization and militarism that stems from, and reinforces, a killing intention. Empathy helps to alleviate these moral—and, importantly, practical—concerns. In this section, I aim to show empathy's resistance to dehumanization and militarism, its role in undermining a killing intention, and its contribution to a right intention. First, I will clarify what I mean by empathy.

Defining Empathy

For the term 'empathy' to warrant our attention, it must meaningfully refer to something. Scholars have applied the term to different phenomena, often in contradictory fashion, and its popular usage commonly equates it to sympathy or compassion.[34] I want to suggest that empathy's distinctive "contribution that

---

32. This comparison to surgery comes from Orend 2006, 106; and Aquinas, *Summa theologiae* II–II q. 64 a. 3.
33. John M. Schofield, "Notes on 'The Legitimate in War,'" *Journal of the Military Service Institution* 2 (1881), 1–10; as quoted by Brian Linn, *The Echo of Battle: The Army's Way of War* (Cambridge, MA: Harvard University Press, 2009), 58.
34. See Batson 2009 for an illustrative summary; for fuller introductions of the term and its history, see Stueber 2006, Coplan and Goldie 2011, Zahavi 2014, and Matravers 2017.

only it makes" is the felt characteristic of another person's experience.[35] This felt characteristic is not restricted to feelings, but includes the feel of things beyond immediate feelings, such as desires, convictions, intentions, worries, commitments—nearly any part of another's mental life, including the feel of her cognitive life (meaning how it feels to maintain a certain belief). If one's friend says, "I just voted for the candidate whom I've been campaigning for over the last several weeks," there are both cognitive and affective states associated with this experience. The friend's cognitive states of, say, believing her preferred candidate is the best one, or believing it is important to exercise one's right to vote, etc., exists concurrently with affective states of hoping for the candidate to follow through on her platform, or fretting about the candidate's chances of winning, or feeling confidence in the campaigning effort, or feeling relief that the campaigning is over, or, more importantly, a complex combination of these. Furthermore, these cognitive and affective states are mutually causative, meaning they may prompt or reinforce each other. Empathy is understanding, to some degree, how this overarching experience of voting (after campaigning) feels for one's friend, given a complex interplay of cognition and affect grounded in specific circumstances and context.[36]

Empathy is not, therefore, just assigning a generic feeling of hope or nervousness to one's friend. As Max Scheler suggests, empathy is not "simply a question of intellectually judging that somebody else is undergoing a certain experience; it is not the mere thought that this is the case..."[37] Empathy is specifically oriented on the other's experience in its phenomenality. In other words, empathy provides a limited understanding of what another experiences; not a description of that experience (which depends, among other things, on the empathizer's ability to verbalize it), but the phenomenal nature of it. As a working definition, then, I endorse Joel Smith's conception of empathy as an experiential understanding of *what* another feels or thinks, not just a propositional or theoretical understanding *that* the other feels or thinks a certain way.[38]

Empathy is thus importantly distinct from sympathy. Empathy is understanding what another thinks or feels, but it is not caring for another's

---

35. Smith 2015, 711.
36. It is important to also note that the accuracy of empathizing increases with one's knowledge about one's friend—whether she is naturally optimistic, or worrisome, etc. This acquaintance can give greater fidelity to the empathetic attempt to understand the friend's mental states.
37. As cited by Zahavi 2014, 118.
38. Smith 2015, 712–713.

wellbeing.[39] As Edmund Husserl observes, "Whereas empathy is a form of understanding, sympathy involves care and concern."[40] The two concepts are related; in fact, empathy may prompt and aid sympathetic concern, and sympathy may prompt attempts at an empathetic understanding of another. Conflating the terms is probably more common because of David Hume's and Adam Smith's usage of "sympathy" in their works on moral theory; the phenomena they describe, however, corresponds to what we now call empathy. Specifically, Hume's conception resembles the mirroring of another's emotions in lower-level empathy, while Smith's conception resembles the imaginative perspective-taking in higher-level empathy.[41] Lower-level empathy is generally considered to be subconscious, automatic, and revealing "surface" mental states of emotion and immediate intentions. Higher-level empathy is seen as conscious, voluntary, and revealing deeper or more enduring mental states, including broad intentions or the meaning behind behavior.[42] Notably, the term "empathy" did not enter the English language until a century after Hume and Smith, which makes it harder to fault them for the confusion.

Research reinforces the intuition that empathy leads to sympathy, but it also shows that it does not necessarily do so.[43] It can, in fact, inhibit sympathy toward some individuals while promoting it for others, given the ease with which we empathize with members of our own culture or other group and the difficulty we can have in empathizing with those outside of these groups. Thus, empathy can introduce a morally problematic partiality. This concern has fueled some to argue against empathy's presumed contribution to morality.[44] It also highlights the difference between empathy and sympathy.[45]

Empathy Reveals the Enemy's Moral Equality

Empathy entails a foundational solidarity with others. It is not a solidarity of opinions, perspectives, judgments, values, or feelings, but only a

---

39. Darwall 1998, 261–270.
40. As cited by Zahavi 2014, 139 (footnote 14).
41. Darwall 1998, 267; Coplan and Goldie 2011, x.
42. Coplan and Goldie 2011, xxxiii.
43. Batson 1991; Darwall 1998, 272–273.
44. Prinz 2011; Bloom 2014.
45. For more extensive discussion on the relation between empathy and sympathy, see Darwall 1998; Coplan and Goldie 2011, x–xi; Gallagher 2012, 360–362; Zahavi 2014, 115–117; Matravers 2017, 115.

solidarity of fundamental personhood. It may contribute to the former, but not necessarily so. Empathy, as an experiential understanding of another person, reveals the humanity that a soldier has in common with his enemy. Empathy humanizes others and, therefore, counters dehumanizing tendencies. Lower-level empathy grounds an intuition of the enemy's human status, something akin to sense perception. This lower-level empathy can be tuned out or interrupted, like closing one's eyes to interrupt sight, but without such action, lower-level empathy occurs automatically. Higher-level empathy builds on this intuition through cognitive processes such as imaginative perspective-taking to reveal insights about the other's experience, including elements of its narrative structure, worldview, values, and intentions. Higher-level empathy is not automatic; it must be consciously initiated. It can, however, be habituated.

As an example, consider the experience of a team of soldiers deployed to Iraq as part of a counterinsurgency campaign. They conducted a raid on the home of a former Iraqi Army colonel who had begun planning and funding the insurgent efforts around his hometown. Upon forcing their way through the front door, a crouched man rushed into the entry room. He was bent over, his hands were hidden, he was lunging forward, and then two of the four soldiers shot him and he fell to the floor. Those were the only shots fired. Thirty seconds later, the house was deemed secure and the team began rendering first aid to the fallen man. He died in front of them—and in front of his wife and young daughter, who had been found in the home and brought to the entry room. The dead man was the Iraqi colonel.[46]

That man's death remained with the soldiers who shot him. One soldier, in particular, wrestled with the loss that he caused. The chain of command agreed that the team's actions were justified, but that did not lessen the weight that the one soldier felt. The man he killed was not carrying anything in his hands. He struggled to understand why the man lunged the way that he did. Was the colonel attempting to protect his family? Was he trying to tackle the lead soldier coming through the door? Was he entering the room to investigate the loud noise? Did he simply trip as he entered to room? The soldier had a wife and a young daughter, and he could not help but wonder what would happen to this colonel's family.

This soldier's struggle is an example of the empathy that commonly occurs in war, even if it goes largely unrecognized in our theorizing about war. It

---

46. This story is drawn from my experience deployed to Iraq with the 4th Infantry Division, US Army, in 2003.

is a natural response to war's regrettable duties, yet military training is too often focused on repressing these reactions to ensure soldiers persist in their duties—better a thoughtless soldier instead of one too thoughtful. I want to resist this conclusion; either extreme is just as detrimental to good soldiering. I propose that, through military training and enculturation, this soldier interrupted his lower-level empathy for the sake of forceful actions in raiding the Iraqi colonel's house. After the forced entry, the shooting of a person who seemed threatening, and the securing of the rest of the house, the soldiers attempted to stabilize the wounded colonel. In the shift from forceful actions to assessing the immediate situation and treating the colonel, the intuition of lower-level empathy returned, particularly to the one soldier, as something received instead of suppressed. His higher-level empathy processed the intuition and expanded on it to foster an understanding of the colonel in his other roles as husband and father. In turn, this understanding spurred the soldier's empathetic understanding of the widow and daughter. In this experiential understanding, this moment of empathy, my soldier also became troubled.

The source of his disturbance was at least partly due to the dead Iraqi's more complicated status. He was no longer purely or simply an enemy combatant to be fought; he was also a dead human being to be mourned. The soldier paused over the fact that he and this colonel were both husbands, and they were both fathers of little girls. It had been easier to peremptorily consider the colonel a criminal, one who was personally responsible for this war in which the soldier found himself. The corresponding hatred for the guilty enemy made it easier to kick in the door and to pull the trigger. Now, however, this hatred had been

> ...interrupted or overridden by a more reflective understanding...the sense that the enemy soldier, though his war may be criminal, is nevertheless as blameless as oneself. Armed, he is an enemy; but he isn't *my* enemy in any specific sense; the war itself isn't a relation between persons but between political entities and their human instruments....[Like me, they find themselves] trapped in a war they didn't make. I find in them my moral equals.[47]

This notion of moral equality, of a moral innocence shared by soldiers on both sides of a war that they did not initiate, is developed further with an

---

47. Walzer 1977, 36.

empathetic thought experiment. It is expressed here in terms of a counter-insurgency situation similar to the recent effort in Iraq. As an extension of the reflective understanding above, a US soldier might ask, "What would it take for *me* to cooperate with a foreign occupying force patrolling my hometown? What behavior on their part would truly win *my* cooperation? How likely might I be to take up arms against the foreign occupying force?" These questions risk an error of projection since they involve self-oriented perspective taking, which incorporates many cultural influences that differ from the average Iraqi. However, self-oriented perspective taking can be an appropriate mode of higher- level empathy "when there is a great deal of overlap between self and other or where the situation is the type that would lead to a fairly universal response."[48] Foreign soldiers patrolling the streets of one's neighborhood prompts a similar concern for the safety of one's family, a similar patriotism, and a similar distrust of strangers from a foreign culture.

Empathy helps soldiers to recognize the moral equality of their enemies. In doing so, empathy provides a "check on a wartime inclination" to dehumanize.[49] It undermines the tendency to see enemies as lesser animals or as so evil that their humanity falls away. They are, instead, perceived as being subject to similar influences of nationalistic fervor, respect for laws of conscription, and a desire to protect their families and fellow country-men. This honesty regarding one's enemies can have two effects. First, it instills greater restraint, such that soldiers more reliably keep acts of force to only those that are genuinely necessary. Second, it lays the groundwork for a disposition toward a just and lasting peace. Moral equality serves as a "reason for returning defeated foes back to their lives, a step toward a return to normalcy and peace—for how can one punish in the enemy what one would have done oneself, if in the same situation?"[50]

Are Terrorists Morally Equal?

A crusading mentality is hard to maintain when one realizes the moral equality of an enemy soldier, but the case is different when considering the proper stance toward a terrorist. Should we empathize with a terrorist and

48. Amy Coplan, "Understanding Empathy: Its Features and Effects," in *Empathy: Philo-sophical and Psychological Perspectives*, ed. Amy Coplan and Peter Goldie (New York: Oxford University Press, 2011), 9.
49. Brough 2007, 151.
50. Brough 2007, 151. This conclusion that one would do the same as the other is not entailed by empathy but is enabled by it. Empathy proffers only understanding, not agreement.

promote this sense of moral equality with him? Is there moral equality? On the one hand, there is a similar influence of culture, recruitment efforts, propaganda, etc., to which the terrorist is subject. Further, if the terrorist is a low-ranking member of his organization, he is subject to orders from his leaders. These orders will be influential, even though they may not carry the legal endorsement and authority of an established and recognized regime. While this fact might be held against the low-ranking terrorist as shirking a proper deference to an established government, it may be that the government in question has lost its legitimacy and right to govern, or that there is no effective government in place. If subordinate enough, such that the low-ranking terrorist does not help in decisions regarding violent means or selection of targets, he may acquire a similar moral innocence to a low-ranking soldier, despite his material participation in the terrorist act. Admittedly, the act would need to be such that this low-ranking participant could not reliably identify moral features of the act (particularly the purposeful targeting of innocent persons) or be subject to relevant pressures that absolve him of culpability. Yet, if this is the case, then the title "terrorist" does not apply to him. He is morally equal to a soldier and, therefore, does not warrant the pejorative label.

A genuine terrorist, though, remains morally different from a soldier due to the nature of terrorism that spawns the title. Terrorism is the deliberate use or threat of violence against noncombatants for political impact.[51] This use of force fails to meet moral demands regarding innocent lives. The genuine terrorist, therefore, is not morally innocent like the soldier, who is bound by principles of *jus in bello* to discriminate between combatants and noncombatants and is prepared for this duty through the emphasis in law, training, and military or societal culture. The terrorist deliberately and avoidably targets innocent persons.[52] It is, therefore, much easier to maintain a crusading mentality toward the terrorist; he *is* a criminal in a way that soldiers are not.

---

51. Bruce Hoffman, *Inside Terrorism,* revised and expanded edition (New York: Columbia University Press, 2006), 26–28. See also United Nations, "Declaration on Measures to Eliminate International Terrorism," annex to UN General Assembly Resolution 49/60, "Measures to Eliminate International Terrorism" (9 December 1994).

52. This parsing between soldier and terrorist helps to reveal the ease with which soldiers can commit terroristic acts. They can deliberately fail to discriminate between combatants and noncombatants or fail to sufficiently protect noncombatants. Given their broadly political ends, these acts begin to resemble the definition of terrorism. See David Rodin's discussion of reckless or negligent force against noncombatants in "Terrorism without Intention," *Ethics* 114 (July 2004), 752–771.

Yet, there is still a diminished, or thinner, equality that a soldier shares with a terrorist.[53] It is the kind that one shares with a culpable wrongdoer, in general. It is a moral equality in human status and value, even if not in moral innocence for one's acts of force. An empathetic understanding of the terrorist underscores this thinner moral equality (as it does, more generally, with wrongdoers as a whole). This equality, like the thicker kind with enemy soldiers above, does not entail agreeing with the terrorist's worldview, moral judgments, or decisions; it merely prompts a proper account of their humanity in one's judgments, despite their own failure in this regard toward their victims.

Through its unveiling of either a thick or thin moral equality, empathy humanizes enemies and, therefore, improves soldiers' judgment. "If states and their soldiers can learn to see the enemy as someone fully human and individually morally equal, they will discern the moral landscape more clearly and avert moral disaster for both sides of the war."[54] It is hard to maintain a militaristic attitude if empathy is present. One cannot ignore the tragedy of war, but must face it, as the soldier above did in wrestling with the loss of the Iraqi colonel.

However, empathy applied selectively can interfere with good judgment. For example, empathy with the victims of aggression can spur perseverance. If taken too far or too exclusively, this perseverance will propel one into a vengeful intention, undermining any notion of moral equality. One avoids this extreme by a further moment of empathy with the aggressors.

Empathy's Relation to Killing

"To our modern mind," Shay observes, "the enemy is detestable—by definition."[55] Maintaining the humanity of the enemy is commonly considered impossible; for many it is a self-evident truth "that men cannot kill an enemy understood to be honorable and like oneself."[56] Contrary to the argument that soldiers *must* dehumanize enemies to kill them, however, there are at least some moments when they *cannot* dehumanize enemies because of intimate encounters with them. Michael Walzer offers some of these instances, drawing on veterans' memoirs in which they describe the

---

53. I take this notion of a thinner moral equality from Brough 2007, 150.
54. Brough 2007, 160.
55. Jonathan Shay, *Achilles in Vietnam: Combat Trauma and the Undoing of Character* (New York: Scribner, 1994), 103.
56. Ibid.

difficulty of firing their weapons at enemy soldiers "who look funny, who are taking a bath, holding up their pants [as they run along a trench], reveling in the sun, [or] smoking a cigarette."[57] Richard Holmes observes that the "concept of a hateful and inhuman enemy rarely survives contact with him as an individual."[58] The troubled soldier's experience above also illustrates the unavoidable empathetic moments of war. These moments are, admittedly, only brief glimpses at the humanity of individuals, glimpses that are often buried under the propaganda of the war effort and the piercing emotions of struggle and loss inherent to war. However, simply stifling these empathetic moments leads to the dangers of dehumanization, militarism, and killing as one's overarching purpose. Right intention is lost.[59] In reconciling the humanity of enemies with the duty to kill them, there must be an alternative to dehumanization, which merely tries to deny the former.[60]

Michael Brough asks this same question: "How, then, should soldiers view the killings they commit in war, and how should nations teach their soldiers to view them? Dehumanization is too costly."[61] Drawing on the research of psychologists David Grossman and Stanley Milgram, Brough concedes a necessity to distance oneself from one's target in order to kill him. This distance may take a physical form, especially as enabled by modern technologies, but it may also take an emotional form, including "social distance (which emphasizes differences in social caste), cultural distance (which accentuates racial and ethnic differences), and moral distance (which envisions

---

57. Walzer 1977, 138–143.

58. Richard Holmes, *Acts of War: The Behavior of Men in Battle* (New York: The Free Press, 1985), 368; as cited by Brough 2007, 157.

59. It also leads to the danger of moral injury, a debilitating sense of betrayal and/or guilt among veterans that is receiving increasing attention. For an introduction, see Jonathan Shay (1994); Nancy Sherman, *Afterwar: Healing the Moral Wounds of our Soldiers* (New York: Oxford University Press, 2015); and David Wood, *What Have We Done: The Moral Injury of Our Longest Wars* (New York: Little, Brown and Company, 2016).

60. The pacifist response is to deny the latter—there is never a duty to kill. While I part ways with the pacifist stance at a certain point, I share Brian Orend's concern that there can be an "embarrassing arrogance" in just war literature regarding pacifism ("A Just War Critique of Realism and Pacifism," *Journal of Philosophical Research*, Vol. XXVI [2001], 435–436). We all ought to have a pacifist commitment to nonviolent conflict resolution as a default. It is a *prima facie* commitment that even soldiers ought to maintain, understanding that their profession remains oriented toward those circumstances that lie past the threshold of this commitment. Various situations require judging whether one is past that threshold or not. In counterinsurgencies, especially, with no clear front lines, this judgment is required of soldiers lower down the chain of command, despite it often being more difficult to make.

61. Brough 2007, 159.

the enemy's moral inferiority)."[62] These latter forms of emotional distance are precisely the dehumanizing tendencies that make enemies either "base, as an animal or insect, or evil, as a monster or demon," and are, therefore, unacceptable.[63] Brough labels these attempts at distance "subhumanization" to denote their denial of an enemy's human worth. In their place, he suggests an alternative form of emotional distance that he calls "nonhumanization." Prompted by the physical distance of modern weaponry, "nonhumanization began with the invention of indirect trajectory artillery, when enemy soldiers became pushpins or pencil dots on maps, or shouted coordinates to a gun section."[64] Perceiving the enemy as nonhuman "blips on a computer screen" has expanded as warfare has increasingly become electronically mediated.[65]

Instead of an emotionally charged belittling of the enemy, nonhumanization involves an emotionless objectifying of the enemy. It may, therefore, be a few moral degrees better than subhumanization, given the violent excesses that the latter invites. However, even though the *non* prefix avoids the connotation of lesser value that *sub* does, it still conveys the sense that the enemy is *un*-human, something other than human. Thus, it still seems a problematic approach to the justified killing in war of other *humans*. Brough is quick to point out this concern, saying that considering enemies nonhuman can deny their moral equality in a similar way to considering enemies subhuman.[66] Given the need for some kind of emotional distance, however, or some way of "making killing easier" in the right moral circumstances, Brough endorses a nonhumanizing moment, though one tightly bounded by a respect for the enemy.[67] The killing of another, he suggests, "does not preclude honoring the dead after the battle. A prayer, a thought, a muttered farewell might suffice as a sign of respect for the fallen." He highlights the therapeutic research that shows how important it is for soldiers to honor fallen adversaries in order to avert "damaging psychological repercussions."[68]

I am sympathetic to Brough's effort, but I want to offer an alternative to nonhumanization. The soldier who finds herself in circumstances such

---

62. Ibid., 160.
63. Ibid.
64. Ibid., 161.
65. Ibid.
66. Ibid.
67. Walzer suggests something similar about killing enemies when he states, "But the alienation [of the enemy] is temporary, the humanity imminent" (1977, 142).
68. Brough 2007, 163. The psychological research is that of Jonathan Shay and David Grossman, and moral injury is one of these repercussions.

that killing the enemy is at least morally permissible, if not obligatory, should keep the humanity of the enemy intact, but detach herself from her empathetic impulse that underscores that humanity. I already suggested this alternative above when I traced the roles of lower-level and higher-level empathy in the experience of the troubled soldier reacting to the death of the Iraqi colonel. This alternative is similar to the surgeon's need to emotionally detach from the patient to best perform a surgery.

Just as the surgeon should not be expected to empathetically perceive or imagine the experience he is causing in the patient, at least in the midst of the surgical act, so the soldier should not be expected to empathetically engage with her enemy during the lethal act. Also just like the surgeon, however, the soldier should not maintain the stoic detachment afterward (and often cannot, as demonstrated most starkly by morally injured soldiers). The parallel exists in the responsibilities of senior soldiers, as well:

> ...it is a necessary part of high military command in the field that a commander should callous himself against the human cost of his plans and orders—otherwise it would be emotionally impossible for him to do his job. This need not make him deficient in care before battle or in compassion after it, however. It need not make him inhumane...[69]

It is possible that I am splitting hairs in trying to distinguish between Brough's nonhumanization and my interruption of one's empathetic impulse. However, it does seem relevant to describe the necessary step not as an actual attribution of nonhuman status to the enemy, but instead as a management of one's mental faculties. Over time, a disposition will develop based on one or the other. It seems better to limit that disposition to how one affectively responds to others rather than forming a habit of objectifying others. The more limited disposition will better enable a soldier to respect deceased enemies in the manner Brough recommends, since their humanity is never set aside. Nonhumanization too easily lends itself to the dangers of a bureaucratic mindset or a checklist approach to *jus in bello*, putting the maintenance of a right intention at risk.

So instead of dehumanizing enemies as either subhuman or nonhuman, I suggest a management of one's empathy that is similar to the management of one's senses. Just as one can attune one's ear to detect certain sounds over others, one can focus one's empathy in selective ways. This empathetic

---

69. Nigel Biggar, *In Defence of War* (Oxford: Oxford University Press, 2013), 127.

attunement already happens in various contexts, and there are immoral moments of it in which we get too selective. This partiality is particularly common in war, where the empathy with one's comrades can drown out the empathy with enemies or noncombatants.

The case of justified killing in war, however, counts as a morally appropriate moment.

Outside of this concession for the justified killing act, empathy should not be suppressed in war. Indeed, it cannot be, at least with any finality, given the instinctive nature of lower-level empathy, the unavoidable empathetic moments that occur even in war, and the introspection that follows combat for most every soldier. Soldiers are humans, and therefore are hardwired for empathy, making the human automaton an impossible goal, even with extensive military training. It is also an immoral goal, since an automaton cannot maintain a disposition to a just and lasting peace but must be equipped with merely a program of activity, and therefore lacks the judgment needed to properly wield lethal force across the range of circumstances a soldier may face. Thirdly, it is a tactically foolish goal: an automaton cannot adapt to genuinely novel circumstances since it is only equipped with a checklist, however elaborate.

What Else Besides Dehumanizing?

Given the unavoidable nature of empathy, the humanization of others that empathy prompts, and the vital moral need to keep others humanized in war, it is important to identify alternatives to the modern view that leave no room for the humanity of the enemy. This modern view suggests that a soldier's valor depends upon, and is even proven by, a disdainful or dismissive degradation of the enemy. Consider, instead, the attitude of the ancient Greeks as portrayed by Homer, or, most tellingly, the attitude of early Christians, which allow for an enemy to be understood as "honorable and like oneself" even when fighting to the death.[70]

In Jonathan Shay's extensive study of Homer's *Iliad*, he finds no instance of Greeks or Trojans dehumanizing each other in their battle over Troy.[71] Neither side referred to the other with derogatory terms, which is a common practice in modern wars. Nor do they express disrespect, more generally. On the contrary, the two sides repeatedly express admiration for the fighting prowess of their adversaries. After an extended duel that ends in a draw, the Trojan warrior Ajax states:

---

70. Shay's phrase from above.
71. Shay 1994, 103–120.

> We'll meet again another time—and fight until the unseen power
> decides between those hosts of ours, awarding one or the other
> victory. Afterwards they'll say, among [Greeks] and Trojans: 'These
> two fought and gave no quarter in close combat, yet they parted
> as friends.'[72]

Shay notes that the "contrast to fighting 'Gooks' in Vietnam cannot be
sharper."[73]

The important exception to this respectful attitude is the appalling
treatment of Hektor's body after Achilles defeats him in battle. Achilles
mutilates the corpse and shamefully drags it on a public display. As Shay
points out, though, this behavior was condemned by Greeks and Trojans
alike, violating deep-seated norms that they shared.[74] What is more, Homer
portrays Achilles as especially respectful and generous toward adversaries
prior to his change of character early in the story, which was spurred by
his commanding officer's betrayal.

Admittedly, the Greeks and Trojans shared a common culture that made
respect easier to maintain. It was not as difficult for one side to view the other
as equal in human status and corresponding value. Shay notes that "later
Greeks did debase foreign, 'barbarian' enemies every bit as much as modern
Americans [did in World War II and Vietnam]."[75] Nonetheless, the Greek
and Trojan example stands as an important exception to the presumed need
for dehumanization to fulfill soldierly duties. As respectably as the Greeks
and Trojans perceived each other, it did not dilute their fighting tenacity.[76]

Shay attributes the contrast between the ancient Greek attitude toward
enemies and its modern counterpart to an inherent tendency to dehumanize
adversaries in biblical religions.[77] The Jewish, Christian, and Islamic traditions,
in Shay's view, emphasize the dehumanization of enemies as an expression
of piety. "When modern American soldiers and their leaders dehumanize
the enemy, they affirm their loyalty to God, expressing a cultural tradition

---

72. Ibid., 108–109.
73. Ibid.
74. Ibid., 29.
75. Ibid., 111, note 6. Shay cites Edith Hall's research in *Inventing the Barbarian* (New York: Oxford University Press, 1991).
76. Nor did it soften the victor's treatment of captured combatants and noncombatants. Both sides understood that if they fell in battle, they would be slaughtered, their towns plundered, and their families possessed as slaves. As awful as these actions might be, it did not stem from viewing the vanquished as subhuman. See Shay 1994, 103.
77. Shay 1994, 103, 111–120.

powerfully engraved by biblical scripture."[78] Shay examines the story of David and Goliath, highlighting speech that compares Goliath to animals and presents him "as a moral monstrosity as well as a physical monster, not conceivable as a counterpart in political settlement..."[79] Shay concludes:

> The Judeo-Christian (and Islamic) world view has triumphed so completely over the Homeric world view that dishonoring the enemy now seems natural, virtuous, patriotic, pious. Yet in the *Iliad* only Achilles disrespects the enemy. In Homer's world, this is not a natural but an inhuman state into which Achilles has tragically fallen. Homer's warriors are never weakened by respecting the enemy.[80]

There is no denying the dehumanization that has been done in the name of God, nor the religious fervor that too often fuels it. Yet, Shay's contention seems lopsided and incomplete. In his analysis of David's comments about and to Goliath, it is not as clear as Shay claims that David reduces Goliath to the lesser status of an animal or monster. David compares the challenge of fighting him to his prior challenges of fighting a lion and a bear, but this comparison is not necessarily demeaning; it may also be read as a complimentary recognition of Goliath's ferocity. David clearly draws courage from his belief of having God's favor, and this presumption can lead to an arrogant and contemptuous view of others, but it is not apparent that David is displaying arrogance or contempt. It could be confidence and a desire to give God the credit of the victory that he anticipates.

Regardless, the bigger concern is Shay's silence on the Jewish, Christian, and Islamic traditions' advocacy for humane treatment of enemies. I will focus on the Christian tradition, both because its early members were foundational to the just war tradition and because the Christian mandate regarding enemies is so drastic: as Jesus famously declared, they are to be loved.[81]

Many find this injunction untenable; it is a contradiction for a soldier to claim that she loves the enemy whom she kills. Perhaps the soldier is motivated by love for the victim as she kills an aggressor, but it seems absurd to claim that she is also acting lovingly toward the aggressor. Instead, the modern intuition of dehumanizing the aggressor begins to take shape as something

---

78. Ibid., 111.
79. Ibid., 112.
80. Shay 1994, 115.
81. Matthew 5:43–45; Luke 6:27–28, 35.

more realistic. Augustine, however, defends the love for the aggressor, partly by identifying love as an inward disposition of the soldier's heart, and partly by suggesting that the forceful restraint of the aggressor benefits him and not merely the victim: "the person from whom is taken away the freedom which he abuses in doing wrong is vanquished with benefit to himself..."[82] Restraining an aggressor who lives to mend his ways is one thing, but Augustine maintains this benefit even if the aggressor is killed, since, in the Christian worldview, each person must answer for wrongs done on this earth, and this aggressor's death prevents his commission of further wrongs.

Augustine offers another answer that does not appeal to an afterlife, nor does it require force short of killing. In a letter to a military commander who expressed doubts about his ability to be both Christian and soldier, Augustine says:

Therefore, even in waging war, cherish the spirit of a peacemaker, that, by conquering those whom you attack, you may lead them back to the advantages of peace; for our Lord says: "Blessed are the peacemakers; for they shall be called the children of God" (Matthew 5:9)....Let necessity, therefore, and not your will, slay the enemy who fights against you. As violence is used towards him who rebels and resists, so mercy is due to the vanquished or the captive, especially in the case in which future troubling of the peace is not to be feared.[83]

There are two pieces of this passage that are particularly germane to sustaining the humanity of enemies in war. Augustine tells this commander to be a peacemaker, which could conceivably mean either the reconciliatory coexistence of a positive peace or the eliminative version of negative peace. The latter is quickly ruled out, though, as Augustine encourages this soldier to "lead [enemies] back to the advantages of peace" and later, to grant mercy "to the vanquished." The peace that Augustine wants this soldier to make involves the enemies' participation, not subjugation or elimination, and therefore respects their humanity.

Secondly, Augustine advises this soldier to "Let necessity, therefore, and not your will, slay the enemy who fights against you." Augustine recommends that this soldier kill regrettably, not wholeheartedly, almost in a manner such that the enemy has to force his hand. Nigel Biggar offers a contemporary version of this idea:

---

82. Augustine, Letter 138 (emphasis added).
83. Augustine, Letter 189.

> Nevertheless, it may be permissible to choose to act in such a way as to cause the death of a human being, provided that what is intended is something other than his death (e.g. defending the innocent), that the possibility (or even certainty) of his death is accepted with an appropriate and manifest reluctance, and that this acceptance is necessary, non-subversive, and proportionate. Morally speaking, deliberately to cause death in this fashion is not the same as intending to kill.[84]

On the face of it, Biggar's suggestion that a soldier have no intention to kill sounds as absurd as loving one's enemies even as one kills them. However, if by "intention" Biggar means overall purpose, then he is simply arguing for soldiers to have the right intention toward a just and lasting peace, instead of a killing intention as their preeminent aspiration.

These summaries of the Greek and Christian outlooks are merely meant to show the viability of maintaining the humanity of one's enemies in the midst of fighting them. They deserve fuller treatment, and no doubt there are other examples that demonstrate a respect for the enemy's humanity,[85] but at this point I will settle for establishing the plausibility of alternatives to dehumanization, and therefore securing empathy's compatibility with soldiering.

Keeping Killing in its Place

Soldiers with empathy are more capable of maintaining the act of killing as a necessary and regrettable task instead of their overarching purpose. Empathy aids soldiers in resisting the dehumanization of others, especially enemies. More specifically, empathy reveals the bare fact of an enemy's humanity, as well as elements of his experience, including values, desires, and intentions. These elements are instrumentally useful for tactical decisions in fighting

---

84. Biggar 2013, 101.

85. I received another promising suggestion, though it requires more extensive study: the attitude toward prey within the hunting ethic of some Native American communities. In the practice of the Ojibwe, for example, a "hunter makes a speech of thankfulness to the animal/spirit world, showing appreciation in advance or after a harvest." Also: "Handling the deer carcass and disposing of unused portions should be done in a way that maintains dignity for the deer's spirit." See Nicholas James Reo, Kyle Powys Whyte, "Hunting and Morality as Elements of Traditional Ecological Knowledge," *Human Ecology*, Vol. 40:1 (February 2012), 15–27. While I hesitate to connect enemy soldiers with prey, the respectful attitude here seems in line with maintaining their humanity. It would be worth further research to confirm that the Ojibwe emphasize this attitude among their warriors doing battle and not merely while hunting. My thanks to Monte Hoover for this reference.

the enemy, but even more importantly, they allow for improved judgments regarding a shared peace and a right intention that pursues that peace.

There should always be an eye kept toward the end goal of peace, even by soldiers. Their conduct in combat affects the prospects for peace. While killing, injuring, incapacitating, threatening, and forcefully detaining others are inherent to combat actions, they must be done in light of the over-arching purpose they are to serve. Furthermore, while soldiers may need to attenuate empathetic impulses to proficiently complete these combat actions, it should be a temporary interruption of one's empathetic faculty, not a denial of the enemy's humanity.

III. Empathy in War-Waging

The above section delineated empathy's support for a right intention among soldiers and how soldiers can maintain an empathetic understanding of enemies in conjunction with their task of justified killing. In this section, I aim to show the specific relevance of empathy to "war-waging" responsibilities, as James Dubik calls them. Empathy is just as relevant to traditional war-fighting principles such as discrimination and proportionality, but for the sake of space I will focus on Dubik's innovative critique of the just war tradition.

Dubik distinguishes between war-*fighting* and war-*waging* to more fully describe the activities within war.[86] War-fighting refers to the range of activities that occur on the battlefield itself, particularly the wielding of lethal force against the enemy through the weaponry at hand. With war-waging, Dubik means the range of activities that precedes, directs, coordinates, and sustains the war-fighting on the battlefield—the comprehensive management of a war and not merely the specific battlefield actions that occur within it.[87]

Empathy has an important role in the activities of war-waging. In this section, I will examine empathy's contribution to strategic planning and assessing progress. As Dubik notes,

> While final decision authority rests on a very small group—
> sometimes a single individual—decisions of this magnitude are
> preceded by detailed analysis of alternatives, feasibility studies, and
> reams of paper reflecting the arguments that had been conducted

---

86. James M. Dubik, *Just War Reconsidered—Strategy, Ethics, and Theory* (Lexington: University Press of Kentucky, 2016), 3–4.
87. Ibid., 15.

by numerous committees and study groups as well as subordinate organizations and staff agencies. The quality of the final decisions often reflected the quality of the preparatory work.[88]

My claim is that empathy improves the preparatory work and the final decision. As a veteran of numerous committees, study groups, and staff sections, I recognize that these roles, and the windowless offices that often accompany them, can stifle empathetic consideration of others (in some ways, more completely than the vagaries of combat). Yet the consequences at stake demand the best in comprehending the worldview and motivations of human actors, in thinking critically and creatively, in rigorously scrutinizing one's assumptions, and assessing progress honestly and meaningfully. Furthermore, in doing this work well, one helps to maintain the legitimacy of the war, at least in one respect. Legitimacy, Dubik points out, is a "function of the righteousness of the war (a *jus ad bellum* issue) and progress toward probable success (a *jus in bello* issue). [It] is tied directly to the competence of senior political and military leaders in executing their war-waging responsibilities."[89] As empathy improves the planning and assessment process, it also helps to secure genuine progress, thus contributing to legitimacy.

Strategic Planning

In Dubik's analysis of the kinds of problems soldiers face in war, he distinguishes between technical problems and adaptive problems.[90] Technical problems are those that soldiers can remedy with their current knowledge and experience; the problems "can be resolved through the application of authoritative expertise and the organization's current structures, procedures, and ways of doing things."[91] Technical problems may be complicated, but their solution is readily discernable. Adaptive problems, on the other hand, fall outside an organization's normal capacities and are usually hard to understand, let alone solve. The context of an adaptive problem is "continually changing," and therefore "the solution changes continually as well."[92] Dubik observes that the tactical challenges in war are generally technical in nature, while the strategic challenges are usually adaptive. Thus, war-waging involves mostly adaptive problems.

---

88. Dubik 2016, 18.
89. Dubik 2016, 155.
90. Dubik 2016, 141–143.
91. Ibid., 141–142.
92. Ibid., 142.

The first, and most important, step in handling adaptive problems is grasping them properly. One of the most basic challenges to this step is recognizing the shortcomings of one's own conceptual frameworks. When an adaptive problem involves human actors, especially enemies, empathetically understanding those humans helps to overcome the faults of preexisting conceptions of them. In other words, empathy helps to overcome cultural, ideological, racial, or social biases and prejudices. For example, an empathetic approach toward the Japanese in World War II would have humanized them and made it harder to underestimate their capabilities. Instead, racist stereotypes had convinced Allied planners early in the war that the Japanese were "too nearsighted and prone to vertigo to fly a combat aircraft; too fearful to fight in jungles, which they supposedly believed were inhabited by ghosts and demons."[93] Underestimating enemies leads to needless loss of lives.

When facing adaptive problems, there can be an overriding temptation to define the problem as a technical one, instead. Especially in military culture with its orientation toward action, the enticing option is to treat an unfamiliar, inconvenient problem with a familiar and convenient solution. As an example of this error, consider the rise and fall of a military planning construct called "Effects-Based Operations," or EBO.[94]

EBO was a planning construct originating with the US Air Force, but employed in one form or another by the other services as well.[95] It derives its name from a strict focus on the damaging effects to be achieved against enemy forces rather than a more generic focus on the amount of resources to apply against the enemy (in terms of units, ammunition, or weapon systems). Air Force planners developed EBO to more efficiently employ resources against key nodes of an enemy's forces. For example, a pilot might target a radar system that provides crucial data to several enemy air defense weapon systems, rather than target each of the air defense systems themselves. Besides using fewer resources, this approach paralyzed the enemy with more selective, simultaneous attacks. EBO saw its first major application in the successful air campaign of 1990 as the initial part of the campaign to drive Saddam's forces out of Kuwait. The construct of EBO

93. Shay 1994, 120.
94. US Armed Forces, Joint Publication 3–0, *Operations* (Washington, DC: Joint Staff, September 2006); superseded in August 2011, then again in January 2017.
95. Gary Cheek, "Effects-Based Operations: The End of Dominant Maneuver?" *Transformation Concepts for National Security in the 21st Century,* ed. Williamson Murray (2002), 73–100.

also produced the "shock and awe" air campaign at the outset of the 2003 invasion of Iraq.

The procedures of EBO guided military planners in accounting for all relevant factors of an enemy force's capabilities. When analyzing a relatively closed system, such as the air defense weapons above, EBO proved useful in highlighting the enemy's vulnerabilities and steering the judicious application of military force. However, the tactical successes resulting from EBO planning prompted the extension of EBO to larger strategic concerns. Planners attempted to capture political, military, economic, and social factors in an ambitious but simplistic information grid, coming to treat "something as complex as human activity [as] an essentially passive and lifeless domain."[96] In the place of air defense radars, for example, tribal leaders became the key nodes to be "targeted" with available resources. EBO thinking drew attention away from traditional considerations of superior combat power or maintaining a reserve force in the case of surprises, and instead promised, with a tantalizing level of certainty and efficiency, a dismantled enemy stymied into submission. By 2008, critiques of this planning construct began to emerge:

> Concepts with such labels as network-centric warfare, rapid decisive operations, shock and awe, and various permutations of effects-based operations embraced what increasingly appeared as a faith-based argument that future war would lie mainly in the realm of certainty and therefore could be won quickly and efficiently, at low cost by small forces.[97]

Later that same year, a senior military commander in charge of doctrine issued a disparaging memorandum that banned US forces from using EBO for military planning.[98] The commander noted that EBO "mechanistically attempts to provide certainty and predictability in an inherently uncertain environment," is "too prescriptive and over-engineered," and "discounts the human dimensions of war (e.g., passion, imagination, willpower and unpredictability)."[99] He agreed that "Elements of [EBO] have proven use-

---

96. Milan Vego, "Systems versus Classical Approach to Warfare," *Joint Force Quarterly* 52 (1st Quarter 2009), 42.
97. H.R. McMaster, "On War: Lessons to be Learned," *Survival* 50:1 (March 2008), 21.
98. General James Mattis (the recent US Secretary of Defense), "USJFCOM Commander's Guidance on Effects-Based Operations," *Joint Force Quarterly* 51 (4th Quarter 2008), 105–108.
99. Ibid., 106–1U.07.

ful in addressing 'closed systems,' such as targeting where effects can be measured per [US Air Force's] deliberate analysis and targeting methods.

However, the concepts have been misapplied by others to operations beyond their original intent, resulting in overextension and confusion."[100]

The title of this planning construct, *Effects-Based* Operations, implies greater wisdom than this critique has allowed. Indeed, focusing on desired effects can make the selection of means both more efficient and more ethically respectable (minimizing collateral damage, for example). However, the application of EBO to larger strategic concerns rested on a hubristic assumption that the military force could actually manipulate certain effects into existence with no need to accommodate unpredictable behavior of the enemy or others, nor a need to garner the cooperation of allies and key groups of noncombatants. This error was, metaphorically speaking, an attempt to *manufacture* effects that could only be *farmed*—military units could not control all the factors (specifically, uncooperative humans) but vainly assumed otherwise. It is an epistemological error, in that soldiers failed to acknowledge the limits of what they could actually control. The mistake was in attempting to turn a tactical planning construct that was suitable against closed systems of material components into a strategic planning construct for open, unpredictable systems with human components. A greater appreciation for empathy, for the understanding that it provides and the respect that it entails, would have prevented the assumption that the desired effects could be manufactured.

Besides the epistemological error in treating an adaptive problem as a technical one, the EBO planning construct involved a moral error in treating humans as things amenable to law-like generalizations. This moral error is a form of dehumanization; it objectifies human actors. In this mode, military planners employ cultural knowledge inappropriately, treating the knowledge as laws of behavior akin to the laws of physics. Planners approach enemies or others in a mechanical fashion and cast simplistic assumptions across whole populations. It is often a bureaucratic dehumanization, not necessarily a visceral subhumanization like in the stress of combat, though it may also stem from the latter. Regardless, it has effects just as troubling morally and practically. This kind of dehumanizing leads to treating war as a physical science and human actors as merely manipulable objects. So, "Effects–Based Operations" is a misleading title because the effects were

---

100. Ibid.

chosen peremptorily from a moment of, at the least, bureaucratic dehumanization. Empathy is an antidote for this dehumanizing predisposition toward war as a physical science and toward cultural knowledge as merely law-like generalizations of others.

Assessment

Empathy improves the assessment of progress by keeping the focus of gauging outputs instead of merely inputs. In dealing with the confusion of the counterinsurgencies in Iraq and Afghanistan, US personnel have faced a constant temptation to assess their progress based exclusively on inputs. While inputs are easier to control, they are obviously unsuitable as a basis for assessing the progress of operations. Nonetheless, one State Department leader of a provincial reconstruction team in Iraq reflected,

> We measured the impact of our projects by their effect on us, not by their effect on the Iraqis. Output was the word missing from the vocabulary of developing Iraq. Everything was measured only by what we put in—dollars spent, hours committed, people engaged…press releases written.[101]

Empathy's nature as a receptive mode toward another's experience steers soldiers from a focus on input to output and incorporates the population's view of military efforts. While the judgments of local citizens should not serve as the sole factor in the assessment of progress, their judgments should comprise one piece of that assessment, especially given the cooperative rebuilding efforts inherent to counterinsurgencies (or in the aftermath of conventional conflicts).

Another reason inputs can dominate assessments is their easy measurement. With the ever-present pressure of time, military planners can easily succumb to this error. Empathy, however, reduces this temptation toward easy measurement because it emphasizes a more holistic assessment of military operations that includes the opinions of allies, neutral parties, and noncombatants. These empathetic understandings should not be the sole consideration in assessing progress, but they remain important, nonetheless.

If caught in a bureaucratic, overly quantitative mindset, planners and leaders fail to assess the war effort accurately. Recall the example of the Vietnam War, in which this kind of mindset combined with a killing inten-

---

101. Peter Van Buren, *We Meant Well: How I Helped Lose the Battle for the Hearts and Minds of the Iraqi People* (New York: Metropolitan Books, 2011), 144.

tion to produce quantitative metrics such as body count to measure progress. One military historian remarked that, when stuck in this mindset, "If you can't count what's important, what you can count becomes important."[102] Empathy, with its humanization of enemies and others, and its spur toward a right intention, helps to offset this error by shifting the focus to a just and lasting peace between warring parties.

As in war-fighting above, a selective empathy can skew the assessment of progress instead of helping it. If leaders attend only to an empathetic understanding of soldiers, at the expense of a similar understanding of others, then the sole assessment criterion can become the safe return of every soldier, regardless of any progress in the mission at hand. This selective empathy can promote an overly risk-averse approach to military operations.

IV. Conclusion

When the nature of soldiering is properly understood as oriented toward establishing a just and lasting peace, the role for empathy becomes clear and crucial. Empathy prompts soldiers to keep this peace as their intention, rather than seeking a negative peace that entails the subjugation or eradication of all adversaries. Empathy helps soldiers fend off the seemingly "universal wartime tradition" of dehumanizing enemy combatants and the civilians associated with them.[103] Instead, soldiers exercise appropriate restraint regarding forceful actions and improved judgment on when they are genuinely necessary. In this manner, soldiers better traditional war-fighting principles like discrimination and proportionality. This same empathetic understanding of others and corresponding right intention also improves soldiers' fulfillment of war-waging responsibilities in planning military campaigns within moral and practical constraints and assessing progress honestly and holistically.[103]

---

102. James Willbanks (Burns documentary, episode 4).
103. Brough 2007, 151.

Works Cited

Aquinas, Thomas. *Summa theologiae.* Translated by Fathers of the English Dominican Province. Second and Revised Edition, 1920. Online Edition Copyright © 2008 by Kevin Knight. <http://www.newadvent.org/summa/>.

Augustine. *The City of God.* Trans. R. Ryson. Cambridge: Cambridge University Press, 1998.

———. *Contra Faustum* XXII, Translated by Richard Stothert. From *Nicene and Post-Nicene Fathers*, First Series, Vol. 4. Edited by Philip Schaff. Buffalo, NY: Christian Literature Publishing, 1887. Revised and edited for New Advent by Kevin Knight. <http://www.newadvent.org/fathers/140622.htm>.

———. Letter 138. Translated by J. G. Cunningham. From *Nicene and Post-Nicene Fathers*, First Series, Vol. 1. Edited by Philip Schaff. Buffalo, NY: Christian Literature Publishing, 1887. Revised and edited for New Advent by Kevin Knight. <http://www.newadvent.org/fathers/1102138.htm>.

———. Letter 189. Translated by J. G. Cunningham. From *Nicene and Post-Nicene Fathers*, First Series, Vol. 1. Edited by Philip Schaff. Buffalo, NY: Christian Literature Publishing, 1887. Revised and edited for New Advent by Kevin Knight. <http://www.newadvent.org/fathers/1102189.htm>.

Batson, C. D. (2009). "These Things Called Empathy." *The Social Neuroscience of Empathy.* Ed. Jean Decety and William Ickes. Cambridge, MA: MIT Press.

———. (1991). *The Altruism Question: Toward a Social-Psychological Answer.* Hillsdale, NJ: Erlbaum.

Bell, Daniel (2009). *Just War as Christian Discipleship: Recentering the Tradition in the Church Rather Than the State.* Grand Rapids, MI: Brazos Press.

Biggar, Nigel (2013). *In Defence of War.* Oxford: Oxford University Press. Bloom, Paul (2016). *Against Empathy.* New York: HarperCollins.

Bolgiano, David, and John Taylor (2017). "Can't Kill Enough to Win? Think Again." *Proceedings Magazine*, Vol. 143/12/1,378. US Naval Institute, December 2017. <https:// www.usni.org/magazines/proceedings/2017-12/cant-kill-enough-win-think-again>.

Brough, Michael (2007). "Dehumanization of the Enemy and the Moral Equality of Soldiers." In *Rethinking the Just War Tradition.* Eds. Michael Brough, John Lango, Harry van der Linden. Albany: State University of New York Press, 149–167.

Burkhardt, Todd (2017). *Just War and Human Rights: Fighting with Right Intention.* Albany, NY: SUNY Press.

Burns, Ken and Lynne Novick (2017). "The Vietnam War." Documentary. Florentine Films and WETA.

CNN Politics. "Troops alone will not yield victory in Afghanistan." CNN.com (10 September 2008). <http://www.cnn.com/2008/POLITICS/09/10/mullen.afghanistan>.

Capizzi, Joseph (2015). *Politics, Justice, and War: Christian Governance and the Ethics of Warfare.* Oxford: Oxford University Press.

Cavanaugh, Matt (2015). "The Military's Purpose is Not to Kill People and Break Things." *War on the Rocks.* 26 August 2015. <https://warontherocks.com/2015/08/the-militarys- purpose-is-not-to-kill-people-and-break-things/>.

Cheek, Gary (2002). "Effects-Based Operations: The End of Dominant Maneuver?" *Transformation Concepts for National Security in the 21st Century*. Ed. Williamson Murray. Strategic Studies Institute, US Army War College, 73–100. <https://ssi.armywarcollege.edu/pubs/display.cfm?pubID=252>.

Coates, A. J. (2016). *The Ethics of War*. 2nd ed. Manchester, UK: Manchester University Press. Coplan, Amy (2011). "Understanding Empathy: Its Features and Effects." *Empathy: Philosophical and Psychological Perspectives*. Eds. Amy Coplan and Peter Goldie. New York: Oxford University Press.

Coplan, Amy and Peter Goldie (2011). "Introduction." *Empathy: Philosophical and Psychological Perspectives*. Eds. Amy Coplan and Peter Goldie. New York: Oxford University Press, ix–xlvii.

Darwall, Stephen (1998). "Empathy, Sympathy, and Care." *Philosophical Studies* 89: 261–282. Dubik, James (2016). *Just War Reconsidered—Strategy, Ethics, and Theory*. Lexington: University Press of Kentucky.

Frowe, Helen (2011). *The Ethics of War and Peace*. London: Routledge.

Gallagher, Shaun (2012). "Empathy, Simulation, and Narrative." *Science in Context*, vol. 25, no. 3, 355–381.

Gourley, Jim (2015). "The military's purpose isn't to break things and kill people, but it should be." *Foreign Policy*. 24 September 2015. <http://foreignpolicy.com/2015/09/24/the- militarys-purpose-isnt-to-break-things-and-kill-people-but-it-should-be/>.

Hoffman, Bruce (2006). *Inside Terrorism*. Revised and expanded edition. New York: Columbia University Press.

Klay, Phil (2017). "What We're Fighting For." *New York Times*. 10 February 2017.

Linn, Brian (2009). *The Echo of Battle: The Army's Way of War*. Cambridge, MA: Harvard University Press.

MacIntyre, Alasdair (2016). *Ethics in the Conflicts of Modernity: An Essay on Desire, Practical Reasoning, and Narrative*. New York: Cambridge University Press.

———. (2007). *After Virtue: A Study in Moral Theory*. 3rd ed. Notre Dame: University of Notre Dame Press.

Matravers, Derek (2017). *Empathy*. Malden, MA: Polity Press.

Mattis, James (2008). "USJFCOM Commander's Guidance on Effects-Based Operations," *Joint Force Quarterly*. Vol. 51 (4th Quarter 2008), 105–108.

McMahan, Jeff (2005). "Just Cause for War." *Ethics and International Affairs* 9:3 (December 2005), 1–21.

McMaster, H. R. (2008). "On War: Lessons to be Learned." *Survival* 50:1 (March 2008), 19–30. Morris, Errol (2003). "The Fog of War: Eleven Lessons from the Life of Robert S. McNamara." Documentary. Sony Pictures Classics.

Orend, Brian (2006). *The Morality of War*. Toronto: Broadview Press.

Orend, Brian (2001). "A Just War Critique of Realism and Pacifism." *Journal of Philosophical Research*, Vol. XXVI, 435–477.

Pickstock, Catherine (1998). *After Writing*. Malden, MA: Blackwell Publishers.

Prinz, Jesse (2011). "Is Empathy Necessary for Morality?" *Empathy: Philosophical and Psychological Perspectives*. Ed. Amy Coplan and Peter Goldie. New York: Oxford University Press, 211–229.

Reo, Nicholas James, and Kyle Powys Whyte (2012). "Hunting and Morality as Elements of Traditional Ecological Knowledge." *Human Ecology*. Vol. 40:1 (February 2012), 15–27.

Rodin, David (2004). "Terrorism without Intention," *Ethics* 114 (July 2004), 752–771.

Ross, Janell (2015). "Mike Huckabee Says the Military's Job Is To 'Kill People and Break Things.' Well, Not Quite." *The Washington Post* (7 August 2015).

Schofield, John M (1881). "Notes on 'The Legitimate in War.'" *Journal of the Military Service Institution*. Vol. 2, 1–10.

Shay, Jonathan (1994). *Achilles in Vietnam: Combat Trauma and the Undoing of Character*. New York: Scribner.

Smith, Joel (2015). "What is Empathy For?" *Synthese*, vol.194, 709–722.

Stueber, Karsten (2006). *Rediscovering Empathy: Agency, Folk Psychology, and the Human Sciences*. Cambridge, MA: MIT Press.

Tacitus, Publius Cornelius. *The Works of Tacitus: The Oxford Translation, Revised with Notes*, Vol. 2. London: Bell and Daldy, 1872.

UNESDOC, UNESCO Digital Library, unesdoc.unesco.org.

United Nations. "Declaration on Measures to Eliminate International Terrorism." Annex to UN General Assembly Resolution 49/60, "Measures to Eliminate International Terrorism." (9 December 1994). <https://www.un.org/documents/ga/res/49/a49r060.htm>.

US Armed Forces. Joint Publication 3-0, *Operations* (Washington, DC: Joint Staff, September 2006); superseded in August 2011, then again in January 2017.

Van Buren, Peter (2011). We Meant Well: How I Helped Lose the Battle for the Hearts and Minds of the Iraqi People. New York: Metropolitan Books.

Vego, Milan (2009). "Systems versus Classical Approach to Warfare." *Joint Force Quarterly*. Vol. 52 (1st Quarter 2009), 40–48.

Walzer, Michael (1977). *Just and Unjust Wars: A Moral Argument with Historical Illustrations*. Philadelphia: Basic Books.

Weinstein, Adam (2017). "No, We Can't Kill Our Way to Victory Despite What 2 Misguided Lieutenant Colonels Might Think." *Task and Purpose* (8 December 2017). <https://taskandpurpose.com/no-cant-kill-way-victory-despite-2-misguided-lieutenant- colonels-might-think/>.

Wood, David (2016). *What Have We Done: The Moral Injury of Our Longest Wars*. New York: Little, Brown and Company, Kindle edition.

Zahavi, Dan (2014). *Self and Other: Exploring Subjectivity, Empathy, and Shame*. New York: Oxford University Press. Notes

Empatía y *Jus in bello*

Kevin Cutright
Lieutenant Colonel, US Army
Traducción al español por: Haydeé Espino

I. La negligencia de la recta intención

El principio de la recta intención es "la adecuada disposición de aquellos [individuos] que luchan en la guerra" hacia una paz justa y duradera.[1] Los primeros teóricos de la guerra justa hacían énfasis en que la recta intención era esencial para la justificación moral de la guerra y la conducta de los soldados que la conformaban.[2] Este principio está destinado a servir como correctivo a los hombres de Estado o a aquellos soldados que pueden tener una causa justificada para la guerra, pero que la utilizan como mera cortina para otros propósitos. A medida que los pensadores modernos delineaban diferencias más claras entre el *jus ad bellum* y el *jus in bello* —y eventualmente el *jus post bellum*—, la recta intención solo se apreciaba en la categoría de *ad bellum*. Supuestamente, aún podría influir en las consideraciones del *in bello* por su presencia en las deliberaciones que provocan la guerra. Sin embargo, la recta intención recibió una atención circunspecta en las discusiones modernas del *jus ad bellum*.[3] Desde entonces, algunos estudiosos han sugerido que la recta intención es redundante o imposible de corroborar y que debe subsumirse al principio de la causa justa.[4]

Otros teóricos se basan en las leyes y reglas para restringir de manera externa a los políticos y los soldados, alejándose de las intenciones y virtudes

---

1. Joseph Capizzi, *Politics, Justice, and War: Christian Governance and the Ethics of Warfare* (Oxford: Oxford University Press, 2015), 108-109.
2. San Agustín fue el primer defensor de la recta intención; véase *The City of God*, trad. R. Ryson (Cambridge: Cambridge University Press, 1998). Tomás de Aquino menciona la recta intención como uno de los tres principios que gobiernan la guerra; véase *Summa theologiae* II-II q. 40 art. 1 y q. 64 art. 3.
3. Daniel Bell marca el comienzo de esta visión oscura con Hugo Grotius; véase *Just War as Christian Discipleship: Recentering the Tradition in the Church rather than the State* (Grand Rapids, MI: Brazos Press, 2009), 56-58.
4. Como ejemplo prominente, véase Jeff McMahan, "Just Cause for War," *Ethics and International Affairs* 9:3, 1-21. Para argumentos en contra del rechazo de la recta intención, véase Capizzi 2015, 71-126; Todd Burkhardt, *Just War and Human Rights: Fighting with Right Intention* (Albany, NY: SUNY Press, 2017); y Bell 2009, 153-158.

que podrían restringirlos de manera interna.[5] A. J. Coates contrasta esta tendencia hacia el "enfoque basado en reglas" con un "enfoque basado en el carácter" más tradicional.[6] Si bien reconoce los méritos de ambos, descubre en el enfoque basado en reglas un antagonismo hacia el enfoque basado en el carácter. El enfoque basado en reglas da prioridad a la reflexión deliberativa de las demandas morales sin las consideraciones disposicionales:

> La moralidad 'reflexiva' no solo es negligente o indiferente a la idea de una vida moral centrada en disposiciones morales; se opone a ella por principio debido a que "la mente sin disposición es por sí sola la fuente del juicio 'racional' y de la conducta 'racional'". La conducta moral es "racional" en el sentido estrictamente concebido de la 'conducta surgida de un previo proceso de "razonamiento", excluyendo la conducta, la cual tiene su origen en 'la autoridad de una tradición, de una costumbre o de un hábito de conducta' sin examinar. Desde un punto de vista reflexivo, los aspectos comunales y habituales de la moralidad tradicional se consideran menos como fuentes de empoderamiento moral que como obstáculos fundamentales para el logro de la autonomía moral. El progreso moral depende de la emancipación del individuo racional con respecto a las influencias heterónomas de la moralidad tradicional.[7]

El principio pre-moderno de la recta intención se ha visto ampliamente relegado como si fuera una de estas cuestionables disposiciones de la moralidad tradicional, o como si fuera irrelevante para la moralidad —como lo son todas las intenciones de la ética consecuencialista— o se le ha redefinido en términos de una regla —como en la ética deontológica—. Como resultado, la recta intención, entendida como una disposición del carácter, está prácticamente ausente en la erudición contemporánea sobre el *jus in bello*.

El impacto de esta negligencia

Un enfoque moral basado en reglas ha contribuido valiosas aportaciones para satisfacer mejores demandas morales tales como la codificación de prin-

---

5. Para un resumen de esta tendencia, véase Brian Orend, *The Morality of War* (Toronto: Broadview Press, 2006), 17-23.
6. A.J. Coates, *The Ethics of War*, 2nd ed. (Manchester, UK: Manchester University Press, 2016), 1-18.
7. Coates 2016, 12. cita a Michael Oakeshott, *Rationalism in Politics* (Londres: Methuen, 1962) 87, 84-85.

cipios morales en el derecho internacional.[8] Además, la reflexión que conlleva un enfoque basado en reglas es vital para el bienestar moral del individuo, probablemente evidenciado por la falta de reflexión contenida en algunos casos de daño moral entre los soldados.[9] Sin embargo, el surgimiento de un marco basado en reglas, con la exclusión de un enfoque basado en el carácter, ha dado como resultado tres deficiencias. En primer lugar, fomenta una técnica hueca de "lista de cotejo" en la ética militar.[10] Una lista de cotejo de las reglas morales nunca puede abarcar las circunstancias imprevistas y de rápido desarrollo a las que se enfrentan los soldados, ni proporcionar la intención a futuro que los soldados necesitan para sortear dichas circunstancias.[11] Como señala Coates, la "ubicuidad de lo imprevisto o imprevisible [en la guerra] impide la reflexión y fortalece los reclamos de la moralidad tradicional".[12] Los soldados precisan de una disposición hacia una paz justa y duradera —lo que, sin duda, implica una comprensión complementaria y reflexiva de esa paz— para cumplir adecuadamente con sus deberes. La restricción extrínseca no puede reemplazar eficazmente a la restricción intrínseca.[13]

En segundo lugar, un enfoque exclusivo en las reglas produce una mentalidad excesivamente burocrática entre los soldados; los hace parecerse al gestor burocrático Alasdair MacIntyre, quien "trata los fines como un hecho, como si estuvieran fuera de sus responsabilidades..."[14] En lugar de una racionalidad orientada hacia los fines, este gestor aplica una burocrática "racionalidad de compaginar los medios con los fines de una forma económica y eficiente", considerando que los fines mismos están "predeterminados".[15]

---

8. Brian Orend, *The Morality of War* (Toronto: Broadview Press, 2006), 20-23.

9. David Wood señala: "El ejército de Estados Unidos. ha invertido años y fortunas en el perfeccionamiento del entrenamiento de combate más realista y completo del mundo. Pero al preparar a los jóvenes estadounidenses para la guerra, ha fracasado en un aspecto flagrante. Nunca se entrena a aquellos a quienes se envía a la guerra a anticipar los predicamentos morales de la muerte a los que se enfrentarán; no se les brinda la oportunidad ni se les incita a pensar o a discutir qué es lo que hace que algunos asesinatos sean moralmente correctos, otros un pecado y que otros sean incluso ilegales "(*What Have We Done: The Moral Injury of our Longest Wars,* [Nueva York: Hachette Book Group 2016], cap. 11 [edición digital]).

10. Orend 2006, 105; Bell 2009, 8.

11. Bell 2009, 73-88.

12. Coates 2016, 14.

13. En este sentido, el enfoque moderno basado en reglas de la moralidad comparte la deficiencia que muchos han señalado a la tradición manualista católica en su intento de codificar la moralidad. Mi agradecimiento a Luis Pinto de Sa por esta deducción.

14. Alasdair MacIntyre, *After Virtue: A Study in Moral Theory,* 3ª ed. Notre Dame: University of Notre Dame Press, 1993.

15. Ibíd., 25.

Hay poco énfasis en la doctrina militar, el entrenamiento o la educación profesional para una genuina comprensión de lo que el mensaje de matar en la guerra pretende promover. El énfasis se hace en las reglas a seguir.[16] La división entre *jus ad bellum* y *jus in bello* —los fines de la guerra y los medios de la guerra— puede reforzar aún más esta racionalidad burocrática puesto que los temas *ad bellum* son, en última instancia, responsabilidad de los líderes políticos. Añadiendo la deferencia del ejército de los Estados Unidos hacia la autoridad civil —tan apropiada como lo es—, y la división analítica de las categorías morales puede intensificarse hasta ocasionar una perturbadora compartimentación que aparentemente exime a los soldados de su obligación de comprender los fundamentos morales de su servicio. En lugar de verse como agentes morales, al igual que los demás, se ven a sí mismos como autómatas.

En tercer lugar, un marco moral estrictamente basado en reglas es deficiente porque el razonamiento por sí solo no induce a la acción, pero requiere de un compromiso afectivo congruente con los principios o valores que conducen a la acción correcta. "La moralidad reflexiva pone su fe en la regla. Descuida la cuestión fundamental de la voluntad y la motivación al asumir —erróneamente— el poder de la automotivación de la razón".[17] Este hecho resulta pertinente especialmente debido a las reacciones afectivas contrarias que las personas tienen en situaciones estresantes como la guerra. La moralidad tradicional, con su enfoque en los rasgos de carácter en lugar de únicamente en la reflexión intelectual, "reconoce que, para que sean efectivos, los juicios morales precisan del apoyo de las disposiciones, sentimientos e inclinaciones morales".[18] Es, en este sentido, más apta para los desafíos de la guerra. El principio de la recta intención enfatiza el *carácter* que se requiere para la consecución de la justicia y no el *estado de las cosas* que se necesita para hacer justicia —como hace el principio de causa justa—. Por lo tanto, la recta intención es un componente indispensable del *jus in bello*.

---

16. Existen algunas excepciones a esta crítica general: todas las academias de servicio exigen un curso básico de ética que incluye varias lecciones dedicadas a la tradición de la guerra justa. El programa del Cuerpo de Capacitación de Oficiales de la Reserva (ROTC) en los campus universitarios, el cual entrena a la mayoría de los oficiales comisionados, exige unas cuantas horas de instrucción en ética militar que también van más allá del tema de las reglas a seguir (aunque escasamente). Estos oficiales comisionados son una minoría pequeña, aunque autorizada, dentro de la vasta población militar. La mayoría de los miembros enlistados en el servicio reciben una instrucción mínima en ética militar. Extraigo estos hechos de mi propia experiencia, pero también los corrobora Burkhardt 2017, 37-38.
17. Coates 2016, 15.
18. Ibíd.

Una peor intención

La lista de cotejo, la mentalidad burocrática, y el mito de la razón por sí solo impulsando a la acción, establecen en conjunto las condiciones para que se desarrolle una disposición concienzuda entre muchos soldados —e indirectamente, entre muchos civiles— de que su propósito esencial es el de matar; matar es su *raison d'etre*. El acto letal no se considera una tarea lamentable que, si bien es necesario, está subordinado al objetivo de una paz justa y duradera. En cambio, el acto llena el vacío en la cultura militar que deja la ausencia de la recta intención como principio rector. Es una confusión de tarea y propósito. Si no se cultiva una disposición hacia una paz justa entonces habrá una disposición hacia otra cosa; un soldado sin disposición es una imposibilidad. En el peor de los casos, se origina una disposición a matar solo por matar, lo que implica una especie de goce siniestro. Con más frecuencia, y sólo marginalmente mejor, es una disposición orientada hacia una "paz negativa", del tipo que se establece al eliminar al enemigo.[19] Es este el objetivo que tenía en mente el antiguo historiador Tácito al afirmar que "donde [los imperios] crean un desierto, lo llaman paz".[20]

Esta paz negativa puede ser legítima en casos extremos de agresores fanáticamente comprometidos con la eliminación de otros. Sin embargo, los soldados —y nuevamente, los civiles— no deberían de tener la *disposición* para esta paz, sino solo adherirse a ella cuando las circunstancias lo exijan. Su disposición debe orientarse hacia una paz que involucre una coexistencia reconciliadora dentro de la comunidad internacional, una armonía entre los cuerpos políticos basada en la justicia, en lugar de orientarse hacia la ausencia de conflicto porque un solo cuerpo político se mantiene activo. Incluso una versión más ligera de esta paz negativa, en la que los adversarios son subyugados en lugar de ser asesinados, rara vez cumple con los estándares de la justicia y, por lo tanto, rara vez debe considerarse como la paz a la que se ha de aspirar. Además de ser injusta, este tipo de paz casi nunca perdura: "La paz de los hombres sometidos no es una paz genuina, sino una paz marcada por una profunda inestabilidad…"[21]

Cuando los soldados comprenden el concepto de paz solo de manera negativa, le dan una importancia prominente al asesinato. El matar se emplea de manera casual y más eficaz de lo que es en realidad, especialmente cuando

---

19. Coates 2016, 293; Capizzi 2015, 7.
20. Publius Cornelius Tacitus, *The Works of Tacitus: The Oxford Translation, Revised with Notes*, vol. 2 (Londres: Bell y Daldy, 1872), 372.
21. Capizzi 2015, 9.

las normas profesionales promueven un uso de los principios morales con la falta de seriedad de una lista de cotejo legalista, la eficiencia mecánica de una burocracia y la indiferencia de un autómata. Un ejemplo aleccionador es el de la guerra de Vietnam, con sus líderes políticos y militares haciendo énfasis en los 8 parámetros cuantificables de los avances, principalmente en el notorio recuento de los muertos.[22] Más recientemente, en un debate sobre las elecciones presidenciales del 2015, el candidato Mike Huckabee comentó: "El propósito de las fuerzas armadas es el de matar gente y romper cosas".[23] Aunque posiblemente lo haya dicho más por su efecto retórico que por ser verdad, su sonido mordaz aún enciende una opinión pública que revela la disposición de muchos soldados hacia una paz meramente negativa y la matanza que esta conlleva.[24] Otro ejemplo: el almirante Michael Mullen, como presidente de la Junta de Jefes de Estado Mayor, en el 2008, advirtió a los miembros del Congreso: "Matar no nos lleva a la victoria" en Afganistán.[25] Dos oficiales militares retirados argumentaron que Mullen estaba equivocado, que los soldados debían sentirse libres de la "timidez" que encerraba el comentario de Mullen para "actuar con el salvajismo y la determinación necesarios para destruir...a los terroristas islámicos en todo el mundo".[26] En la revisión del historial militar de los oficiales retirados, para apoyar su punto, el crear un desierto y llamarlo paz parece ser lo único que debe buscarse con el uso de las fuerzas militares. Cabe mencionar que estos dos oficiales se desempeñaban como abogados militares en Irak

---

22. Robert McNamara transfirió su enfoque altamente cuantitativo de la industria automotriz a su nuevo rol como Secretario de Defensa (en el cargo de 1961 a 1968). Sin embargo, unos años después del conflicto de Vietnam, expresó en privado al presidente Johnson sus dudas sobre su idoneidad. Es una crítica interna que los historiadores revelaron hace relativamente poco tiempo, debido en parte a la desclasificación reciente del material. Véase Ken Burns y Lynne Novick, "The Vietnam War," Florentine Films y WETA (2017), episodio 6; y Errol Morris, "The Fog of War: Eleven Lessons from the Life of Robert S. McNamara," Sony Pictures Classics (2003).
23. Janell Ross, "Mike Huckabee says the military's job is to 'kill people and break things'. Well, not quite", *The Washington Post*, 7 de agosto de 2015.
24. Para una muestra del debate, véase Matt Cavanaugh, "The Military's Purpose is not to Kill People and Break Things," *War on the Rocks*, 26 de agosto de 2015; Jim Gourley, "The military's purpose isn't to break things and kill people, but it should be," *Foreign Policy* (24 de septiembre de 2015).
25. CNN Politics, "Troops alone will not yield victory in Afghanistan," CNN.com, 10 de septiembre de 2008.
26. David Bolgiano, John Taylor, "Can't Kill Enough to Win? Think Again," *Proceedings Magazine*, Vol. 143/12/1,378 (U.S. Naval Institute, Diciembre de 2017). Para una opinión disidente, véase Adam Weinstein, "No, We Can't Kill Our Way To Victory Despite What 2 Misguided Lieutenant Colonels Might Think," *Task and Purpose* (8 de diciembre de 2017).

y Afganistán asesorando a los comandantes de campo sobre las reglas de enfrentamiento y obligaciones bajo el derecho internacional —que, según afirman, deberían inclinarse a favor de sus propias fuerzas—.[27]

Una lectura solidaria de su argumento precisa el distinguir entre dos nociones de victoria. Supuestamente, Mullen se refiere a la victoria del esfuerzo general para instituir un régimen afgano estable que resista los disturbios de grupos extremistas violentos y provea de lo necesario a sus ciudadanos de manera que los extremistas no encuentren en ellos refugio ni apoyo. Los dos oficiales, sin embargo, se centran en la victoria táctica en combate. Es más, parecen definir la victoria a cualquier escala en términos del conflicto táctico. La postura de estos oficiales revela una suposición subyacente de que, generalmente, las relaciones internacionales, y las guerras algunas veces estas generan, son siempre juegos de suma cero. Si bien los momentos de combate real cuentan, es importante no perder nunca de vista el contexto externo de esos violentos enfrentamientos donde la ganancia de otro no se traduce necesariamente en la pérdida propia y donde existe la posibilidad de algo mejor que una paz negativa. Cuando esta mejor paz sea una opción, estaremos moral y prudentemente obligados asumirla. Esta obligación es lo que se entiende por recta intención. Es una disposición hacia una paz positiva, una insistencia a no perder de vista su posibilidad, incluso en medio de concesiones contrarias.[28]

Una disposición hacia una paz negativa y su correspondiente fijación por matar es más fácil de mantener si se considera a los enemigos menos humanos. Podría decirse que los adversarios infrahumanos, animales o insectos no justifican el tipo de restricciones que uno ejerce sobre otros seres humanos, ni tampoco el mismo nivel de compromiso con un futuro conjunto. Además de las influencias sociales del nacionalismo, del racismo o de los estereotipos culturales negativos, la aparente justicia de la guerra puede imposibilitar que se mire al enemigo "como algo más que un criminal, y como tal, está sujeto a todo lo que se le presente".[29] Esta mentalidad de cruzada es una

---

27. Bolgiano, Taylor 2017.
28. El grado y alcance de esta obligación varía según la posición y los deberes de cada uno. En el fragor del combate los soldados no deberían concentrarse en cuáles términos de paz podrían conceder los líderes políticos opositores. Deben, sin embargo, estar atentos a la posibilidad de que la contraparte enemiga se rinda. El grado de cumplimiento de esta obligación es mayor para aquellos soldados que no están inmersos en el fragor del combate, sino en las operaciones más calculadoras de determinar los objetivos estratégicos, la planificación de las campañas para lograr dichos objetivos y la de evaluar el progreso de la guerra.
29. Capizzi 2015, 121.

presión más para deshumanizar a los enemigos y a los no combatientes con quienes se les relaciona. Sin embargo, en lugar de categorizar a los enemigos bajo el estado infrahumano de un insecto, la mentalidad de las cruzadas los considera como monstruos moralmente malvados.[30] El matar se vuelve una obligación moral central independientemente del nivel de paz que genere.

Además, una intención de matar es más fácil de sostenerse con una visión militarista de guerra. Si se considera que la guerra posee un valor intrínseco, un honor sin el reconocimiento de su tragedia, entonces no se lamentan los asesinatos que conlleva, sino que se aceptan. Esta postura militarista es con frecuencia un mecanismo de supervivencia para los soldados confrontados con la tensión entre la inmoralidad *prima facie* del asesinato y el deber *prima facie* de asesinar. En lugar de trabajar a través de esta tensión —la cual podría impulsar a un soldado hacia el principio de la recta intención—, este podría ignorar la primera y decidirse por la segunda, generalmente con la ayuda de otros que se encuentren en una situación similar y debido también a las fuerzas culturales en general. Como lo describe un veterano: "Una vez que aprendes a lidiar con conductas inmorales, todo se vuelve más fácil".[31]

La intención de matar, la deshumanización y el militarismo se refuerzan mutuamente en una cultura militar que no está arraigada en una disposición hacia una paz justa y duradera. Una analogía con la cirugía puede ayudar a ilustrar el peligro de distorsionar el propósito global del soldado.[32] Nadie desea ser el paciente de un cirujano obsesionado con la cirugía, ignorando lo que contribuiría realmente a una salud plena. Por muy hábil que sea el cirujano con el bisturí, su propósito esencial sigue siendo el de promover el bienestar físico. El cirujano no debe realizar la cirugía solo porque tiene la autoridad y la habilidad para hacerlo. Debe reconocer plenamente cuándo y de qué manera el uso del bisturí contribuirá al mejoramiento de la salud. Así mismo, debe poder adaptarse a detalles imprevistos o a complicaciones que surjan durante la cirugía. De la misma forma, los soldados deben hacer uso de la fuerza letal de manera experta, pero también deben comprender la paz justa que se supone que el acto de matar promueve, comprender

---

30. Tomo estas dos categorías infrahumanas, "base, como un animal o insecto, o malvado, como un monstruo o demonio", de Michael Brough, "La deshumanización del enemigo y la moral igualitaria de los soldados", en *Rethinking the Just War Tradition* , eds. Michael Brough, John Lango, Harry van der Linden (Albany, NY: State University of New York Press, 2007), 160.

31. Wood 2016, ch. 1.

32. Esta comparación con la cirugía fue tomada de Orend 2006, 106; y Aquino, *Summa theologiae* II-II q. 64 a. 3.

cuándo el uso de la fuerza letal podría socavarla, y adaptar sus acciones a circunstancias inesperadas para lograrla a pesar de todo. Como señalara el general estadounidense John Schofield en 1881: "El objetivo y el fin de la guerra *no* es el de 'matar'. Este es sólo uno de los *medios* necesarios para ese fin....El objetivo de la guerra es el de conquistar una paz honorable, ventajosa y duradera".[33] Cuando los soldados no valoran este tipo de paz ni se comprometen con ella, de acuerdo con el principio de la recta intención, están peligrosamente mal equipados para hacer un uso sabio de la fuerza letal.

II. Reviviendo la recta intención

Hasta este momento he destacado la falta de aplicación de la recta intención como un principio del *jus in bello*, el vacío resultante permite que en su lugar se desarrolle una intención de matar, así como la deshumanización y el militarismo que se derivan y refuerzan en ella. La empatía ayuda a aminorar estas preocupaciones morales —y lo que es más importante— prácticas. En esta sección, pretendo demostrar la resistencia de la empatía a la deshumanización y el militarismo, su papel en el debilitamiento de una intención de matar y su aportación a una recta intención. Primero, aclararé a qué me refiero con la palabra empatía.

Definiendo la empatía

Para que el término 'empatía' merezca nuestra atención, debe referirse significativamente a algo. Los académicos han aplicado el término a diferentes fenómenos, con frecuencia de manera contradictoria, y su uso popular lo equipara comúnmente con la simpatía o la compasión.[34] Quisiera sugerir que la distintiva "contribución de la empatía que solo ella logra" es la característica sensible de la experiencia de otra persona.[35] Esta experiencia sensible no se limita a los sentimientos, sino que incluye la sensación de cosas más allá de los sentimientos inmediatos, como los deseos, las convicciones, las intenciones, las preocupaciones, los compromisos —casi cualquier parte de la vida mental de alguien más, incluyendo la sensación de su vida cognitiva —es decir, cómo se siente al mantener una creencia determinada—. Si un amigo dice: "Acabo de votar por el candi-

---

33. John M. Schofield, "Notes on 'The Legitimate in War'", *Journal of the Military Service Institution* 2 (1881), 1-10; citado por Brian Linn, *The Echo of Battle: The Army's Way of War* (Cambridge, MA: Harvard University Press, 2009), 58.
34. Véase Batson 2009 para un resumen ilustrativo. Para una introducción más completa de este término y su historia, véase Stueber 2006, Coplan y Goldie 2011, Zahavi 2014 y Matravers 2017.
35. Smith 2015, 711.

dato por el que he estado haciendo campaña durante las últimas semanas", significa que existen estados tanto cognitivos como afectivos asociados a esta experiencia. Los estados cognitivos del amigo, digamos, de creer que su candidato preferido es el mejor o que es importante ejercer el derecho al voto, etc., existen simultáneamente con los estados afectivos de desear que el candidato avance en su plataforma política, de preocuparse por las posibilidades de triunfo del candidato, de la sensación de confianza en el esfuerzo de la campaña, de la sensación de alivio de que la campaña haya terminado o, lo que es más importante, de una compleja combinación de estos. Además, estos estados cognitivos y afectivos son mutuamente caus- ativos, lo que significa que pueden impulsarse o reforzarse mutuamente. La empatía es el comprender, hasta cierto punto, cómo se siente el amigo luego de esta experiencia global de votar —después de haber hecho campaña—, debido a una compleja interacción cognitiva y afectiva de acuerdo con las circunstancias y contextos específicos.[36]

La empatía no es, por tanto, el simple hecho de asignar un sentimiento genérico de esperanza o de nerviosismo a un amigo. Tal y como plantea Max Scheler, la empatía no es "simplemente una cuestión de juzgar intelec- tualmente una determinada experiencia por la que otros estén pasando; no es el mero pensamiento de que ese sea el caso…"[37] La empatía se orienta específicamente a la experiencia del otro en su fenomelanismo. En otras palabras, la empatía proporciona una comprensión limitada de las experi- encias del otro y no una descripción de esa experiencia —la cual depende, entre otras cosas, de la habilidad del empatizador para verbalizarla—, sino de la naturaleza fenomenal de la misma. Entonces, como definición práctica, apoyo el concepto de empatía de Joel Smith como una comprensión experi- encial de *qué* siente o piensa otra persona, no únicamente una comprensión proposicional o teórica de *lo que* el otro siente o si piensa de cierta manera.[38]

Por lo tanto, la empatía difiere mucho de la simpatía. La empatía es el comprender lo que piensa o siente el otro, pero no se preocupa por su bienestar.[39] Según señala Edmund Husserl, "Mientras que la empatía es una forma de comprensión, la simpatía involucra cuidado e interés".[40] Los

---

36. También es importante considerar que la precisión de la empatía aumenta con el conocimiento que uno mismo tenga sobre el amigo, y si éste fuese naturalmente optimista, inquieto, etc. Dicha familiaridad puede brindar mayor fidelidad a la tentativa empática de comprender los estados mentales del amigo.
37. Según lo citado por Zahavi 2014, 118.
38. Smith 2015, 712-713.
39. Darwall 1998, 261-270.
40. Según lo cita Zahavi 2014, 139 (nota al pie 14)

dos conceptos están relacionados. De hecho, la empatía puede propiciar y ayudar a la preocupación por la simpatía, y la simpatía puede impulsar tentativas de comprensión empática hacia los demás. La fusión de los términos es probablemente más común gracias al uso que David Hume y Adam Smith hacen de "la simpatía" en sus obras sobre teoría de la moral; los fenómenos que describen, sin embargo, corresponden a lo que ahora llamamos empatía. Específicamente, la concepción de Hume se asemeja al reflejo de las emociones de la otra persona en una empatía de nivel inferior, mientras que la concepción de Smith se asemeja a la postura de perspectiva imaginativa en una empatía de nivel superior.[41] Generalmente, una empatía de nivel inferior se considera como subconsciente, automática y reveladora de estados mentales de emoción "superficial" e intenciones inmediatas. Una empatía de nivel superior se considera como consciente, voluntaria y reveladora de estados mentales más profundos o duraderos, incluyendo intenciones más amplias o el sentido que encierra el comportamiento.[42] En particular, el término "empatía" no se incorporó al idioma inglés sino hasta un siglo después de las obras de Hume y Smith, lo que hace difícil el responsabilizarlos por la confusión.

La investigación refuerza la intuición de que la empatía conduce a la simpatía, pero también demuestra no ser necesariamente así.[43] De hecho, puede inhibir la simpatía hacia algunos individuos mientras la impulsa hacia otros debido a la facilidad con la que empatizamos con los miembros de nuestra propia cultura u otro grupo y a la dificultad que podríamos tener de sentir empatía hacia otros grupos ajenos a estos. Por lo tanto, la empatía puede introducir una parcialidad moralmente problemática. Esta preocupación ha alimentado el debate en contra de la supuesta aportación de la empatía a la moralidad.[44] Destaca asimismo la diferencia entre la empatía y la simpatía.[45]

La empatía revela la igualdad moral del enemigo

La empatía implica una solidaridad fundacional con los demás. No se trata de una solidaridad de opiniones, perspectivas, juicios, valores o sentimientos, sino sólo de una solidaridad de la individualidad fundamental.

---

41. Darwall 1998, 267; Coplan y Goldie 2011, x.
42. Coplan y Goldie 2011, xxxiii.
43. Batson 1991; Darwall 1998, 272-273.
44. Prinz 2011; Bloom 2014.
45. Para una discusión más amplia sobre la relación entre la empatía y la simpatía, véase Darwall 1998; Coplan y Goldie 2011, x-xi; Gallagher 2012, 360-362; Zahavi 2014, 115-117; Matravers 2017, 115.

La empatía puede contribuir a la primera, aunque no necesariamente. La empatía, como una comprensión experiencial de otra persona, revela la calidad humana que un soldado tiene en común con el enemigo. La empatía humaniza a los demás y, por lo tanto, contrarresta las tendencias deshumanizantes. Una empatía de nivel inferior fundamenta una intuición del estado humano del enemigo, que es algo comparable a la percepción sensorial. Esta empatía de nivel inferior se puede desconectar o interrumpir, como el cerrar los ojos para no ver, pero sin tal acción, la empatía de nivel inferior se produce automáticamente. La empatía de nivel superior se erige sobre dicha intuición gracias a procesos cognitivos como la postura de una perspectiva imaginativa para revelar información sobre la experiencia del otro, incluidos elementos de su estructura narrativa, su cosmovisión, sus valores y sus intenciones. La empatía de nivel superior no es automática; debe propiciarse conscientemente. Sin embargo, uno puede habituarse a ella.

Tomemos como ejemplo la experiencia de un equipo de soldados desplegados en Irak como parte de una campaña contrainsurgente. Los soldados llevaron a cabo una redada en la casa de un ex coronel del ejército iraquí, quien había comenzado a planificar y financiar los movimientos de insurgencia en su localidad. Tras abrirse paso por la puerta principal, un hombre acuclillado ingresó rápidamente en el zaguán. Estaba agachado, con las manos ocultas, se abalanzaba hacia adelante y, entonces, dos de los cuatro soldados le dispararon, y cayó al suelo. Esos fueron los únicos disparos realizados. Treinta segundos después, la casa fue declarada segura y el equipo comenzó a brindar los primeros auxilios al hombre caído. El hombre murió en presencia de los soldados, y de su esposa y su pequeña hija, a quienes se les había encontrado en la casa y se les había conducido hasta el zaguán. El hombre muerto era el coronel iraquí.[46]

El recuerdo de la muerte de ese hombre permaneció en la memoria de los soldados que le dispararon. Uno de ellos, particularmente, se sintió atormentado con la baja que ocasionó. La cadena de mando determinó que las acciones del equipo se justificaban, pero eso no aminoró la pesadumbre del soldado. El hombre al que mató no llevaba nada en las manos. El soldado luchó por comprender por qué el hombre se había abalanzado de tal forma. ¿Acaso intentaba el coronel proteger a su familia? ¿Intentaba derribar al soldado líder que entraba por la puerta? ¿Estaba entrando en la habitación para saber por qué había fuertes ruidos? ¿Simplemente se había tropezado

---

46. Esta historia se basa en mi propia experiencia cuando me enviaron a Irak con la 4ta División de Infantería del Ejército de los Estados Unidos en el año 2003.

al entrar en la habitación? El soldado tenía esposa y una hija pequeña, y no pudo evitar el preguntarse qué iba a ser de la familia de este coronel.

El conflicto de este soldado es un ejemplo de la empatía que comúnmente ocurre durante la guerra, aunque no se le reconozca plenamente en nuestra teorización sobre la misma. Es una respuesta natural a los penosos deberes de la contienda. Aun así, el entrenamiento militar se enfoca muy frecuentemente en reprimir estas reacciones para garantizar que los soldados persistan en sus deberes — es mejor un soldado irreflexivo que uno demasiado reflexivo—. Quiero resistirme a dicha conclusión; cualquiera de los dos extremos resulta igualmente perjudicial para un buen soldado.

Propongo que, a través del entrenamiento militar y la inculturación, este soldado interrumpió su empatía de nivel inferior en aras de las acciones coercitivas al participar en la redada de la casa del coronel iraquí. Luego de ingresar por la fuerza, del disparo de una persona que parecía amenazante y del aseguramiento del resto de la casa, los soldados intentaron estabilizar al malherido coronel. En la transición de las acciones coercitivas para evaluar la situación inmediata y brindar auxilio al coronel, la intuición de la empatía de nivel inferior resurgió, particularmente en este único soldado, como algo que se admite en lugar de reprimirse.

Su empatía de nivel superior procesó la intuición y la expandió para propiciar la comprensión de la situación del coronel en cada uno de sus otros roles como esposo y padre. A su vez, dicha comprensión estimuló la comprensión empática del soldado con respecto a la viuda y a la hija. Durante esta comprensión experiencial, en este momento de empatía, mi soldado también se siente atormentado.

La fuente de su perturbación se debió, al menos parcialmente, al estatus más complejo del iraquí muerto. Dejó de ser pura o simplemente un combatiente enemigo contra el que se debía luchar; era también un ser humano sin vida que habría de ser llorado. El soldado se detuvo ante el hecho de que él mismo y este coronel eran esposos y ambos tenían hijas pequeñas. Habría sido más fácil considerar perentoriamente al coronel como un criminal, como a alguien personalmente responsable de la guerra en la que el soldado se encontraba. El correspondiente odio por el enemigo culpable hizo que el patear la puerta y el apretar el gatillo fuera más fácil. Ahora, sin embargo, este odio había sido…

> …interrumpido o anulado por una comprensión más reflexiva…la sensación de que el soldado enemigo, aunque su guerra fuera criminal, era, sin embargo, tan inocente como uno mismo.

> Armado, él es un enemigo; pero no es *mi* enemigo en ningún
> sentido estricto; la guerra en sí no es una relación entre personas
> sino entre entidades políticas y sus instrumentos humanos....[que
> como yo, se encuentran] atrapados en una guerra que no declara-
> ron. Veo en ellos a mis homólogos morales.[47]

Esta noción de la igualdad moral, de una inocencia moral compartida
por soldados de ambos lados de una guerra que no iniciaron, se desarrolla
aún más con un experimento del pensamiento empático. Lo que se expresa
aquí en términos de una situación de una contrainsurgencia similar al
reciente esfuerzo bélico en Irak. Como una extensión de la comprensión
reflexiva antes mencionada, un soldado estadounidense podría preguntarse:
"¿Qué tendría que pasar para que *yo* cooperara con una fuerza de ocupación
extranjera que patrulla mi localidad? ¿Qué comportamiento por parte de
ellos les haría ganar *mi* cooperación? ¿Qué posibilidades habría de que me
levantara en armas contra las fuerzas de ocupación extranjera? Estas pregun-
tas corren el riesgo de presentar un error de proyección ya que requieren
de una perspectiva orientada hacia uno mismo, la cual incorpora a su vez
numerosas influencias culturales que son diferentes a las del iraquí promedio.
Sin embargo, el tener una perspectiva orientada hacia uno mismo puede
ser un modo adecuado de empatía de nivel superior "cuando existe una
gran superposición entre uno mismo y los demás o cuando la situación es
del tipo que conduciría a una respuesta lo suficientemente universal".[48] Los
soldados extranjeros que patrullan las calles del vecindario generan una
preocupación similar por la seguridad de la familia, un patriotismo similar
y una desconfianza similar hacia esos extraños de cultura extranjera.

La empatía ayuda a los soldados a reconocer la igualdad moral de sus
enemigos. De esta forma, la empatía "frena la inclinación en tiempos de
guerra" a deshumanizar.[49] Debilita la tendencia de ver al enemigo como
un animal de nivel menor o como si el enemigo fuese tan vil que se des-
prendiera de su calidad humana. En cambio, se le percibe como si estuviera
sujeto a influencias similares de fervor nacionalista, de respeto a las leyes de
reclutamiento y al deseo de proteger a su familia y a sus compatriotas. Esta
honestidad con respecto al enemigo puede tener dos efectos. En primer lugar,

---

47. Walzer 1977, 36
48. Amy Coplan, "Understanding Emphaty: Its Features and Effects", en *Empathy: Philo-sophical and Psychological Perspectives*, ed. Amy Coplan y Peter Goldie (Nueva York: Oxford University Press, 2011), 9.
49. Brough 2007, 151.

infunde un mayor autocontrol de modo que los soldados limitan sus actos coercitivos, de manera más confiable, a solo aquellos que sean realmente necesarios. En segundo lugar, sienta las bases para una disposición hacia una paz justa y duradera. La igualdad moral funge como una "razón por enviar al enemigo derrotado de regreso a su vida habitual, un paso hacia el regreso a la normalidad y la paz —porque ¿cómo puede castigarse en el enemigo lo que habría hecho uno mismo de haber estado en la misma situación?[50]

¿Son los terroristas moralmente iguales?

Es difícil mantener una mentalidad de cruzada cuando uno se percata de la igualdad moral de un soldado enemigo, pero el caso es diferente cuando se considera la postura adecuada hacia un terrorista. ¿Debemos sentir empatía hacia un terrorista y promover este sentido de igualdad moral con él? ¿Existe la igualdad moral? Por una parte, existe una influencia similar de la cultura, los esfuerzos de reclutamiento, la propaganda, etc., a los que el terrorista está sujeto. Además, si el terrorista es un miembro de bajo rango en su organización, estará sujeto a las órdenes de sus líderes. Estas órdenes serán influyentes aun cuando no estén legalmente respaldadas por la autoridad de un régimen establecido y reconocido. Mientras que este hecho podría ser utilizado en contra del terrorista de bajo rango por eludir una debida deferencia hacia un gobierno establecido, puede ser que el gobierno en cuestión ya haya perdido su legitimidad y su derecho a gobernar o que no exista un gobierno efectivo. Si su subordinación es tal que el terrorista de bajo rango no participa en la toma de decisiones relacionadas con medidas de violencia o la selección de objetivos, este terrorista puede adquirir una inocencia moral similar a la de un soldado de bajo rango a pesar de su participación material en el acto terrorista. Es cierto que el acto tendría que ser de tal naturaleza que este participante de bajo rango no pudiera identificar de manera confiable las características morales de dicho acto —particularmente el ataque intencional a personas inocentes—, o el estar sujeto a presiones de tal magnitud que lo absuelvan de su culpabilidad. Sin embargo, de ser así, entonces el título de "terrorista" no aplicaría en su caso. Él es moralmente igual a un soldado y, por tanto, no se merece tal etiqueta peyorativa.

Sin embargo, un auténtico terrorista sigue siendo moralmente diferente a un soldado debido a la naturaleza terrorista que genera este título. El

---

50. Brough 2007, 151. Esta conclusión de que uno haría lo mismo en el lugar del otro no se debe a la empatía, pero esta la hace posible. La empatía solo brinda comprensión y no un acuerdo.

terrorismo es el uso deliberado o una amenaza de violencia contra no combatientes para lograr un impacto político.[51] Este uso de la fuerza no satisface las demandas morales con respecto a las vidas inocentes. El terrorista auténtico, por lo tanto, no es moralmente inocente como el soldado, quien por los principios del *jus in bello* está obligado a discriminar entre los combatientes y los no combatientes, para lo está preparado mediante el énfasis en la ley, en el entrenamiento y en la cultura militar o social. El terrorista tiene como objetivo deliberado y evitable a personas inocentes.[52] Por lo tanto, es mucho más fácil mantener una mentalidad de cruzada hacia el terrorista; él *es* un criminal de una manera en que los soldados no lo son.

Aun así, existe una igualdad disminuida, o más delgada, que un soldado comparte con un terrorista.[53] En general, es del tipo que uno tiene en común con un malhechor que es culpable. Es una igualdad moral en el estatus y el valor humanos, aunque no lo sea en la inocencia moral de los actos de fuerza de cada uno. Una comprensión empática del terrorista subraya esta igualdad moral más delgada —como lo hace, de manera más general, con los malhechores en su conjunto—. Esta igualdad, como del tipo más grueso con los soldados enemigos ya mencionados, no implica el estar de acuerdo con la visión del mundo, los juicios morales o las decisiones del terrorista; simplemente suscita una explicación idónea de su humanidad según el juicio de uno mismo, a pesar del propio fracaso de los enemigos, en este sentido, con respecto hacia sus víctimas.

A través de la revelación de una igualdad moral ya sea delgada o gruesa, la empatía humaniza a los enemigos y, por lo tanto, fortalece el juicio de los soldados. "Si los estados y sus soldados pueden aprender a ver al enemigo como alguien completamente humano e individual y moralmente homólogo, discernirán el paisaje moral más claramente y evitarán un desastre moral

---

51. Bruce Hoffman, *Inside Terrorism,* edición revisada y ampliada, (Nueva York: Columbia University Press, 2006), 26-28. Véase también Naciones Unidas, "Declaración sobre medidas para eliminar el terrorismo internacional", anexo a la resolución 49/60 de la Asamblea General de las Naciones Unidas, "Medidas para eliminar el terrorismo internacional" (9 de diciembre de 1994).

52. Este análisis entre el soldado y el terrorista ayuda a revelar la facilidad con la que los soldados pueden cometer actos terroristas. Los soldados pueden deliberadamente no discriminar entre los combatientes y los no combatientes, o no proteger debidamente a los no combatientes. Debido a sus fines ampliamente políticos, dichos actos comienzan a parecerse a la definición de terrorismo. Véase la discusión de David Rodin sobre la fuerza imprudente o negligente contra los no combatientes en "Terrorism without Intention", *Ethics* 114 (julio de 2004), 752-771.

53. Tomo esta noción de una igualdad moral más delgada de Brough 2007, 150.

para ambos lados de la guerra".[54] Es difícil mantener una actitud militarista cuando hay empatía. No se puede ignorar la tragedia de la guerra, pero debe enfrentarse, tal y como hizo el soldado antes mencionado, al lidiar con la muerte del coronel iraquí.

Sin embargo, la empatía aplicada selectivamente puede interferir con el buen juicio. Por ejemplo, la empatía hacia las víctimas de la agresión puede estimular la perseverancia. Si se lleva demasiado lejos o de manera demasiado exclusiva, esta perseverancia empujará al individuo a una intención vengativa, quebrantando cualquier noción de igualdad moral. Uno evita este extremo gracias a un nuevo momento de empatía hacia los agresores.

La relación de la empatía con matar

"Para nuestra mente moderna", señala Shay, "el enemigo es detestable, por definición".[55] El mantener la calidad humana del enemigo se considera generalmente imposible; para muchos es una verdad manifiesta el "que los hombres no pueden matar a un enemigo que consideran honorable y como ellos mismos".[56] Sin embargo, contrario al argumento de que los soldados *deben* deshumanizar a los enemigos para matarlos, hay al menos algunos momentos en los que *no pueden* deshumanizarlos debido al contacto íntimos con ellos. Michael Walzer presenta algunos de estos casos basándose en las memorias de veteranos en las que estos describen la dificultad para disparar sus armas contra los soldados enemigos "quienes se ven graciosos, quienes están duchándose, subiéndose los pantalones [mientras corren por una trinchera], están disfrutando del sol, [o] fumando un cigarrillo".[57] Richard Holmes advierte que "el concepto de un enemigo odioso e inhumano rara vez subsiste cuando se tiene contacto con él como un individuo".[58] La experiencia del soldado atormentado mencionado anteriormente ilustra asimismo los inevitables momentos de empatía en la guerra. Estos momentos son, ciertamente, sólo breves vislumbres de la humanidad del individuo, vislumbres a menudo soterrados bajo la propaganda del esfuerzo bélico y las penetrantes emociones de lucha y pérdida inherentes a la guerra. Sin embargo, el simplemente sofocar estos momentos de empatía conduce a

---

54. Brough 2007, 160.
55. Jonathan Shay, *Achilles in Vietnam: Combat Trauma and the Undoing of Character* (Nueva York: Scribner, 1994), 103.
56. Ibíd.
57. Walzer 1977, 138-143.
58. Richard Holmes, *Acts of War: The Behavior of Men in Battle* (Nueva York: The Free Press, 1985), 368; citado por Brough 2007, 157.

los peligros de la deshumanización, del militarismo y del asesinato como propósito primordial. Se pierde la recta intención.[59] Al reconciliar la naturaleza humana de los enemigos con el deber que se tiene de matarlos debe existir alguna otra alternativa a la deshumanización, la cual simplemente intenta negar la naturaleza humana.[60]

Michael Brough plantea la misma pregunta: "¿Entonces cómo deben ver los soldados los asesinatos que cometen en la guerra, y cómo deben las naciones instruir a sus soldados a ese respecto? La deshumanización es demasiado costosa".[61] Basándose en la investigación de los psicólogos David Grossman y Stanley Milgram, Brough reconoce la necesidad de distanciarse del objetivo para poder matarlo. Esta distancia puede tomar una forma física, especialmente como lo permiten las tecnologías modernas, pero también puede tomar una forma emocional, incluyendo la "distancia social —la cual enfatiza las diferencias de la casta social—, la distancia cultural —la cual acentúa las diferencias raciales y étnicas—, y la distancia moral —la cual visualiza la inferioridad moral del enemigo—".[62] Estas últimas formas de distancia emocional son precisamente las tendencias deshumanizantes que convierten a los enemigos ya sea en "seres sin importancia, como un animal o un insecto, o en malvados, como un monstruo o un demonio", y que son, por lo tanto, inaceptables.[63] Brough etiqueta estos intentos de "infrahumanización" a distancia para denotar su negación del valor humano del enemigo. En su lugar sugiere una forma alternativa de distancia emocional a la que se refiere como "no humanización". Impulsada por la distancia

---

59. Lleva también al peligro de daño moral, una debilitante sensación de traición y / o culpa entre los veteranos, la cual está captando una mayor atención. Para una introducción, véase Jonathan Shay (1994); Nancy Sherman, *Afterwar: Healing the Moral Wounds of our Soldiers* (Nueva York: Oxford University Press, 2015); y David Wood, *What Have We Done: The Moral Injury of Our Longest Wars* (Nueva York: Little, Brown and Company, 2016).

60. La respuesta pacifista es la de negar esto último — no existe el deber de matar—. Si bien me alejo de la postura pacifista hasta cierto punto, comparto la preocupación de Brian Orend de que podría haber una "arrogancia vergonzosa" en la literatura de guerra justa con respecto al pacifismo ("A Just War Critique of Realism and Pacifism", *Journal of Philosophical Research*, Vol. XXVI [2001], 435-436). Por default, todos deberíamos tener un compromiso pacifista con la resolución no violenta de conflictos. Es un compromiso *prima facie* que incluso los soldados deben de mantener, en el entendido de que su profesión continúa orientada hacia aquellas circunstancias que traspasan el umbral de este compromiso. Varias situaciones precisan de juzgar si uno ha traspasado o no ese umbral. En las contrainsurgencias, especialmente, sin vanguardias definidas, se requiere de este juicio por parte de los soldados que están más abajo en la cadena de mando, aunque a menudo resulte más difícil.

61. Brough 2007, 159.

62. Ibíd., 160.

63. Ibíd.

física del armamento moderno, "la no humanización surgió a raíz de la invención de la artillería de trayectoria indirecta, cuando los soldados enemigos se convirtieron en chinchetas o trazos de lápiz en mapas, o gritaban coordenadas a una sección de armas".[64] La percepción del enemigo no humano "como un punto luminoso en la pantalla de una computadora" se ha expandido a medida que la guerra se ha ido ejecutando más y más de forma electrónica.[65]

En lugar de menospreciar al enemigo con una carga emocional, la no humanización implica el tratar al enemigo como un objeto sin emociones. Por lo tanto, puede estar unos grados de la moral por encima de la infra-humanización debido a los excesos violentos que esta última suscita. Sin embargo, a pesar de que el prefijo *"no"* evita la connotación de menor valor en comparación con el prefijo *"infra"*, transmite la sensación de que el enemigo es un *in* humano, algo distinto a un humano. En consecuencia, todavía así parece ser un enfoque problemático para la muerte justificada de otros *seres humanos* en guerra. Brough se apresura a resaltar esta inquietud diciendo que considerar como no humanos a los enemigos puede negar su igualdad moral de forma similar a la consideración de los enemigos como infrahumanos.[66] Sin embargo, dada la necesidad de algún tipo de distancia emocional o de alguna forma de "hacer que matar sea más fácil" en las circunstancias morales adecuadas, Brough respalda un momento no humanizante, aunque fuertemente limitado por el respeto por el enemigo.[67] El matar a otra persona, según él, "no impide el honrar a los muertos después de la batalla. Una oración, un pensamiento o el musitar una despedida pueden ser muestras de respeto suficientes ante los caídos". Brough destaca la investigación terapéutica que demuestra cuán importante es para los soldados el honrar a sus adversarios caídos con el fin de evitar "repercusiones psicológicas dañinas".[68]

Yo simpatizo con esta propuesta de Brough, pero deseo aportar una alternativa a la no humanización. El soldado que se encuentra en circunstancias tales en las que el matar al enemigo sea al menos moralmente permisible, si no es que obligatorio, debe mantener intacta la humanidad del

---

64. Ibíd., 161.
65. Ibíd.
66. Ibíd.
67. Walzer sugiere algo similar con respecto a matar al enemigo cuando afirma: "Pero la alienación [del enemigo] es temporal, la humanidad es inminente" (1977, 142).
68. Brough 2007, 163. La investigación psicológica es la de Jonathan Shay y David Grossman, y el daño moral es una de estas repercusiones.

enemigo, pero también debe desprenderse del impulso empático que destaca esa humanidad. Anteriormente sugerí esta alternativa cuando describí los roles de una empatía de nivel inferior y una superior en la experiencia del soldado atormentado y su reacción ante la muerte del coronel iraquí. Dicha alternativa es similar a la necesidad del cirujano de alejarse emocionalmente del paciente para realizar mejor una cirugía. Así como no es de esperarse que el cirujano perciba o imagine con empatía la experiencia que está produciendo en el paciente, al menos durante el acto quirúrgico, tampoco debe de esperarse que el soldado se enfrente a su enemigo con empatía durante el acto letal. Sin embargo, al igual que el cirujano, el soldado no debe mantener el alejamiento estoico posteriormente —y a menudo no puede, como se demuestra crudamente con aquellos soldados moralmente dañados—. El paralelo existe también en las responsabilidades de los soldados más experimentados:

> …es una parte necesaria del alto mando militar en el campo de batalla el que un comandante se endurezca hacia el coste humano de sus planes y órdenes —de lo contrario sería emocionalmente imposible para él el desempeñar su trabajo—. Sin embargo, lo anterior no tiene por qué volverlo deficiente con respecto al cuidado previo a la batalla o a la compasión posterior a ella. No tiene por qué volverlo inhumano…[69]

Es posible que me ande con sutilezas al tratar de distinguir entre la no humanización de Brough y mi concepto de interrupción del impulso empático. Sin embargo, sí parece relevante el describir este paso necesario, no como una atribución real al enemigo de un estatus no humano, sino como la gestión de las facultades mentales de uno mismo. Con el tiempo se desarrollará una disposición basándose ya sea en uno o en el otro. Parece que es mejor limitar esa disposición sobre cómo responde uno afectivamente hacia los demás, en lugar de formarse el hábito de considerar a los demás como objetos. La disposición más limitada hará posible que el soldado respete a los enemigos fallecidos de la forma que Brough recomienda, puesto que su calidad humana nunca ha sido ignorada. La no humanización se presta muy fácilmente a los peligros de una mentalidad burocrática o al de una aproximación al *jus in bello* de lista de cotejo, arriesgando el mantenimiento de una recta intención.

---

69. Nigel Biggar, *In Defense of War* (Oxford: Oxford University Press, 2013), 127.

Entonces, en lugar de deshumanizar a los enemigos ya sea como infra-humanos o como no humanos, sugiero un manejo de la empatía de uno mismo que sea similar al uso de los sentidos. Así como puede educarse el oído para detectar unos sonidos en lugar de otros, así puede enfocarse la empatía de manera selectiva. Esta armonización empática ya tiene lugar en varios contextos y tiene momentos inmorales en los que nos volvemos demasiado selectivos. Esta parcialidad es particularmente común en la guerra, donde la empatía hacia los camaradas puede ahogar la empatía hacia enemigos o los no combatientes. Sin embargo, el caso del asesinato justificado en la guerra cuenta como un momento moralmente apropiado.

Fuera de esta excepción con respecto al acto de matar justificado, la empatía no debe reprimirse en la guerra. De hecho, no se puede, al menos no definitivamente, debido a la naturaleza instintiva de la empatía de nivel inferior, a los inexorables momentos de empatía que tienen lugar incluso durante la guerra y a la introspección posterior al combate como le sucede a la mayoría de los soldados. Los soldados son seres humanos y, por lo tanto, están programados para sentir empatía, lo que hace del autómata humano un objetivo imposible de lograr incluso con un extenso entrenamiento militar. Es también un objetivo inmoral puesto que un autómata no puede mantener una disposición hacia una paz justa y duradera, sino que simple-mente debe estar equipado con un programa de actividad y, por lo tanto, carece del juicio necesario para ejercer adecuadamente la fuerza letal en todas las circunstancias a las que un soldado se enfrenta. En tercer lugar, es una meta tácticamente desatinada: un autómata no puede adaptarse a circunstancias realmente nuevas puesto que solo está equipado con una lista de cotejo, por muy elaborada que sea esta.

¿Y qué más además de deshumanizar?

Dada la inevitable naturaleza de la empatía, la humanización de los individuos que impulsa y la vital necesidad moral de ver a los demás como humanizados durante la guerra, es importante el identificar alternativas a la visión moderna, la cual no da cabida a la humanidad del enemigo. Esta visión moderna sugiere que el valor de un soldado depende de, e incluso se comprueba por medio una degradación desdeñosa o despectiva del enemigo. Considérese, en cambio, la actitud de los antiguos griegos retratada según Homero o, lo que resulta aún más revelador, la actitud de los primeros cristianos, quienes permitían que el enemigo fuera visto como alguien tan "honorable y como uno mismo" incluso cuando se luchara a muerte.[70]

---

70. La frase de Shay antes mencionada.

Jonathan Shay, en su extenso estudio sobre la *Ilíada*, de Homero, no identifica ningún ejemplo en el que los griegos o los troyanos se deshumanicen entre sí durante la guerra de Troya.[71] Ninguna de las partes se refiere a la otra en términos despectivos, una práctica común en las guerras modernas. Tampoco se expresan irrespetuosamente, de manera más general. Por el contrario, las dos partes expresan repetidamente su admiración por la destreza en combate de sus adversarios. Luego de un prolongado duelo que culmina en empate, el guerrero troyano Ajax afirma:

> Volveremos a encontrarnos en otro momento, y lucharemos hasta que el poder invisible decida entre nuestros anfitriones, otorgando a uno o al otro la victoria. Posteriormente se dirá entre [griegos] y troyanos:'Estos dos se batieron cuerpo a cuerpo sin piedad, pero se separaron como amigos'.[72]

Shay señala que el "contraste con la lucha contra los 'Gooks' en Vietnam no podría ser más marcado".[73]

La principal excepción a esta respetuosa actitud es el trato horroroso que se le da al cuerpo de Héctor luego de que Aquiles lo venciera en la batalla. Aquiles mutila el cadáver y lo arrastra de forma vergonzosa para exhibirlo públicamente. Todavía así, como señala Shay, este comportamiento fue condenado por griegos y troyanos por igual, por violar normas profundamente arraigadas que compartían.[74] Es más, Homero retrata a Aquiles como especialmente respetuoso y generoso con sus adversarios antes de cambiar de parecer al principio de la historia, lo cual fue provocado por la traición de su oficial al mando.

Es cierto que los griegos y los troyanos tenían una cultura común que hacía que el respeto fuera más fácil de mantener. No era tan difícil para una de las partes ver a la otra como igual en su condición humana y en su valor correspondiente. Shay señala que "los griegos posteriores degradaron a los 'bárbaros' enemigos extranjeros de la misma forma en que los estadounidenses modernos lo hicieron [en la Segunda Guerra Mundial y Vietnam]".[75] No obstante, el ejemplo de Grecia y Troya constituye una importante excepción

---

71. Shay 1994, 103-120.
72. Ibíd., 108-109.
73. Ibíd.
74. Ibíd., 29.
75. Ibíd., 111, nota 6. Shay cita la investigación de Edith Hall en *Inventing the Barbarian* (Nueva York: Oxford University Press, 1991).

a la supuesta necesidad de la deshumanización para el cumplimiento de los deberes militares. Aunque los griegos y los troyanos se percibían con mucho respeto entre sí, eso no diluyó la tenacidad de su lucha.[76]

Shay atribuye el contraste entre la actitud de los antiguos griegos hacia sus enemigos y su contraparte moderna a una tendencia inherente a deshumanizar a los adversarios en las religiones bíblicas.[77] Las tradiciones judía, cristiana e islámica, según Shay, hacen énfasis en la deshumanización de los enemigos como una expresión de piedad. "Cuando los soldados estadounidenses modernos y sus líderes deshumanizan al enemigo, afirman su lealtad hacia Dios expresando una tradición cultural poderosamente grabada en las escrituras bíblicas".[78] Shay analiza la historia de David y Goliat, destacando el pasaje donde se compara a Goliat con animales y lo presenta "como una monstruosidad moral al igual que como un monstruo físico, no concebible como una contraparte en un acuerdo político…"[79] Shay concluye:

> La cosmovisión judeocristiana —e islámica— ha triunfado completamente sobre la cosmovisión homérica de tal manera que el deshonrar al enemigo ahora parece natural, virtuoso, patriótico, piadoso. Sin embargo, en la *Ilíada* solo Aquiles irrespeta al enemigo. En el mundo de Homero, este no es un estado natural sino uno inhumano en el que Aquiles ha caído trágicamente. Los guerreros de Homero nunca se debilitan por respetar al enemigo.[80]

No puede negarse la deshumanización que se ha llevado a cabo en el nombre de Dios, ni el fervor religioso que con mucha frecuencia la alimenta. Sin embargo, la afirmación de Shay parece desequilibrada e incompleta. En su análisis de los comentarios de David sobre Goliat y hacia Goliat mismo, no queda muy claro, como afirma Shay, que David rebaja a Goliat al estado inferior de un animal o un monstruo. David compara el desafío de luchar contra él con sus desafíos anteriores de luchar contra un león o un oso, pero esta comparación no es necesariamente degradante; también

---

76. Tampoco minimizó el trato del vencedor hacia los combatientes y no combatientes capturados. Ambas partes sabían que si morían en la batalla serían masacrados, sus ciudades serían saqueadas y sus familias serían esclavizadas. Por horribles que fueran estos actos, no fue el resultado de considerar a los vencidos como infrahumanos. Véase Shay 1994, 103.
77. Shay 1994, 103, 111-120.
78. Ibíd., 111.
79. Ibíd., 112.
80. Shay 1994, 115.

puede leerse como un reconocimiento laudatorio de la ferocidad de Goliat.
David saca valor claramente de su creencia de contar con el favor de Dios,
y esta presunción puede conducir a una visión arrogante y despectiva de los
demás, pero no es evidente que David demuestre arrogancia o desprecio.
Podría tratarse de su confianza en sí mismo y un deseo de darle a Dios el
crédito de la victoria anticipada.

A pesar de todo, lo más preocupante es el silencio de Shay sobre la
defensa del trato humano de los enemigos en las tradiciones judía, cristiana e islámica. Me enfocaré en la tradición cristiana porque sus antiguos
integrantes fueron los cimientos de la tradición de la guerra justa y porque
el mandato cristiano con respecto a los enemigos es muy drástico: como
declaró Jesucristo, hay que amarlos.[81]

Muchos consideran que este mandato es insostenible; resulta contradic-
torio para un soldado afirmar que ama al enemigo al que le causa la muerte.
Quizás el soldado se sienta motivado por el amor a la víctima cuando mata
a un agresor, pero parece absurdo afirmar que también actúa amorosamente
hacia el agresor. En cambio, la intuición moderna de deshumanizar al agresor
comienza a perfilarse como algo más realista. Sin embargo, San Agustín
defiende el amor por el agresor, parcialmente identificando el amor como
una disposición interior del corazón del soldado, y parcialmente sugiriendo
que el control coercitivo del agresor lo beneficia a él mismo y no solamente
a la víctima: "Es útil la derrota para *aquellos* a quienes se les quita la licencia
de la iniquidad…"[82] Restringir a un agresor que vive para enmendar su
camino es una cosa, pero San Agustín sustenta este beneficio incluso si el
agresor es asesinado, ya que, en la cosmovisión cristiana, cada quien debe
rendir cuentas por los agravios cometidos en este mundo, y la muerte de
este agresor le impide a este cometer otros agravios.

San Agustín proporciona otra respuesta que no apela a la ultratumba, ni
requiere fuerza sin matar. En una carta a un comandante militar que expresó
dudas sobre su capacidad para ser cristiano y soldado, San Agustín dice:

> Sé, pues, pacífico aun cuando combates, para llevar, al vencerlos,
> al bien de la paz a aquellos mismos contra quienes luchas. Porque
> el Señor dijo: "Bienaventurados los pacíficos, porque ellos serán
> llamados hijos de Dios" (Mateo 5: 9)….Sea la necesidad, y no la
> voluntad, la que extermine al enemigo en armas. Así como se

---

81. Mateo 5: 43-45; Lucas 6: 27-28, 35.
82. Agustín, Carta 138 (énfasis añadido).

contesta con la violencia al que se rebela y resiste, así se le debe
la misericordia al vencido y prisionero, especialmente cuando
no se teme de él la perturbación de la paz.[83]83

Hay dos partes de este pasaje que son particularmente sustanciales para
sostener la calidad humana de los enemigos en la guerra. Agustín pide a este
comandante que sea un pacífico, lo que posiblemente podría significar la
coexistencia reconciliatoria de una paz positiva o la versión eliminatoria de
la paz negativa. Sin embargo, esto último se descarta rápidamente, ya que San
Agustín anima a este soldado a "llevar [a los enemigos] de vuelta a las ventajas
de la paz" y luego, a tener misericordia "hacia los vencidos". La paz que San
Agustín espera de este soldado implica la participación de los enemigos, no
su sometimiento o eliminación, por lo que respeta su calidad humana.

En segundo lugar, San Agustín aconseja a este soldado: "Sea la necesidad, y no la voluntad, la que extermine al enemigo en armas". Agustín
recomienda a este soldado que mate con remordimiento, no de corazón,
casi como si el enemigo mismo tuviera que forzarle la mano. Nigel Biggar
propone una versión contemporánea de la misma idea:

> Sin embargo, puede permitirse la opción de actuar de tal manera
> que provoque la muerte de un ser humano, siempre que lo que se
> pretenda sea algo distinto a su muerte (por ejemplo, el defender
> a un inocente), que la posibilidad (o incluso la certeza) de su
> muerte se acepte con la debida y manifiesta renuencia, y que
> dicha aceptación sea necesaria, no subversiva, y proporcionada.
> Moralmente hablando, provocar la muerte deliberadamente de
> este modo no es lo mismo que hacerlo con la intención de
> matar.[84]

A primera vista, la sugerencia de Biggar de que un soldado no tiene la
intención de matar suena tan absurdo como el amar a los propios enemigos
incluso como se les da muerte. Sin embargo, si por "intención" Biggar
se refiere a un propósito general, entonces simplemente defiende que los
soldados tengan como su principal aspiración una recta intención hacia una
paz justa y duradera en lugar de una intención de matar.

Esta recapitulación de las perspectivas griega y cristiana está destinada
simplemente a mostrar la viabilidad de mantener la calidad humana de

---

83. Agustín, Carta 189.
84. Biggar 2013, 101.

los enemigos cuando se lucha contra ellos. Merecen un tratamiento más completo, y sin duda existen otros ejemplos que demuestran el respeto por la calidad humana del enemigo,[85] pero en este punto me conformaré con establecer la plausibilidad de las alternativas a la deshumanización y, por lo tanto, el aseguramiento de la compatibilidad de la empatía con el soldado.

Manteniendo a la muerte en su lugar

Los soldados con empatía son más capaces de mantener el acto de matar como una tarea necesaria y lamentable que como su propósito general. La empatía ayuda a los soldados a no deshumanizar a los demás, especialmente al enemigo. Más específicamente, la empatía revela el simple hecho de la calidad humana del enemigo, así como elementos de su experiencia, incluyendo valores, deseos e intenciones. Estos elementos son instrumentalmente útiles para las decisiones tácticas en la lucha contra el enemigo, más aun, permiten realizar juicios perfeccionados con respecto a una paz conjunta y a una recta intención que intenta alcanzar esa paz.

Nunca debe perderse de vista el objetivo final de la paz, incluso por parte de los soldados pues su conducta en combate afecta la posibilidad de alcanzar la paz. Si bien las acciones de matar, herir, incapacitar, amenazar y retener a otros por la fuerza son inherentes al combate, deben realizarse a la luz del propósito general a cumplirse. Además, si bien los soldados pueden verse en la necesidad de atenuar los impulsos de empatía para completar diestramente estas acciones de combate, esta debe ser una interrupción temporal de la facultad de la empatía del individuo, no una negación de la calidad humana del enemigo.

III. Empatía en la guerra

En la sección anterior se delineó el apoyo de la empatía con respecto a la recta intención en los soldados y cómo los soldados pueden mantener

---

85. Recibí otra sugerencia prometedora, aunque requiere de un estudio más extenso: la actitud hacia la presa dentro de la ética de la caza de algunas comunidades nativas en Estados Unidos. En la práctica de los Ojibwe, por ejemplo, un "cazador hace un discurso de agradecimiento al mundo animal y espiritual, mostrando aprecio ya sea antes o después de una cosecha". Además: "El manejo del cuerpo del venado y la eliminación de las partes no utilizadas deben realizarse de manera que se mantenga la dignidad del espíritu del venado". Véase Nicholas James Reo, Kyle Powys Whyte, "Hunting and Morality as Elements of Traditional Ecological Knowledge," *Human Ecology,* Vol. 40:1 (Febrero de 2012), 15-27. Aunque no me atrevo a relacionar a los soldados enemigos con presas, esta respetuosa actitud parece alinearse con el mantenimiento de su humanidad. Valdría la pena investigar más para confirmar que los Ojibwe hacen énfasis en esta actitud entre sus guerreros durante la batalla y no solo mientras cazan. Mi agradecimiento a Monte Hoover por esta referencia.

una comprensión empática del enemigo junto con su justificada tarea de matar. En esta sección, pretendo demostrar la relevancia específica de la empatía en relación con las responsabilidades de "librar la guerra", como las denomina James Dubik. La empatía es tan importante para los principios tradicionales de la guerra como la discriminación y la proporcionalidad, pero por cuestiones de espacio me centraré en la innovadora crítica que hace Dubik de la tradición de la guerra justa.

Dubik distingue entre *lucha de la guerra* y el *librar la guerra* para describir con más detalle las actividades que la componen.[86] Lucha de la guerra se refiere a las diferentes actividades que tienen lugar en el campo de batalla mismo, particularmente el uso de fuerza letal contra el enemigo usando el armamento con que se disponga. Dubik se refiere a librar una guerra como la gama de actividades que precede, dirige, coordina y mantiene la lucha de la guerra en el campo de batalla: es la gestión integral de una guerra y no simplemente las acciones pertinentes al campo de batalla.[87]

La empatía tiene un papel importante en las actividades del libramiento de la guerra. En esta sección, examinaré la contribución de la empatía a la planificación estratégica y la evaluación del progreso. Como señala Dubik:

> Si bien la autoridad de la decisión final descansa en un grupo muy pequeño —a veces en un solo individuo— las decisiones de tal magnitud tienen como antecedente un análisis detallado de alternativas, estudios de factibilidad y pilas de documentos que reflejan los razonamientos que han sido expuestos por numerosos comités y grupos de estudio, así como por organismos subordinados y agencias de personal. La calidad de las decisiones finales a menudo reflejaba la calidad del trabajo preparatorio.[88]

Mi propuesta es que la empatía mejora el trabajo preparatorio y la decisión final. Como veterano de numerosos comités, grupos de estudio y secciones de personal, reconozco que estos roles, y las infaltables oficinas sin ventanas en las que se reúnen, pueden reprimir la consideración empática por los demás —hasta cierto punto, de manera más completa que los caprichos del combate—. Sin embargo, las consecuencias que están en juego exigen lo mejor en lo que se refiere a la comprensión de la cosmovisión y las

---

86. James M. Dubik, *Just War Reconsidered - Strategy, Ethics, and Theory* (Lexington: University Press of Kentucky, 2016), 3-4.
87. Ibíd., 15.
88. Dubik 2016, 18.

motivaciones de los actores humanos, al pensamiento crítico y creativo, al escrutinio riguroso de las propias suposiciones y de la evaluación de los avances, y a la guerra de manera honesta y significativa. Además, al realizar este trabajo de la mejor manera se ayuda a mantener la legitimidad de la guerra, al menos en este aspecto. La legitimidad, señala Dubik, es una "función de la justicia de la guerra —un asunto del *jus ad bellum*— y avanza hacia un éxito probable —un asunto del *jus in bello*—. [Este] se vincula directamente con la competencia de los líderes políticos y militares de alto nivel para ejecutar sus responsabilidades en la guerra".[89] A medida que la empatía mejora el proceso de planificación y evaluación, ayuda también al aseguramiento de un progreso auténtico, contribuyendo así a la legitimidad.

La planificación estratégica

En el análisis de Dubik de los tipos de problemas que los soldados enfrentan en la guerra, se distingue entre los problemas técnicos y los problemas de adaptación.[90] Los problemas técnicos son aquellos que los soldados pueden solucionar con el conocimiento y experiencia que poseen; los problemas "pueden resolverse mediante el uso de expertos autorizados, de las estructuras y procedimientos actuales, y la forma de hacer las cosas en la organización".[91] Los problemas técnicos pueden ser complicados, pero su solución es fácilmente discernible. Los problemas de adaptación, por otra parte, no se consideran dentro de las capacidades normales de una organización y, por lo general, son difíciles de entender, no se diga resolver. El contexto de un problema adaptativo es que "cambia continuamente" y, por eso, "la solución también cambia continuamente".[92] Dubik señala que los retos tácticos en la guerra son generalmente de naturaleza técnica, mientras que los retos estratégicos suelen ser adaptativos. Por lo tanto, el librar la guerra conlleva principalmente problemas de adaptación.

El primer paso, y el más importante, en el manejo de los problemas de adaptación es el de comprenderlos plenamente. Uno de los desafíos más básicos de este paso es el de reconocer las deficiencias de los marcos conceptuales de uno mismo. Cuando un problema de adaptación involucra a actores humanos, sobre todo si trata de enemigos, el comprender con empatía a esos seres humanos contribuye a superar las fallas de las concepciones preexistentes que se tiene de ellos. En otras palabras, la empatía contribuye a romper las

---

89. Dubik 2016, 155.
90. Dubik 2016, 141-143.
91. Ibíd., 141-142.
92. Ibíd., 142.

preconcepciones y prejuicios culturales, ideológicos, raciales o sociales. Por ejemplo, un enfoque empático hacia los japoneses durante la Segunda Guerra Mundial los habría humanizado y así habría sido más difícil subestimar sus capacidades. En cambio, al principio de la guerra, los planificadores aliados estaban convencidos, gracias a estereotipos racistas, de que los japoneses eran "demasiado miopes y propensos al vértigo como para volar un avión de combate; demasiado temerosos para luchar en las selvas, las cuales estaban supuestamente habitadas por fantasmas y demonios".[93] La subestimación del enemigo conduce a la pérdida innecesaria de vidas humanas.

Al enfrentarse a problemas de adaptación, puede existir la imperiosa tentación de definir el problema como si fuese de naturaleza técnica. Especialmente en la cultura militar, orientada hacia la acción, la opción más atractiva es la de resolver un problema desconocido e inconveniente con una solución conocida y conveniente. Para ilustrar este error, considérese el auge y el declive de una estrategia de planificación militar denominada "Operaciones Basadas en Efectos" o EBO, por sus siglas en inglés.[94]

La EBO era una estrategia de planificación que se originó en la Fuerza Aérea de los Estados Unidos, pero que también se utilizó de una u otra forma en otros sectores militares.[95] La EBO debe su nombre a un enfoque riguroso en los efectos destructivos contra las fuerzas enemigas, en lugar de un enfocarse en otro más genérico como la cantidad de recursos a usarse contra el enemigo —en términos de unidades, municiones o sistemas de armas—. Los planificadores de la Fuerza Aérea desarrollaron la EBO para utilizar recursos contra los nodos clave de las fuerzas enemigas de manera más eficiente. Por ejemplo, en lugar de que un piloto eligiera individualmente cada uno de los sistemas de defensa aérea como blanco, elegiría un sistema de radar que proporciona datos cruciales a diferentes sistemas de armas de la defensa aérea del enemigo. Además de utilizar menos recursos, este enfoque paralizó al enemigo con ataques simultáneos más selectivos. La EBO se aplicó por primera vez de manera importante en la exitosa campaña aérea de 1990, como parte inicial de la campaña para expulsar de Kuwait a las fuerzas de Saddam Hussein. La estrategia EBO produjo asimismo la campaña aérea conocida como "conmoción y pavor" al comienzo de la invasión de Irak en el año 2003.

---

93. Shay 1994, 120.
94. U.S. Armed Forces, Joint Publication 3-0, *Operations* (Washington, DC: Joint Staff, septiembre de 2006); remplazada en agosto de 2011, y luego nuevamente en enero de 2017.
95. Gary Cheek, "Effects-Based Operations: the End of Dominant Maneuver?" *Transformation Concepts for National Security in the 21st Century,* ed. Williamson Murray (2002), 73-100.

Los procedimientos de la EBO guiaron a los planificadores militares para que consideraran todos los factores relacionados con las capacidades de la fuerza enemiga. Al analizar un sistema relativamente cerrado, como las armas de defensa aérea mencionadas, la EBO resultó de utilidad para identificar los puntos vulnerables del enemigo y encauzar el uso juicioso de la fuerza militar. Sin embargo, los éxitos tácticos derivados de la planificación EBO provocaron que se extendiera su uso a objetivos estratégicos más importantes. Los planificadores intentaron captar factores políticos, militares, económicos y sociales dentro una ambiosa y sencilla red de información, llegando a tratar "algo tan complejo como la actividad humana [como] si fuera básicamente un campo pasivo y sin vida".[96] En lugar de que los radares de defensa aérea fueran el blanco de los ataques, los líderes de las tribus, por ejemplo, se volvieron los nodos clave para ser atacados con los recursos disponibles. La mentalidad EBO desvió la atención de los preceptos del poder superior de combate tradicionales o del mantenimiento de fuerzas de reserva en caso de ataques sorpresa, y con un gran nivel de expectación, certeza y eficiencia prometía, en cambio, desarmar y obstaculizar al enemigo hasta someterlo. Para el año 2008, comenzaron a surgir críticas contra esta estrategia de planificación:

> Conceptos con etiquetas como la guerra centrada en la red, operaciones rápidas y decisivas, conmoción y pavor, y diversas variantes de las operaciones basadas en efectos adoptaron lo que parecía cada vez más un argumento basado en la creencia de que la guerra del futuro descansaría principalmente en el ámbito de la certeza y, por lo tanto, se podría ganar de manera rápida y eficiente, a un bajo costo con fuerzas militares reducidas.[97]

Más adelante, en ese mismo año, un alto comandante militar que estaba a cargo de la doctrina emitió un degradante memorando en el que se prohibía a las fuerzas estadounidenses la utilización de la EBO en la planificación militar.[98] El comandante señaló que la EBO "intenta mecánicamente brindar certeza y previsibilidad en un entorno inherentemente incierto", es "demasiado prescriptiva y está sobredimensionada", así mismo "descarta

---

96. Milan Vego, "Systems versus Classical Approach to Warfare," *Joint Force Quarterly* 52 (1er trimestre 2009), 42.
97. HR McMaster, "On War: Lessons to be Learned", *Survival 50* : 1 (marzo de 2008), 21.
98. General James Mattis (el reciente comandante de Defensa de los Estados Unidos), "USJFCOM Commander's Guidance on Effects- Based Operations," *Joint Force Quarterly* 51 (4to trimestre 2008), 105-108.

las dimensiones humanas de la guerra —por ejemplo, la pasión, la imaginación, la fuerza de voluntad y la imprevisibilidad—".[99] Admitió que "los elementos de [la EBO] han demostrado ser útiles para abordar 'sistemas cerrados', como la focalización donde los efectos pueden medirse según el análisis deliberado y los métodos de focalización [de la Fuerza Aérea de los Estados Unidos].

Sin embargo, los conceptos han sido mal utilizados por terceros para realizar operaciones más allá de su intención original, lo que ha dado como resultado una extensión excesiva de dichos conceptos y confusión".[100]

El título de esta estrategia de planificación, *Operaciones Basadas en Efectos*, requiere de una mayor sabiduría de la que se ha permitido esta crítica. De hecho, el centrarse en los efectos deseados puede hacer que la selección de los medios sea más eficiente y éticamente respetable —por ejemplo, minimizando los daños colaterales—. Sin embargo, la utilización de la EBO en asuntos estratégicos de mayor envergadura se basaba en una arrogante suposición de que las fuerzas militares podrían verdaderamente manipular ciertos efectos para hacerlos posibles sin necesidad de adaptarse al comportamiento impredecible del enemigo o el de los demás, y sin necesidad de obtener la cooperación de aliados y grupos clave de no combatientes. Este error fue, metafóricamente hablando, un intento por *fabricar* efectos que solo podían *cultivarse*: las unidades militares no podían controlar todos los factores —específicamente, a los individuos que no cooperaban— pero en vano se asumía lo contrario. Es un obstáculo epistemológico, ya que los soldados no reconocían los límites de lo que podían controlar en realidad. El error fue el de intentar convertir una estrategia de planificación táctica que era adecuada contra los sistemas cerrados de componentes materiales en un precepto para la planificación estratégica de sistemas abiertos e impredecibles con componentes humanos. Una mayor apreciación por la empatía, por la comprensión que brinda y por el respeto que conlleva, habría impedido suponer que los efectos deseados podían ser fabricados.

Además del obstáculo epistemológico al tratar un problema adaptativo como uno técnico, la estrategia de planificación EBO implicaba la comisión de un error moral por tratar a los seres humanos como objetos susceptibles a generalizaciones rigurosas. Este error moral es una forma de deshumanización; trata como objetos a los actores humanos. En esta

---

99. Ibíd., 106-107.
100. Ibíd.

modalidad, los planificadores militares aplican el conocimiento cultural de manera inapropiada, emplean el conocimiento como si fueran leyes de comportamiento similares a las leyes de la física. Los planificadores se aproximan a los enemigos u otros individuos de una forma mecánica y aplicando suposiciones simplistas a poblaciones enteras. A menudo se trata de una deshumanización burocrática y no necesariamente de una infra-humanización visceral como en el estrés del combate, aunque también puede derivarse de este último. A pesar de todo, tiene efectos igualmente preocupantes de tipo moral y práctico. Este tipo de deshumanización lleva a un manejo de la guerra como si fuera una ciencia física y a los actores humanos como si fueran simplemente objetos manipulables. Por lo tanto, "Operaciones Basadas en Efectos" es un nombre engañoso debido a que los efectos se escogieron perentoriamente a raíz de un momento de, como mínimo, deshumanización burocrática. La empatía es un antídoto para esta predisposición deshumanizadora hacia la guerra como ciencia física, y hacia el conocimiento cultural, como simples generalizaciones rigurosas de las demás personas.

Evaluación

La empatía mejora la evaluación del progreso al enfocarse en la medición de las salidas en lugar de enfocarse simplemente en las entradas. Al lidiar con la confusión de las contrainsurgencias en Irak y Afganistán, el personal estadounidense se ha enfrentado a la tentación constante de evaluar su progreso basándose exclusivamente en las entradas. Si bien las entradas son más fáciles de controlar, obviamente no sirven como una base para evaluar el progreso de las operaciones. No obstante, el líder de un equipo de recon-strucción de provincia en Irak, del Departamento de Estado, reflexionó:

> Medimos el impacto de nuestros proyectos por el efecto que estos tienen sobre nosotros, no por el efecto que tienen sobre los iraquíes. *Salida* era la palabra que faltaba en el vocabulario para el desarrollo de Irak. Todo se medía solo por lo que invertíamos: dólares gastados, horas prometidas, personas empleadas…comu-nicados de prensa escritos.[101]

La naturaleza de la empatía como un modo receptivo hacia la experiencia de los demás dirige a los soldados de un enfoque en entradas a uno de salidas

---

101. Peter Van Buren, *We Meant Well: How I Helped Lose the Battle for the Hearts and Minds of the Iraqi People* (Nueva York: Metropolitan Books, 2011), 144.

e incorpora el punto de vista de la población sobre los esfuerzos militares. Si bien los juicios de los lugareños no deben ser el único factor para la evaluación del progreso, sus juicios deben formar parte de dicha evaluación, especialmente dados los esfuerzos de reconstrucción cooperativa inherentes a las contrainsurgencias —o después de conflictos convencionales—.

Otra razón por la que las entradas pueden dominar las evaluaciones es su fácil medición. Con la constante presión del tiempo, los planificadores militares pueden sucumbir fácilmente ante este error. Sin embargo, la empatía reduce esta tentación hacia una medición fácil porque hace énfasis en una evaluación más holística de las operaciones militares, la cual integra las opiniones de los aliados, la de las partes neutrales y la de los no combatientes. Estas comprensiones empáticas no deben ser la única consideración para evaluar el progreso. Sin embargo, siguen siendo importantes.

Los planificadores y los líderes no evalúan con precisión el esfuerzo de la guerra si están atrapados en una mentalidad burocrática y excesivamente cuantitativa. Basta recordar el ejemplo de la guerra de Vietnam, en la que este tipo de mentalidad se mezcló con una intención de matar para producir parámetros cuantitativos, tales como el número de muertos, para medir el progreso. Un historiador militar comentó que, cuando se está atrapado en esta mentalidad, "si no puedes contar lo que es importante, lo que sí puedes contar se vuelve importante".[102] La empatía, con su humanización de los enemigos y de los demás, y su aliciente hacia una la recta intención, ayuda a compensar este error transfiriendo el enfoque hacia una paz justa y duradera entre las partes en conflicto.

Como en la lucha de la guerra antes mencionada, una empatía selectiva puede sesgar la evaluación del progreso en lugar de contribuir a su ejecución. Si los líderes solo prestan atención a la comprensión empática de los soldados, a costa de una comprensión similar de los demás, entonces el único criterio de evaluación puede significar el regreso seguro de cada soldado, independientemente de los avances de la misión en cuestión. Esta empatía selectiva puede promover un enfoque demasiado cauteloso de las operaciones militares.

IV. Conclusión

Cuando se entiende correctamente que la naturaleza del ser soldado está orientada a establecer una paz justa y duradera, el papel de la empatía se

---

102. James Willbanks (documental de Burns, episodio 4).

vuelve claro y crucial. La empatía impulsa a los soldados a mantener esta paz como su intención, en lugar de buscar una paz negativa que implique la subyugación o la erradicación de todos los adversarios. La empatía ayuda a los soldados a defender la "tradición aparentemente universal de los tiempos de guerra" de deshumanizar a los combatientes enemigos y a los civiles con los que se relacionan.[103] En cambio, los soldados ejercen con moderación el uso de las acciones coercitivas y toman mejores decisiones sobre cuándo utilizarlas. De esta manera, los soldados redefinen los principios tradicionales de la lucha de la guerra tales como la discriminación y la proporcionalidad. Esta misma comprensión empática de los demás y la correspondiente recta intención contribuye asimismo a mejorar el cumplimiento de las responsabilidades bélicas de los soldados al planificar campañas militares dentro de las limitaciones morales y prácticas y al evaluar el progreso de la guerra de manera honesta y holística.

---

103. Brough 2007, 151

Obras Citadas

Aquinas, Thomas. *Summa theologiae.* Translated by Fathers of the English Dominican Province. Second and Revised Edition, 1920. Online Edition Copyright © 2008 by Kevin Knight. <http://www.newadvent.org/summa/>.

Augustine. *The City of God.* Trans. R. Ryson. Cambridge: Cambridge University Press, 1998.

————. *Contra Faustum* XXII, Translated by Richard Stothert. From *Nicene and Post-Nicene Fathers*, First Series, Vol. 4. Edited by Philip Schaff. Buffalo, NY: Christian Literature Publishing, 1887. Revised and edited for New Advent by Kevin Knight. <http://www.newadvent.org/fathers/140622.htm>.

————. Letter 138. Translated by J. G. Cunningham. From *Nicene and Post-Nicene Fathers*, First Series, Vol. 1. Edited by Philip Schaff. Buffalo, NY: Christian Literature Publishing, 1887. Revised and edited for New Advent by Kevin Knight. <http://www.newadvent.org/fathers/1102138.htm>.

————. Letter 189. Translated by J. G. Cunningham. From *Nicene and Post-Nicene Fathers*, First Series, Vol. 1. Edited by Philip Schaff. Buffalo, NY: Christian Literature Publishing, 1887. Revised and edited for New Advent by Kevin Knight. <http://www.newadvent.org/fathers/1102189.htm>.

Batson, C. D. (2009). "These Things Called Empathy." *The Social Neuroscience of Empathy.* Ed. Jean Decety and William Ickes. Cambridge, MA: MIT Press.

————. (1991). *The Altruism Question: Toward a Social-Psychological Answer.* Hillsdale, NJ: Erlbaum.

Bell, Daniel (2009). *Just War as Christian Discipleship: Recentering the Tradition in the Church Rather Than the State.* Grand Rapids, MI: Brazos Press.

Biggar, Nigel (2013). *In Defence of War.* Oxford: Oxford University Press. Bloom, Paul (2016). *Against Empathy.* New York: HarperCollins.

Bolgiano, David, and John Taylor (2017). "Can't Kill Enough to Win? Think Again." *Proceedings Magazine,* Vol. 143/12/1,378. US Naval Institute, December 2017. <https:// www.usni.org/magazines/proceedings/2017-12/cant-kill-enough-win-think- again>.

Brough, Michael (2007). "Dehumanization of the Enemy and the Moral Equality of Soldiers." In *Rethinking the Just War Tradition.* Eds. Michael Brough, John Lango, Harry van der Linden. Albany: State University of New York Press, 149–167.

Burkhardt, Todd (2017). *Just War and Human Rights: Fighting with Right Intention.* Albany, NY: SUNY Press.

Burns, Ken and Lynne Novick (2017). "The Vietnam War." Documentary. Florentine Films and WETA.

CNN Politics. "Troops alone will not yield victory in Afghanistan." CNN.com (10 September 2008). <http://www.cnn.com/2008/POLITICS/09/10/mullen. afghanistan>.

Capizzi, Joseph (2015). *Politics, Justice, and War: Christian Governance and the Ethics of Warfare.* Oxford: Oxford University Press.

Cavanaugh, Matt (2015). "The Military's Purpose is Not to Kill People and Break Things." *War on the Rocks.* 26 August 2015. <https://warontherocks.com/2015/08/ the-militarys- purpose-is-not-to-kill-people-and-break-things/>.

Cheek, Gary (2002). "Effects-Based Operations: The End of Dominant Maneuver?" *Transformation Concepts for National Security in the 21st Century.* Ed. Williamson Murray. Strategic Studies Institute, US Army War College, 73–100.

<https://ssi.armywarcollege.edu/pubs/display.cfm?pubID=252>.

Coates, A. J. (2016). *The Ethics of War.* 2nd ed. Manchester, UK: Manchester University Press. Coplan, Amy (2011). "Understanding Empathy: Its Features and Effects." *Empathy:*

Philosophical and Psychological Perspectives. Eds. Amy Coplan and Peter Goldie. New York: Oxford University Press.

Coplan, Amy and Peter Goldie (2011). "Introduction." *Empathy: Philosophical and Psychological Perspectives.* Eds. Amy Coplan and Peter Goldie. New York: Oxford University Press, ix–xlvii.

Darwall, Stephen (1998). "Empathy, Sympathy, and Care." *Philosophical Studies* 89: 261–282. Dubik, James (2016). *Just War Reconsidered—Strategy, Ethics, and Theory.* Lexington: University Press of Kentucky.

Frowe, Helen (2011). *The Ethics of War and Peace.* London: Routledge.

Gallagher, Shaun (2012). "Empathy, Simulation, and Narrative." *Science in Context,* vol. 25, no. 3, 355–381.

Gourley, Jim (2015). "The military's purpose isn't to break things and kill people, but it should be." *Foreign Policy.* 24 September 2015. <http://foreignpolicy. com/2015/09/24/the- militarys-purpose-isnt-to-break-things-and-kill-people-but-it-should-be/>.

Hoffman, Bruce (2006). *Inside Terrorism.* Revised and expanded edition. New York: Columbia University Press.

Klay, Phil (2017). "What We're Fighting For." *New York Times.* 10 February 2017.

Linn, Brian (2009). *The Echo of Battle: The Army's Way of War.* Cambridge, MA: Harvard University Press.

MacIntyre, Alasdair (2016). *Ethics in the Conflicts of Modernity: An Essay on Desire, Practical Reasoning, and Narrative.* New York: Cambridge University Press.

———. (2007). *After Virtue: A Study in Moral Theory.* 3rd ed. Notre Dame: University of Notre Dame Press.

Matravers, Derek (2017). *Empathy.* Malden, MA: Polity Press.

Mattis, James (2008). "USJFCOM Commander's Guidance on Effects-Based Operations," *Joint Force Quarterly.* Vol. 51 (4th Quarter 2008), 105–108.

McMahan, Jeff (2005). "Just Cause for War." *Ethics and International Affairs* 9:3 (December 2005), 1–21.

McMaster, H. R. (2008). "On War: Lessons to be Learned." *Survival* 50:1 (March 2008), 19–30. Morris, Errol (2003). "The Fog of War: Eleven Lessons from the Life of Robert S. McNamara." Documentary. Sony Pictures Classics.

Orend, Brian (2006). *The Morality of War.* Toronto: Broadview Press.

Orend, Brian (2001). "A Just War Critique of Realism and Pacifism." *Journal of Philosophical Research,* Vol. XXVI, 435–477.

Pickstock, Catherine (1998). *After Writing.* Malden, MA: Blackwell Publishers.

Prinz, Jesse (2011). "Is Empathy Necessary for Morality?" *Empathy: Philosophical and Psychological Perspectives.* Ed. Amy Coplan and Peter Goldie. New York: Oxford University Press, 211–229.

Reo, Nicholas James, and Kyle Powys Whyte (2012). "Hunting and Morality as Elements of Traditional Ecological Knowledge." *Human Ecology.* Vol. 40:1 (February 2012), 15–27.

Rodin, David (2004). "Terrorism without Intention," *Ethics* 114 (July 2004), 752–771.

Ross, Janell (2015). "Mike Huckabee Says the Military's Job Is To 'Kill People and Break Things.' Well, Not Quite." *The Washington Post* (7 August 2015).

Schofield, John M (1881). "Notes on 'The Legitimate in War.'" *Journal of the Military Service Institution.* Vol. 2, 1–10.

Shay, Jonathan (1994). *Achilles in Vietnam: Combat Trauma and the Undoing of Character.* New York: Scribner.

Smith, Joel (2015). "What is Empathy For?" *Synthese,* vol. 194, 709–722.

Stueber, Karsten (2006). *Rediscovering Empathy: Agency, Folk Psychology, and the Human Sciences.* Cambridge, MA: MIT Press.

Tacitus, Publius Cornelius. *The Works of Tacitus: The Oxford Translation, Revised with Notes,* Vol. 2. London: Bell and Daldy, 1872.

United Nations. "Declaration on Measures to Eliminate International Terrorism." Annex to UN General Assembly Resolution 49/60, "Measures to Eliminate International Terrorism." (9 December 1994). <https://www.un.org/documents/ga/res/49/a49r060.htm>.

US Armed Forces. Joint Publication 3-0, *Operations* (Washington, DC: Joint Staff, September 2006); superseded in August 2011, then again in January 2017.

Van Buren, Peter (2011). We Meant Well: How I Helped Lose the Battle for the Hearts and Minds of the Iraqi People. New York: Metropolitan Books.

Vego, Milan (2009). "Systems versus Classical Approach to Warfare." *Joint Force Quarterly.* Vol. 52 (1st Quarter 2009), 40–48.

Walzer, Michael (1977). *Just and Unjust Wars: A Moral Argument with Historical Illustrations.* Philadelphia: Basic Books.

Weinstein, Adam (2017). "No, We Can't Kill Our Way to Victory Despite What 2 Misguided Lieutenant Colonels Might Think." *Task and Purpose* (8 December 2017). <https://taskandpurpose.com/no-cant-kill-way-victory-despite-2-misguided-lieutenant- colonels-might-think/>.

Wood, David (2016). *What Have We Done: The Moral Injury of Our Longest Wars.* New York: Little, Brown and Company, Kindle edition.

Zahavi, Dan (2014). *Self and Other: Exploring Subjectivity, Empathy, and Shame.* New York: Oxford University Press.

Empathie et *Jus in bello*

Kevin Cutright
Lieutenant Colonel, US Army

I. Mise à l'écart de la bonne intention

Le principe de la bonne intention est « la disposition adéquate de ceux qui mènent des guerres » en vertu d'une paix juste et durable.[1] Les premiers théoriciens de la guerre juste ont souligné que la bonne intention est essentielle à l'unité morale de la guerre et à la bonne conduite des soldats.[2] Ce principe est destiné à servir de rempart contre les intentions d'hommes d'État ou de soldats qui peuvent avoir une cause légitime de faire la guerre, mais qui instrumentalisent cette cause pour légitimer d'autres fins. Lorsque les théoriciens modernes de la guerre juste raffinaient les concepts de *jus ad bellum* (droit à la guerre) et de *jus in bello* (droit dans la guerre) (et la catégorie du *jus post bellum*, droit après la guerre), la bonne intention ne figurait que dans le droit à la guerre. Par ailleurs, on peut toujours présumer de l'influence de la bonne intention sur le droit dans la guerre lorsqu'elle est mentionnée dans les délibérations précipitant un conflit. Cependant, la bonne intention n'a souvent été évoquée qu'avec circonspection dans les débats contemporains autour de la notion de *jus ad bellum*[3]. Il a été suggéré depuis par certains chercheurs que la bonne intention est redondante ou impossible à prouver et, qu'en tant que telle, elle devrait être subsumée en vertu du principe de la juste cause.[4]

---

1. Joseph Capizzi, *Politics, Justice, and War: Christian Governance and the Ethics of Warfare* (Oxford: Oxford University Press, 2015), 108-109.
2. Saint Augustin fut le premier défenseur de la bonne intention ; voir *La cité de Dieu, The City of God*, trans. R. Ryson (Cambridge : Cambridge University Press, 1998). Saint Thomas d'Aquin cite la bonne intention comme l'un de ses trois principes régissant la guerre ; voir *Summa theologiae* II-II q. 40 art. 1 et q. 64 art. 3.
3. Daniel Bell marque le début de cette vision pessimiste avec Hugo Grotius; voir *Just War as Christian Discipleship: Recentering the Tradition in the Church rather than the State* (Grand Rapids, MI: Brazos Press, 2009), 56-58.
4. À titre d'exemple, voir Jeff McMahan, « Just Cause for War », *Ethics and International Affairs* 9:3, 1-21. Pour les arguments contre le rejet de la bonne intention, voir Capizzi 2015, 71-126; Todd Burkhardt, *Just War and Human Rights: Fighting with Right Intention* (Albany, NY: SUNY Press, 2017); et Bell 2009, 153-158.

D'autres se sont penchés sur les lois et les réglementations qui permettent de contraindre légalement les actions des politiciens et des soldats, au détriment d'intentions et de qualités humaines qui auraient pu encadrer moralement leurs actions.[5] A.J. Coates oppose une conception traditionnelle « fondée sur le caractère » à la tendance actuelle qui privilégie une conception « fondée sur des règles ».[6] Bien qu'il accorde ses justes mérites à chacune, il considère que la conception fondée sur le droit de la guerre oppose une résistance à la conception humanitaire. En effet, la conception légaliste met en avant une réflexion délibérative au sujet des exigences morales de la guerre sans entrer dans aucune considération liée à des dispositions et des penchants humains :

> La morale « délibérative » n'est pas seulement oublieuse de l'idée d'une vie morale centrée sur des dispositions morales, elle n'est pas non plus indifférente à cette idée, elle s'y oppose par principe puisque « l'esprit *sans disposition* est à lui seul le ressort du jugement « rationnel » et d'une conduite « rationnelle ». La conduite morale est « rationnelle » dans le sens étroit de « conduite découlant d'un processus antérieur de « raisonnement », à l'exclusion du type de conduite trouvant ses origines dans « l'autorité non remise en question d'une tradition, d'une coutume ou d'une habitude de comportement ». D'un point de vue délibératif, les aspects communaux et habituels de la morale traditionnelle sont moins considérés comme des moyens d'autonomisation morale que comme des obstacles fondamentaux à la réalisation de l'autonomie morale. Le progrès moral dépend de l'émancipation de l'individu rationnel par rapport aux influences hétéronomes de la morale traditionnelle.[7]

Le principe prémoderne de la bonne intention a été largement soit mis à l'écart comme l'une de ces dispositions douteuses de la morale traditionnelle, soit comme étant sans rapport avec elle (comme l'est toute intention dans l'éthique conséquentialiste), soit encore elle a été transformée en règle (comme dans l'éthique déontologique). En conséquence, la bonne intention,

---

5. Pour un résumé de ces tendances, voir Brian Orend, *The Morality of War* (Toronto: Broadview Press, 2006), 17–23.

6. A.J. Coates, *The Ethics of War*, 2e éd. (Manchester, Royaume-Uni: Manchester University Press, 2016), 1–18.

7. Coates 2016, 12. Il cite Michael Oakeshott, *Rationalism in Politics* (Londres: Methuen, 1962) 87, 84–85.

comprise comme une disposition de caractère, est pratiquement absente dans la littérature contemporaine au sujet du *jus in bello*.

De l'impact de cette mise à l'écart

Les apports d'une conception de la morale fondée sur le droit permettent de mieux répondre à certaines exigences morales, dont la codification des principes moraux dans le droit international.[8] En outre, la réflexion issue d'une perception fondée sur des règles précises est essentielle au bien-être moral d'une personne, ce qui est évident dans le constat de certains cas de préjudice moral chez les soldats.[9] Cependant, l'émergence d'un cadre fondé sur le droit, à l'exclusion d'une perception humanitaire, a entraîné trois lacunes. Tout d'abord, ce cadre privilégie dans l'éthique militaire une technique superficielle « du catalogage ».[10] Un catalogue de règles morales ne peut en aucun cas tenir compte de circonstances imprévues, et à l'évolution très rapide, auxquelles les troupes sont confrontées sur le terrain, ni préparer les soldats à anticiper ces circonstances pour qu'ils puissent s'y adapter.[11] Comme l'observe Coates, « l'omniprésence de l'imprévu ou de l'imprévisible [dans la guerre] entrave la réflexion, renforçant donc les préceptes de la morale traditionnelle ».[12] Les soldats ont besoin d'une inclination pour une paix juste et durable (ce qui, sans nul doute, implique une compréhension approfondie et posée de cette paix) afin d'être en mesure d'accomplir leur devoir de façon satisfaisante. Une retenue extrinsèque ne peut remplacer efficacement cette retenue intrinsèque.[13]

Deuxièmement, ce recentrage sur les règles seules engendre un état d'esprit excessivement bureaucratique parmi les soldats. Ils en viennent à adhérer à la mentalité de gestionnaire bureaucratique d'Alasdair MacIntyre

---

8. Brian Orend, *The Morality of War* (Toronto: Broadview Press, 2006), 20-23.

9. David Wood observe : « L'armée américaine a passé des années et dépensé une fortune pour perfectionner l'entraînement au combat le plus pragmatique et le plus complet au monde. Mais en préparant les jeunes Américains à la guerre, elle a échoué de manière flagrante dans un des aspects majeurs de l'entraînement. Ceux que nous envoyons à la guerre ne sont jamais formés pour anticiper les dilemmes moraux provoqués par les meurtres auxquels ils seront confrontés ; on ne leur donne pas l'occasion ni ne les encourage à réfléchir et à débattre de ce qui fait de certains meurtres des actes moraux et d'autres meurtres un péché ou même un acte illégal » (*What Have We Done: The Moral Injury of our Longest Wars,* [New York: Hachette Book Group 2016], ch. 11 [édition numérique]).

10. Orend 2006, 105; Bell 2009, 8.

11. Bell 2009, 73-88.

12. Coates 2016, 14.

13. À cet égard, la perception moderne fondée sur les règles de la morale partage la lacune que beaucoup ont nivelée à la tradition manualiste catholique dans sa tentative de codifier la morale. Mes remerciements vont à Luis Pinto de Sa pour sa remarque à cet effet.

qui « traite les finalités comme étant acquises, et échappant à sa portée…»[14] Au lieu de privilégier une rationalité orientée vers des finalités précises, ce gestionnaire met en pratique une « rationalité bureaucratique consistant à faire coïncider la fin et les moyens dans un souci d'efficacité et d'économie », et considérant que les fins en elles-mêmes sont « prédéterminées »[15]. Il est vrai que la doctrine, la formation et l'enseignement professionnel militaires accordent peu d'importance à une compréhension réelle de ce que les meurtres en temps de guerre sont censés promouvoir. En revanche, l'accent est mis sur les règles à suivre.[16] La franche séparation entre le *jus ad bellum* et le *jus in bello* (respectivement droit *à* la guerre et droit *dans* la guerre) vient renforcer cette rationalité bureaucratique, car les questions liées au *ad bellum* dépendent en tout et pour tout de la responsabilité des dirigeants politiques. En ajoutant à cela la déférence de l'armée américaine à l'égard de l'autorité civile (si appropriée qu'elle soit), le fossé analytique entre les catégories morales ne peut que s'agrandir pour aboutir à un cloisonnement inquiétant qui, selon toute vraisemblance, exempte les soldats de l'obligation de comprendre les fondements moraux de leur engagement. Au lieu d'être considérés comme des agents moraux dans la guerre, les soldats sont perçus pratiquement comme des automates par les regards extérieurs. Cette vision correspond d'ailleurs au regard qu'ils portent sur eux-mêmes.

Troisièmement, un cadre moral strictement fondé sur des règles est insuffisant parce que le raisonnement seul n'incite pas à agir : il exige un engagement affectif correspondant aux principes ou aux valeurs qui conduisent à une action juste. « La morale délibérative place toute sa foi dans la règle. Elle néglige la question fondamentale de la volonté et de la motivation en présumant (à tort) du fort pouvoir d'autosuggestion exercé par la raison. »[17]

---

14. Alasdair MacIntyre, *After Virtue: A Study in Moral Theory,* 3rd ed. (Notre Dame: University of Notre Dame Press, 2007), 30.

15. Alasdair MacIntyre, *After Virtue: A Study in Moral Theory,* 3e éd. (Notre Dame: University of Notre Dame Press, 2007), 25.

16. Il y a quelques exceptions à cette critique assez générale : toutes les académies militaires imposent un cours d'introduction à l'éthique comprenant plusieurs leçons consacrées à la tradition de la guerre juste. Le programme du Corps de formation des officiers de réserve (ROTC) dans les campus universitaires, d'où est émoulue la majorité des officiers commissionnés, requiert quelques heures d'enseignement en éthique militaire qui vont également au-delà du sujet des règles à suivre (quoique de manière très superficielle). Ces officiers commissionnés sont une petite minorité assez influente au sein de la population militaire. La majorité des militaires enrôlés bénéficient de bien moins d'instruction en éthique militaire. Je tire ces faits de ma propre expérience, mais ils sont également corroborés par Burkhardt 2017, 37–38.

17. Coates 2016, 15.

Ce fait est particulièrement pertinent étant donné les réactions affectives contradictoires que connaissent les humains dans des situations stressantes comme la guerre. La morale traditionnelle, qui met l'accent sur les traits de caractère plutôt que sur la seule réflexion intellectuelle, « reconnaît que, pour être efficaces, les jugements moraux exigent le soutien de dispositions morales, de sentiments et d'inclinations ».[18] À cet égard, une perception totale est alors plus apte aux défis présentés par la guerre. Le principe de la bonne intention met l'accent sur le *caractère* requis en vertu de la quête de la justice, et non sur *l'état de chose* nécessaire pour rendre la justice (tout comme le principe de la juste cause). Ainsi la bonne intention est-elle une composante indispensable du *jus in bello*.

Une pire intention

Le catalogage, l'état d'esprit bureaucratique et le mythe de la raison à eux seuls, en tant qu'incitation à l'action, posent les jalons d'une disposition profondément ancrée chez de nombreux soldats (et, indirectement, de nombreux civils) les convainquant que le but essentiel d'un soldat est de tuer – faisant du meurtre sa *raison d'être*. L'acte létal n'est donc pas considéré comme une action regrettable, bien que nécessaire, qui serait subordonnée à l'objectif d'une paix juste et durable. Au lieu de cela, l'action létale comble un vide laissé dans la culture militaire par l'absence de la bonne intention en tant que principe directeur. Il y a donc confusion entre tâche et but. En ne prenant pas le soin de cultiver une réelle disposition à une paix juste, une disposition à autre chose aura tout le cours de s'exprimer, car un soldat sans disposition aucune est une impossibilité. Dans le pire des cas, une disposition au meurtre peut s'imposer, impliquant une sorte de goût sombre pour la mort. Le plus souvent, et ce n'est que guère mieux, s'installe une disposition à une « paix négative » rendue possible par l'élimination de l'ennemi.[19] C'est ce que l'historien antique Tacite avait à l'esprit en remarquant : « Là où [les empires] ont fait un désert, ils disent qu'ils ont fait la paix. »[20]

Cette paix négative peut être légitime dans les cas extrêmes où des agresseurs sont fanatiquement engagés dans l'élimination de leurs ennemis. Toutefois, les soldats (et, encore une fois, les civils) ne devraient pas être *disposés* à cette paix, mais plutôt s'en accommoder lorsque ce type de circonstances se présente. Leur disposition devrait s'inscrire en faveur d'une

---

18. Coates 2016, 15.
19. Coates 2016, 293; Capizzi 2015, 7.
20. Publius Cornelius Tacitus, *The Works of Tacitus: The Oxford Translation, Revised with Notes*, Vol. 2 (Londres : Bell et Daldy, 1872), 372.

paix entraînant une coexistence réconciliatrice au sein d'une communauté internationale et une harmonie entre des organes politiques fondés sur la justice, et non en faveur d'une absence de conflit due au fait qu'une seule entité politique parmi celles impliquées dans la guerre ait survécu. Même une version plus édulcorée de cette paix négative, résultant de la reddition des adversaires et non de leur meurtre au nom de la guerre, répond rarement aux normes légales et ne devrait donc pas être entérinée comme une forme de paix envisageable. En plus d'être injuste, une semblable paix ne durera probablement pas : « La paix des hommes réduits à la défaite n'est pas une paix authentique, mais une paix marquée par une profonde instabilité…» [21]

Lorsque les soldats ont essentiellement une compréhension négative de la paix, ils ont tendance à encenser le meurtre. Le fait d'ôter la vie est alors traité de manière délibérément efficace et désinvolte, surtout lorsque les normes professionnelles encouragent l'application de principes moraux avec l'insuffisance caractérisée d'un catalogage légaliste, l'efficacité mécanique d'une bureaucratie et l'indifférence détachée d'un automate. Un triste exemple est celui de la guerre du Vietnam, durant laquelle des dirigeants politiques et militaires s'attachaient à mettre en valeur les mesures quantifiables du progrès de la guerre, et surtout le nombre de victimes.[22] Plus récemment, lors d'un débat durant l'élection présidentielle de 2015, le candidat Mike Huckabee a déclaré : « Le but de l'armée est de tuer des gens et de détruire des choses. »[23] Bien que cette courte phrase ait pu être dite dans le but de ménager un effet rhétorique plus que pour la vérité pure, elle a tout de même déclenché un débat public dévoilant la disposition de nombreux soldats au sujet de la paix négative et des meurtres qui y sont rattachés.[24] Autre exemple : l'amiral Michael Mullen, qui lorsqu'il était président des chefs d'état-major interarmées

---

21. Capizzi 2015, 9.

22. Robert McNamara a adapté sa perspective très quantitative héritée de l'industrie automobile à son nouveau rôle de secrétaire à la Défense (1961-1968). Cependant, quelques années après le début du conflit au Vietnam, il a exprimé ses doutes en privé au président Johnson au sujet de cette perspective. C'est une critique d'initié que les historiens ont révélé relativement récemment, en partie en raison de la déclassification récente de certains documents. Voir Ken Burns et Lynne Novick, "La guerre du Vietnam", Florentine Films et WETA (2017), épisode 6; et Errol Morris, « The Fog of War: Eleven Lessons from the Life of Robert S. McNamara », Sony Pictures Classics (2003).

23. Janell Ross, "Mike Huckabee says the military's job is to 'kill people and break things.' Well, not quite," *The Washington Post*, 7 août 2015.

24. Pour lire un extrait du débat, voir Matt Cavanaugh, "The Military's Purpose is not to Kill People and Break Things," *War on the Rocks*, 26 August 2015; Jim Gourley, "The military's purpose isn't to break things and kill people, but it should be," *Foreign Policy* (24 septembre 2015).

en 2008, a fait savoir aux membres du Congrès qu' « on ne peut pas paver de meurtres le chemin vers la victoire » en Afghanistan.[25] Cette déclaration a entraîné la réponse d'officiers militaires en retraite soutenant qu'il avait tort, et que les soldats devaient être libérés de l' « hésitation timide » du commentaire de Mullen afin d'« agir avec la sauvagerie et la détermination nécessaires pour annihiler…les terroristes islamistes dans le monde entier. »[26] De l'examen de l'histoire militaire effectué par ces officiers en retraite afin de défendre leur point de vue, on retient que faire un désert et dire avoir fait la paix semble être la seule chose qui se puisse obtenir auprès des forces militaires. Il convient de noter que les deux officiers en question étaient, en Irak et en Afghanistan, des avocats militaires chargés du conseil des commandants sur le terrain concernant les règles d'engagement et leurs obligations en vertu du droit international (lequel, selon eux, devrait être assoupli en faveur des forces militaires).[27]

Une appréciation charitable de leur argument requiert la capacité de distinguer deux notions de la victoire. On peut supposer que Mullen faisait référence au succès de l'effort global visant à établir un régime afghan stable qui pouvait résister à la pression des groupes extrémistes violents et subvenir aux besoins de ses citoyens, de sorte que les extrémistes ne puissent plus trouver ni refuge ni soutien. Cependant, les deux officiers en question centraient leur propos sur la victoire tactique au combat. Qui plus est, ils semblaient ne vouloir définir la victoire, à n'importe quelle échelle, qu'en termes de conflit tactique. La position de ces officiers met en exergue l'hypothèse sous-jacente que les relations internationales, en général, et les guerres qu'elles engendrent parfois, sont toujours des jeux à somme nulle. Bien que les moments de combat réel confirment ce point, il est également important de ne jamais perdre de vue le contexte en marge des affrontements violents, où le gain de l'adversaire ne signifie pas nécessairement sa propre perte, et où quelque chose de plus concluant qu'une paix négative est possible. Là où une paix positive est possible, on est tenu par une obligation morale et prudentielle de la rechercher. Cette obligation est ce que l'on entend par la notion de bonne intention. C'est une disposition à une

25. CNN Politics, « Troops alone will not yield victory in Afghanistan », CNN.com, 10 septembre 2008.

26. David Bolgiano, John Taylor, "Can't Kill Enough to Win? Think Again," *Proceedings Magazine*, Vol. 143/12/1,378 (U.S. Naval Institute, décembre 2017). Pour une opinion divergente, voir Adam Weinstein, "No, We Can't Kill Our Way to Victory Despite What 2 Misguided Lieutenant Colonels Might Think," *Task and Purpose* (8 décembre 2017).

27. Bolgiano, Taylor 2017.

paix positive, une forme d'insistance consistant à repérer la possibilité de son existence, même au vu de concessions allant dans un sens différent.[28]

La disposition à une paix négative – qui comprend une fixation sur le meurtre – est plus facile à perpétuer si les ennemis sont considérés comme moins qu'humains. Les adversaires qui entrent dans la catégorie des sous-hommes, tels les animaux ou les insectes, ne justifient sans doute ni le niveau de retenue que l'on accorde à d'autres humains, ni le même engagement envers un avenir commun. En marge des influences sociales du nationalisme, du racisme ou des stéréotypes culturels négatifs, la légitimité manifeste d'une guerre peut empêcher de voir l'ennemi « comme autre chose qu'un criminel qui, en tant que tel, sera soumis à tout ce qu'on doit pouvoir lui faire subir ».[29] Cette mentalité teintée d'une détermination péremptoire exerce une pression supplémentaire en vertu de la déshumanisation des ennemis, ainsi que des non-combattants qui leur sont naturellement associés. Elle n'attribue pas à l'ennemi un statut de sous-homme semblable à celui d'un insecte, mais s'attache à le présenter comme un monstre moralement malfaisant.[30] Ainsi, le tuer devient une obligation morale centrale, quelle que soit la nature de la paix qui pourra en résulter.

De plus, il est aisé d'entretenir l'intention de tuer en partant d'une vision militariste de la guerre. Si la guerre est considérée comme ayant une valeur intrinsèque, une sorte de noblesse sans reconnaissance de sa tragédie, alors le meurtre qu'elle entraîne n'est pas regrettable, mais pleinement consenti. Cette position militariste sert avant tout de mécanisme d'adaptation pour les soldats confrontés à la relation tendue entre l'immoralité *prima facie* (à première vue) de tuer et, en même temps, au devoir *prima facie* de tuer. Au lieu de trouver une résolution à cette tension (qui pourrait d'ailleurs le pousser vers le principe de la bonne intention), le soldat peut refuser le premier et centrer

---

28. Le degré et l'étendue de cette obligation varient en fonction de sa position et de ses fonctions. Les soldats dans le feu des combats ne devraient pas avoir à considérer les termes de la paix que les dirigeants politiques du camp opposé pourraient accepter. Ils devraient toutefois considérer la possibilité que leurs homologues ennemis décident de leur reddition. Le degré d'obligation augmente pour les soldats impliqués non pas dans le feu du combat, mais dans les efforts plus calmes de choix des objectifs stratégiques, de planification des campagnes pour sécuriser ces objectifs, et d'évaluation des progrès vers une issue de la guerre.

29. Capizzi 2015, 121.

30. Ces deux catégories de sous-hommes, "de base, à laquelle appartiennent animaux et insectes, ou monstrueuse, à laquelle appartiennent monstres et démons," sont empruntées à Michael Brough, "Dehumanization of the Enemy and the Moral Equality of Soldiers," dans *Rethinking the Just War Tradition*, eds. Michael Brough, John Lango, Harry van der Linden (Albany, NY: State University of New York Press, 2007), 160.

sa perspective sur le second, généralement avec la complicité de ses pairs qui font l'expérience de la même situation, et grâce à des pressions d'ordre culturel. Comme le décrit un ancien combattant : « Une fois que vous apprenez à vous accommoder d'un comportement immoral, ça devient plus facile. »[31]

Intention meurtrière, déshumanisation et militarisme se renforcent mutuellement au sein d'une culture militaire qui est loin d'être ancrée dans une disposition à une paix juste et durable. On peut faire une analogie avec la chirurgie qui permet d'illustrer le danger d'une déformation de l'objectif global du soldat.[32] Personne ne veut évidemment tomber aux mains d'un chirurgien obsédé par son art et entendant ignorer tout autre traitement adapté pour que son patient puisse recouvrer sa pleine santé. Même si ce chirurgien est habile au maniement du scalpel, son but essentiel devrait être avant tout d'assurer le bien-être physique de son patient. Ainsi ne devrait-il pas tenter la chirurgie simplement parce qu'il en a l'autorité et la compétence. Il lui faut bien comprendre quand et de quelle façon brandir son scalpel pour contribuer de la meilleure manière possible à cette bonne santé. Il doit également être en mesure de parer à des imprévus ou à des complications survenues au cours de l'intervention chirurgicale. De la même façon, le soldat a le devoir d'exercer sa force létale, mais en comprenant les tenants de la paix juste censés être promus par l'acte de tuer et en sachant quand la force létale peut venir la compromettre ; enfin, il doit adapter ses actions à des circonstances inattendues afin d'obtenir la paix désirée. Comme l'a remarqué le général américain John Schofield en 1881 : « l'objet et la finalité de la guerre *ne sont pas* de « tuer », qui n'est que l'un des *moyens* nécessaires à cette finalité....L'objet de la guerre est d'amener une paix honorable, avantageuse et durable. »[33] Lorsque les soldats n'ont aucune appréciation pour cette paix, ni d'engagement personnel à son égard, ils sont dangereusement mal équipés pour exercer une force létale à bon escient comme en témoigne le principe de la bonne intention.

II. Rétablir l'influence de la bonne intention

Jusqu'à présent, j'ai souligné que la mise à l'écart de la bonne intention en tant que principe du *jus in bello* génère un vide qui peut faire place à une

---

31. Wood 2016, ch. 1.
32. Cette comparaison avec la chirurgie est empruntée à Orend 2006, 106 et à Saint Thomas d'Aquin, *Summa theologiae* II-II q. 64 a. 3.
33. John M. Schofield, "Notes on 'The Legitimate in War,'" *Journal of the Military Service Institution* 2 (1881), 1–10; cité par Brian Linn, *The Echo of Battle: The Army's Way of War* (Cambridge, MA: Harvard University Press, 2009), 58

intention meurtrière, et que la déshumanisation et le militarisme qui en découlent viennent renforcer. L'empathie contribue à atténuer ces préoccupations morales, surtout dans leurs aspects pratiques. Dans la partie suivante, j'entends montrer la résistance opposée par l'empathie à la déshumanisation et au militarisme, pour en souligner le rôle dans le désamorçage d'une intention meurtrière ainsi que dans le rétablissement de l'influence de la bonne intention. En premier lieu, je vais expliquer ce que j'entends par empathie.

Définir l'empathie

Pour que le terme « empathie » puisse attirer attention, il doit faire référence à quelque chose de significatif. Certains érudits ont appliqué le terme à différents phénomènes, souvent de manière contradictoire, et l'emploi commun du mot en assimile généralement le sens à la sympathie ou à la compassion.[34] Je voudrais suggérer que l'empathie offre une « contribution distinctive qu'elle seule peut ménager » et qui tient à un ressenti partagé de l'expérience d'une autre personne.[35] Ce ressenti ne se limite pas aux sentiments, car il inclut l'impression des choses qui résident au-delà des sentiments immédiats, tels que les désirs, les convictions, les intentions, les soucis, les engagements – soit presque tout l'éventail de la vie mentale d'autrui, y compris une perception de sa vie cognitive (c'est-à-dire l'impression que produit chez lui le maintien d'une certaine croyance). Si un ami annonce la chose suivante : « Je viens de voter pour le candidat en faveur duquel je fais campagne depuis quelques semaines », il y a évidemment des états cognitifs et affectifs associés à cette expérience. Les états cognitifs de cet ami, qui croit fermement que son candidat préféré est le meilleur, ou qu'il est important d'exercer son droit de vote, etc., existent en même temps que les états affectifs qui consistent par exemple à espérer que le candidat suive son programme, à se préoccuper de ses chances de remporter l'élection, à croire aux effets positifs de la campagne électorale, ou à ressentir un certain soulagement que la campagne soit terminée, ou, plus important encore, une combinaison complexe impliquant certains de ces états affectifs. En outre, ces états cognitifs et affectifs sont mutuellement inclusifs, ce qui signifie qu'ils peuvent s'inciter ou se renforcer mutuellement. Ici l'empathie consiste à comprendre, dans une certaine mesure, comment cette expérience globale du vote (après campagne) touche cette

---

34. Voir Batson 2009 pour un résumé illustratif ; pour des introductions plus complètes du terme et de son histoire, voir Stueber 2006, Coplan et Goldie 2011, Zahavi 2014 et Matravers 2017.
35. Smith 2015, 711.

personne, compte tenu d'un jeu complexe de cognition et d'affect fondé sur un contexte et des circonstances spécifiques.[36]

L'empathie ne réside donc pas simplement dans l'attribution à cet ami d'un sentiment générique d'espoir ou de nervosité. Comme le suggère Max Scheler, l'empathie n'est pas « simplement la question d'émettre un jugement intellectuel sur le fait que quelqu'un d'autre soit soumis à une expérience donnée ; ce n'est pas la simple pensée que c'est le cas…» [37] L'empathie est spécifiquement orientée sur l'expérience de l'autre dans sa phénoménalité. En d'autres termes, l'empathie fournit une compréhension limitée de l'expérience d'autrui ; il ne s'agit pas d'une description de cette expérience en soi (qui dépend, entre autres, de la capacité de la personne empathique à la verbaliser) mais de la nature phénoménale de l'expérience en question. Dans le but de forger une définition de travail, je soutiens donc la conception de l'empathie énoncée par Joel Smith comme une compréhension expérientielle de *ce que* les autres ressentent ou pensent, et pas seulement une compréhension propositionnelle ou théorique *du fait que* l'autre ressent ou pense d'une certaine façon.[38]

L'empathie se distingue donc très clairement de la sympathie. L'empathie, c'est comprendre ce qu'autrui pense ou ressent, mais ce n'est pas prendre soin du bien-être d'autrui. [39] Comme l'observe Edmund Husserl, « alors que l'empathie est une forme de compréhension, la sympathie implique le soin et la préoccupation. »[40] Les deux concepts sont liés; en fait, l'empathie peut susciter et entraîner des attitudes sympathiques alors que la sympathie peut inciter à des tentatives de compréhension empathique d'autrui. La confusion de ces termes est probablement assez commune en raison de l'emploi du mot « sympathie » que font David Hume et Adam Smith dans leurs travaux respectifs sur la théorie morale. Cependant, les phénomènes qu'ils décrivent correspondent à ce que l'on nomme de nos jours l'empathie. En d'autres termes, la conception de Hume renvoie au miroir des émotions d'autrui quand il évoque une empathie de base, tandis que la conception de Smith décrit l'adoption imaginative de la perspective d'autrui dans l'empathie de

---

36. Il est également important de noter que la justesse de l'empathie augmente avec la connaissance que l'on peut avoir de l'ami en question- s'il est naturellement optimiste, inquiet, etc. Cette connaissance peut donner une plus grande acuité à la tentative empathique dédiée à la compréhension des états mentaux de l'ami en question.
37. Cité par Zahavi 2014, 118.
38. Smith 2015, 712-713.
39. Darwall 1998, 261-270.
40. Cité par Zahavi 2014, 139 (note en bas de la page 14).

niveau supérieur.[41] L'empathie de base est généralement vue comme incon-sciente, automatique et révélatrice d'états mentaux concernant l'émotion et les intentions immédiates « de surface ». En revanche, l'empathie de niveau supérieur est considérée comme consciente, délibérée et révélatrice d'états mentaux plus profonds ou plus durables, et comprend des intentions générales ainsi que le sens dissimulé derrière un comportement.[42] On note que le terme d'« empathie » n'est entré dans la langue anglaise qu'un siècle après les travaux de Hume et de Smith ; cette confusion très commune entre les deux termes ne peut donc pas leur être attribuée.

La recherche corrobore l'intuition que l'empathie conduit à la sympathie, mais montre également que ce lien n'est pas systématique.[43] Il peut, au contraire, inhiber la sympathie envers certaines personnes et l'accentuer pour d'autres, comme le montrent la facilité avec laquelle on peut compatir avec les membres de sa propre culture ou d'un autre groupe et la difficulté qu'on peut ressentir à sympathiser avec ceux qui sont en marge de ces groupes. De ce fait, l'empathie peut introduire une partialité moralement problématique. Cette préoccupation alimente certains arguments contre la contribution présumée de l'empathie à la morale.[44] Elle met également en évidence la différence entre l'empathie et la sympathie.[45]

L'empathie révèle l'égalité morale de l'ennemi

L'empathie implique une solidarité fondamentale avec autrui. Il ne s'agit pas d'une solidarité d'opinions, de perspectives, de jugements, de valeurs ou de sentiments, mais simplement d'une solidarité fondamentale de personne à personne. Celle-ci peut d'ailleurs parfois contribuer aux autres formes de solidarité citées plus haut. L'empathie, en tant que compréhension empirique d'une autre personne, laisse s'exprimer l'humanité qu'un soldat a en commun avec son ennemi. Elle permet de reconnaître l'humanité d'autrui et, par conséquent, de contrarier toute tendance à sa déshumanisation. L'empathie de base permet l'enracinement d'une intuition qui confirme le statut humain de l'ennemi ; en cela, elle s'apparente à une perception sensorielle. Cette empathie de base peut être délibérément ignorée ou interrompue, comme

---

41. Darwall 1998, 267; Coplan et Goldie 2011, x
42. Coplan et Goldie 2011, xxxiii.
43. Batson, 1991; Darwall 1998, 272-273.
44. Prinz 2011; Bloom 2014.
45. Pour une discussion plus approfondie au sujet de la relation entre l'empathie et la sym-pathie, voir Darwall 1998; Coplan et Goldie 2011, x-xi; Gallagher 2012, 360-362; Zahavi 2014, 115-117; Matravers 2017, 115.

quand on ferme les paupières pour ne rien voir, à savoir toutefois que quand elle ne connaît pas d'obstacle, son expression est systématique. L'empathie de niveau supérieur est construite sur cette intuition primordiale à travers des processus cognitifs comme l'adoption imaginative de la perspective d'autrui pour dévoiler un aperçu de son existence--dont des éléments de la structure narrative de ses expériences, ainsi que sa vision du monde, ses valeurs et ses intentions. Ainsi l'empathie de niveau supérieur n'est-elle pas naturelle ; elle doit être sciemment mise en œuvre, mais peut toutefois être conditionnée.

À titre d'exemple, il est intéressant de se pencher sur une aventure qui est arrivée à un groupe de soldats déployé en Irak dans le cadre d'une campagne contre-insurrectionnelle. Ils étaient censés mener un raid contre la maison d'un ancien colonel de l'armée irakienne qui avait entrepris de coordonner et de financer les efforts d'insurgés dans sa ville. Lorsque les soldats ont eu forcé l'entrée de la demeure, un homme baissé s'est précipité dans le vestibule. Il était penché, on ne pouvait pas voir ses mains, il a fait un mouvement subit vers l'avant. Alors, deux soldats parmi les quatre qui étaient présents l'ont visé et il est tombé à terre. Il n'y a pas eu d'autres coups de feu. Trente secondes plus tard, le lieu était sécurisé et l'équipe a commencé à prodiguer les premiers soins à l'homme gisant au sol. Il est mort devant eux et devant sa femme et sa fille encore très jeune, qui avaient été retrouvées dans la maison et conduites jusqu'au vestibule. Le colonel irakien était mort.[46]

La mort de cet homme est restée ancrée dans la mémoire des soldats qui l'ont abattu. L'un d'entre eux a eu beaucoup de mal à accepter cette mort qu'il avait en partie causée. La chaîne de commandement a convenu que les actions de l'équipe étaient justifiées, mais cela n'a pas allégé le poids de la culpabilité ressentie par ce soldat. L'homme qui avait été tué n'avait rien dans les mains. Le soldat avait du mal à comprendre pourquoi il s'était jeté devant lui. Le colonel essayait-il de protéger sa famille ? Avait-il même tenté de s'attaquer au soldat qui avait franchi la porte en tête du groupe ? Est-ce qu'il essayait d'entrer dans la pièce pour connaître l'origine du bruit ? Avait-il simplement trébuché en entrant dans la pièce ? Le soldat avait lui aussi une femme et une fille en bas âge et ne pouvait s'empêcher de se demander ce qu'il adviendrait de la famille du colonel.

Les difficultés éprouvées par ce soldat constituent un exemple de l'empathie qui a cours lors d'un conflit, même si celle-ci passe largement inaperçue dans la théorisation que l'on fait couramment de la guerre. Le trouble de ce

---

46. Cette histoire est tirée de mon déploiement en Irak en 2003 avec la 4e Division d'infanterie de l'armée américaine.

soldat est une réaction bien naturelle aux tristes devoirs de la guerre, mais l'entraînement militaire reste trop souvent axé sur la répression de ce type d'émotions, car il faut assurer que les soldats continuent d'assumer leurs fonctions : mieux vaut un soldat sans cervelle qu'un soldat avec trop de cervelle. Je voudrais résister à cette conclusion, mais l'un ou l'autre extrême est tout aussi préjudiciable aux qualités nécessaires à un bon soldat.

Je soutiens que l'entraînement et l'enculturation militaire de ce soldat l'ont conditionné à mettre un terme à son empathie de base au nom d'actions énergiques nécessaires dans le contexte du raid de la maison du colonel irakien. Après l'entrée en force, les tirs sur une personne qui semblait menaçante, et la sécurisation de la maison, les soldats ont tenté de stabiliser le colonel blessé. Dans le changement de perspective nécessaire pour pouvoir passer de l'action énergique à l'évaluation de la situation immédiate et des soins à apporter au colonel, l'empathie intuitive de base, chez ce soldat en particulier, n'a pas été supprimée, mais a repris l'avantage sur son empathie de niveau supérieur comme par réflexe conditionné. Par la suite, l'empathie de niveau supérieur du soldat s'est appuyée sur cette intuition pour forger une compréhension pragmatique du rôle du colonel en tant que mari et père. À son tour, cette compréhension a stimulé la réaction empathique du soldat pour la veuve du colonel et sa fille. Mon équipier est sorti troublé de cette compréhension empirique, de ce moment d'empathie.

La source de ses troubles était due, au moins en partie, au statut complexe de l'Irakien qui avait perdu la vie. Il n'était plus purement et simplement un ennemi à combattre ; il était aussi un être humain disparu dont il fallait faire le deuil. Le soldat ne pouvait pas se détacher du fait que ce colonel, tout comme lui, avait une épouse et était père d'une petite fille. Il avait été plus facile de considérer péremptoirement le colonel comme un criminel, comme celui qui était personnellement responsable de la guerre dans laquelle le soldat se trouvait pris. La haine ressentie envers l'ennemi coupable avait rendu tellement plus facile d'enfoncer la porte et d'appuyer sur la gâchette. Cependant, à ce moment-là, cette haine avait été…

> … interrompue ou remplacée par une compréhension plus réfléchie…le sentiment que le soldat ennemi, bien que sa guerre puisse être criminelle, est néanmoins aussi irréprochable qu'on l'est soi-même. Armé, c'est un ennemi ; mais il n'est pas *mon* ennemi au sens strict ; la guerre elle-même n'est pas une relation entre des personnes, mais entre des entités politiques et leurs instruments humains.…[Comme moi, ils se retrouvent] pris au

piège d'une guerre qu'ils n'ont pas initiée. Je trouve en eux des
égaux d'un point de vue moral.[47]

Cette notion d'égalité morale, d'une innocence morale partagée dans
les deux camps opposés par des soldats impliqués dans une guerre qu'ils
n'ont pas initiée, se développe grâce à une expérience concrète de la pensée
empathique. Cette expérience se déroule ici dans une situation de contre-
insurrection semblable aux récentes initiatives militaires en Irak. Dans le
prolongement de la compréhension réfléchie d'une situation semblable, un
soldat américain pourrait soulever les questions suivantes : « Que faudrait-
il pour me convaincre de coopérer avec une force d'occupation étrangère
patrouillant dans ma ville natale ? Quel comportement de la part de leurs
troupes pourrait vraiment les assurer de ma *propre* coopération ? Quelle serait
la probabilité que je puisse prendre les armes contre cette force d'occupation
étrangère ? Il faut noter que ces questions pourraient aboutir à une erreur
de projection puisqu'elles font intervenir une optique centrée sur soi, c'est-
à-dire comprenant de nombreuses influences culturelles différentes de celles
qui régissent la vie de l'Irakien moyen. Toutefois, cette perspective peut
aussi s'imposer en tant que mode d'empathie de niveau supérieur « lorsqu'il
y a de multiples chevauchements entre soi et autrui ou lorsque la situation
pourrait induire une réponse assez universelle ». [48] Des troupes étrangères
patrouillant dans les rues d'un quartier feront l'objet de préoccupations
concernant la sécurité des familles, ainsi que d'un patriotisme et d'une
méfiance envers ces étrangers venant d'une culture différente.

L'empathie encourage les soldats à prendre en compte l'égalité morale
de leurs ennemis. Ce faisant, elle permet d'assurer un « contrôle sur une
tendance de la guerre » à déshumaniser l'ennemi.[49] En effet, l'empathie
sape la tendance bien ancrée qui amène à considérer les ennemis comme
des animaux inférieurs ou des êtres si mauvais qu'ils en seraient dénués
d'humanité. Les ennemis sont alors perçus comme étant soumis aux mêmes
tendances sécuritaires qui existent dans chaque pays et qui appellent au
respect des lois de la conscription et au désir de protéger leurs familles et
leurs compatriotes. Cette clairvoyance par rapport à la nature de l'ennemi
peut avoir deux effets positifs. Premièrement, elle insuffle une plus grande

---

47. Walzer en 1977, 36.
48. Amy Coplan, « Understanding Empathy: Its Features and Effects », dans *Empathy: Philosophical and Psychological Perspectives*, éd. Amy Coplan et Peter Goldie (New York: Oxford
University Press, 2011), 9.
49. Brough 2007, 151.

retenue aux soldats, de sorte qu'ils soient plus enclins à limiter l'usage de la force au strict nécessaire. Deuxièmement, elle jette les bases d'une disposition vers une paix juste et durable. L'égalité morale sert de « raison pour ramener les ennemis vaincus à leur vie d'avant, comme un pas vers un retour à la normalité et à la paix – car comment peut-on s'arroger le droit de punir chez l'ennemi ce que l'on aurait soi-même fait dans la même situation ? »[50]

De la possible égalité morale des terroristes

Il est difficile de conserver une détermination péremptoire quand on se rend compte de l'égalité morale d'un soldat ennemi, mais le cas est différent lorsque l'on considère la position à adopter envers un terroriste. Doit-on pratiquer l'empathie envers un terroriste et promouvoir un sentiment d'égalité morale avec lui ? De même, l'égalité morale avec un terroriste peut-elle exister ? D'une part, le terroriste est lui aussi soumis à l'influence d'une culture, à des techniques de recrutement, à une certaine propagande, et autres. De plus, si c'est un membre de rang inférieur dans l'organisation à laquelle il appartient, il est soumis aux ordres de ses supérieurs qui seront décisifs, même en n'étant pas porteurs de l'approbation juridique et de l'autorité d'un régime établi et reconnu. Bien que cela puisse être retenu contre le terroriste comme un manquement grave à l'égard d'un gouverne-ment officiel, il se peut que le gouvernement en question ait perdu toute légitimité, et avec elle le droit de gouverner, ou qu'il n'y ait pas de pouvoir politique reconnu dans le pays. Si le terroriste est un subordonné ne disposant d'aucun pouvoir décisionnaire quant à l'emploi de moyens violents ou à la sélection des cibles, il peut faire montre d'une innocence morale semblable à celle d'un soldat de rang inférieur, malgré sa participation matérielle à l'acte terroriste. Certes, l'acte terroriste devrait être tel que ce subalterne ne puisse pas en identifier avec certitude les caractéristiques morales (en particulier le ciblage délibéré de personnes innocentes), ni être soumis à des pressions pouvant l'exonérer de toute culpabilité. Pourtant, si tel est le cas, la dénomination de « terroriste » ne s'applique pas à lui. Il est moralement l'égal d'un soldat et, par conséquent, cette étiquette péjorative est injustifiée.

Un véritable terroriste demeure moralement différent d'un soldat en raison de la nature même du terrorisme qui engendre sa dénomination en tant que tel. Le terrorisme recourt à l'emploi délibéré de la violence ou à sa menace

---

50. Brough 2007, 151. A noter que cette conclusion selon laquelle un individu ferait la même chose qu'un autre n'est pas entraînée par l'empathie qui ne fait que permettre à cette conclusion d'exister. L'empathie est facteur de compréhension et non d'accord.

contre des non-combattants à des fins politiques.[51] Cet emploi délibéré de la force ne répond pas aux exigences morales s'appliquant à des vies innocentes. Le véritable terroriste n'est donc pas moralement innocent comme l'est le soldat qui, lié aux principes du *jus in bello,* est forcé de distinguer les combattants des non-combattants, et prêt à s'acquitter de son devoir rendu possible par une connaissance de la loi, une formation, et une culture militaire ou sociétale. Le terroriste, lui, cible délibérément des innocents alors que ce n'est pas indispensable.[52] Il est donc beaucoup plus facile d'adopter une mentalité délibérément militante contre les terroristes dont les faits criminels sont bien différents de ceux des soldats à la solde d'un gouvernement.

Pourtant, le soldat et le terroriste ont en commun une forme d'égalité diluée ou plus ténue[53] qui s'apparente à celle d'un criminel coupable. C'est une égalité morale du point de vue du statut humain et des valeurs, mais qui ne peut s'inscrire dans une innocence morale à cause des actes de force perpétrés des deux côtés. Une compréhension empathique du terroriste met en valeur la forme d'égalité morale la plus ténue (comme elle le fait, en général, avec les criminels dans leur ensemble). Cette égalité ténue, au même titre que l'égalité plus consistante décrite ci-avant au sujet des soldats ennemis, n'implique pas un accord avec la vision du monde des terroristes, avec leurs jugements moraux ou leurs décisions ; elle ne fait que rendre compte de l'humanité des terroristes à travers leurs jugements, malgré leur échec à cet égard envers leurs victimes.

Par la mise en lumière d'une égalité morale consistante ou ténue, l'empathie humanise les ennemis et, par conséquent, améliore la capacité de jugement des soldats. « Si les États et leurs soldats peuvent apprendre à considérer l'ennemi comme pleinement humain et moralement égal à eux, ils discerneront plus clairement l'étendue possible de la morale et, ainsi, éviteront un désastre moral pour les deux camps opposés dans la guerre. »[54] Il

---

51. Bruce Hoffman, *Inside Terrorism*, édition révisée et élargie, (New York: Columbia University Press, 2006), 26-28. Voir aussi Nations Unies, « Déclaration sur les mesures visant à éliminer le terrorisme international », annexe à la résolution 49/60 de l'Assemblée générale des Nations Unies, « Mesures visant à éliminer le terrorisme international », (9 décembre 1994).

52. Cette analyse comparant soldat et terroriste suffit à révéler la facilité avec laquelle le soldat peut commettre des actes terroristes. Il peut délibérément mettre de côté la distinction entre combattants et non-combattants ou ne pas protéger suffisamment les non-combattants. Compte tenu de leurs objectifs largement politiques, ces actes s'apparentent à la définition du terrorisme. Voir la discussion de David Rodin sur la force imprudente ou négligente contre les non-combattants dans « Terrorism without Intention », *Ethics* 114 (juillet 2004), 752-771.

53. Cette notion d'une égalité morale plus ténue est empruntée à Brough 2007, 150.

54. Brough 2007, 160.

est difficile de maintenir une attitude purement militariste quand l'empathie est présente. On ne peut ignorer la tragédie de la guerre, on ne peut que s'y confronter, comme a dû le faire le soldat au décès du colonel irakien.

Cependant, l'empathie appliquée de manière sélective peut influer sur un bon jugement. Par exemple, l'empathie avec les victimes d'une agression peut engendrer une capacité à la persévérance. Toutefois, en étant prise avec trop de distance ou de manière trop exclusive, cette persévérance pourra précipiter certains dans une optique vengeresse, sapant ainsi toute notion d'égalité morale. Il est possible d'éviter cet extrême grâce à un moment d'empathie ménagée envers les agresseurs.

De la relation de l'empathie avec le meurtre

« Dans notre esprit moderne, observe Shay, l'ennemi est, par définition, détestable. » [55] Ainsi, conserver à l'ennemi son humanité est généralement considéré comme impossible ; pour beaucoup, il s'agit d'une vérité évidente « que les hommes ne peuvent pas tuer un ennemi considéré comme honorable autant que soi-même ».[56] Contrairement à l'argument selon lequel les soldats doivent absolument déshumaniser l'ennemi pour pouvoir le tuer, il y a quelques moments de rencontres intimes avec lui qui rendent sa déshumanisation impossible. Michael Walzer en décrit quelques exemples, s'appuyant sur les souvenirs d'anciens combattants qui racontent la difficulté de tirer son arme face à des soldats ennemis « qui sont drôles, qui prennent un bain, ou tenant leur pantalon [alors qu'ils courent le long d'une tranchée], profitant du soleil, [ou] fumant une cigarette. »[57] Richard Holmes observe que « le concept d'un ennemi haineux et inhumain survit rarement aux contacts directs qu'on peut avoir avec lui en tant qu'individu ».[58] L'expérience du soldat troublé décrite plus haut illustre d'une autre manière les inévitables moments d'empathie vécus dans la guerre. Certes, ces moments sont seulement de brefs aperçus de l'humanité des individus, des impressions fragmentaires souvent enterrées sous la propagande de l'effort de guerre et sous le poids des émotions déchirantes liées à la lutte et à des pertes inhérentes à la guerre. Cependant, le simple fait d'étouffer ces moments empathiques conduit aux dangers de la déshumanisation de

---

55. Jonathan Shay, *Achilles in Vietnam: Combat Trauma and the Undoing of Character* (New York: Scribner, 1994), 103.
56. Ibid.
57. Walzer 1977, 138-143.
58. Richard Holmes, *Acts of War: The Behavior of Men in Battle* (New York: The Free Press, 1985), 368; cité par Brough 2007, 157.

l'individu, du militarisme et du meurtre en tant qu'objectif primordial de
la guerre. Toute bonne intention est alors perdue.[59] En cherchant une forme
de réconciliation entre l'humanité des dits ennemis et le devoir de les tuer,
on pourrait probablement trouver une solution à cette déshumanisation.[60]

Michael Brough pose la même question : « Comment les soldats devraient-
ils percevoir les meurtres qu'ils commettent en temps de guerre, et de quelle
manière les nations pourraient-elles enseigner à leurs soldats comment
appréhender ces meurtres ? Car le choix de privilégier la déshumanisation
est trop coûteux. »[61] S'appuyant sur les recherches des psychologues David
Grossman et Stanley Milgram, Brough évoque la nécessité de se distancier
d'une cible humaine afin de pouvoir la tuer. Cette mise à distance peut
être physique, d'autant plus que les technologies modernes le permettent,
mais elle peut aussi prendre une forme émotionnelle, faisant intervenir «
la distanciation sociale (qui met l'accent sur les différences entre les classes
sociales), la distanciation culturelle (qui accentue les différences raciales et
ethniques) et la distanciation morale (qui présume de l'infériorité morale de
l'ennemi). »[62] Ces formes de mise à distance émotionnelle sont précisément
les tendances déshumanisantes qui réduisent l'ennemi à un état « de base,
comme un animal ou un insecte, ou monstrueux, comme un monstre ou
un démon », et sont en cela inacceptables.[63] Brough qualifie ces tentatives
de mise à distance de « sous-humanisation » afin de désigner leur déni de la
valeur humaine de l'ennemi. Il suggère à la place une autre forme de mise

---

59. Il conduit également au danger du sentiment de préjudice moral, à un sentiment
invalidant de trahison et / ou de culpabilité chez les anciens combattants qui reçoivent
désormais une attention croissante. Pour introduction, voir Jonathan Shay (1994); Nancy
Sherman, *Afterwar: Healing the Moral Wounds of our Soldiers* (New York: Oxford University
Press, 2015); et David Wood, *What Have We Done: The Moral Injury of Our Longest Wars*
(New York: Little, Brown and Company, 2016).

60. La réponse pacifiste est de nier ce dernier – il ne peut exister de devoir de tuer. Bien
que je veuille m'éloigner quelque peu de la position pacifiste, je partage la préoccupation
de Brian Orend au sujet d'une « arrogance embarrassante » dans la littérature de la guerre
juste concernant le pacifisme (« Une critique du réalisme et du pacifisme de la guerre juste
», *journal de recherche philosophique*, vol. XXVI [2001], 435-436). Nous devrions tous nous
engager pacifiquement par défaut en faveur d'une résolution non violente des conflits. Il
s'agit d'un engagement *prima facie* que même les soldats devraient maintenir, en comprenant que leur profession demeure orientée vers des circonstances qui dépassent les limites
de cet engagement. Diverses situations exigent qu'on puisse juger si l'on a ou non dépassé
ces limites. Dans les contre-insurrections, en particulier, quand il n'y a pas de lignes de
front établies, ce jugement est exigé de soldats d'un rang inférieur dans la chaîne de commandement, bien qu'il soit souvent des plus difficiles.

61. Brough 2007, 159.

62. Brough 2007, 160.

63. Ibid

à distance émotionnelle qu'il appelle la « non-humanisation ». Issue de la distance physique permise par les armes modernes, « la non-humanisation a débuté avec l'invention de l'artillerie à trajectoire indirecte, réduisant l'image qu'on pouvait avoir des soldats ennemis à des épingles ou des marques au crayon sur des cartes militaires, ou encore à des coordonnées criées à la hâte à un groupe de fusiliers. »[64] La perception des ennemis en tant que simples « points de lumière [non-humains] sur un écran d'ordinateur » s'est étendue au fur et à mesure que l'électronique s'imposait en tant que technologie médiatrice de la guerre.[65]

La non-humanisation implique non pas une forme de dénigrement empreint d'une forte charge émotionnelle, mais une réification de l'ennemi totalement dénuée d'émotion. Par conséquent, la non-humanisation peut se situer à quelques degrés de morale au-dessus de la sous-humanisation, compte tenu des violents excès inhérents à cette dernière. Cependant, même si le préfixe négatif *non* évite la connotation de moindre valeur indiquée par le préfixe *sous*, il transmet tout de même le sentiment que l'ennemi est *non*-humain, c'est-à-dire différent de l'humain. En cela, il se dégage de ce préfixe une perspective problématique du meurtre d'autres *humains* tel qu'il est justifié dans la guerre. Brough est prompt à souligner ce point, en affirmant que considérer l'ennemi comme non-humain peut aboutir à la négation totale de son égalité morale, de la même manière qu'en le considérant comme sous-humain.[66] Cependant, étant donnée la nécessité d'une prise de distance émotionnelle ou d'une façon de « rendre le meurtre plus facile » dans les circonstances morales adéquates, Brough approuve l'existence d'un moment non humanisant à condition qu'il soit étroitement délimité par le respect dû à l'ennemi.[67] Le meurtre d'autrui, suggère-t-il, « n'exclut pas d'honorer les morts après la bataille. Une prière, une pensée, un adieu murmuré peuvent suffire pour signifier le respect dû aux morts. » Brough met ainsi en valeur la recherche thérapeutique qui montre combien il est important pour les soldats d'honorer les adversaires tombés au combat afin de pouvoir éviter des « répercussions psychologiques dommageables ».[68]

---

64. Ibid., 161.
65. Ibid
66. Brough 2007, 161.
67. Walzer suggère quelque chose de semblable à propos du meurtre de l'ennemi lorsqu'il déclare : « Alors que l'aliénation [de l'ennemi] est éphémère, son humanité est imminente » (1977, 142).
68. Brough 2007, 163. La recherche psychologique est celle de Jonathan Shay et David Grossman ; le préjudice moral est l'une de ces répercussions.

Quoiqu'étant personnellement favorable à l'optique de Brough, je tiens également à proposer une alternative à la non-humanisation en tant que solution au meurtre dans la guerre. Le soldat se trouvant dans des circonstances telles qu'il est permis, sinon obligatoire, de tuer l'ennemi, devrait conserver intacte l'humanité de l'ennemi, tout en se détachant de l'impulsion empathique qui souligne cette humanité. Je l'ai suggéré précédemment en décrivant le rôle de l'empathie de base et de l'empathie de niveau supérieur dans la réaction du soldat à la mort du colonel irakien. Cette alternative est semblable au besoin du chirurgien de se détacher émotionnellement d'un patient pour mener à bien une intervention chirurgicale. Tout comme on ne devrait pas s'attendre à ce que le chirurgien perçoive ou imagine avec empathie l'expérience que fait le patient de son acte chirurgical, du moins pendant qu'il a cours, il ne faut pas s'attendre à ce que le soldat face à l'ennemi s'implique personnellement de manière empathique pendant l'acte mortel. De même, le soldat ne devrait pas se murer dans un détachement stoïque à la suite du meurtre (et d'ailleurs, ne le peut souvent pas, comme le démontre de façon très brutale le cas des soldats victimes de blessures morales). Un parallèle peut également être fait concernant les responsabilités des soldats de rang supérieur :

> …c'est nécessaire au sein du haut commandement sur le terrain qu'un chef militaire accepte de se confronter au coût humain lié à ses plans et à ses ordres – sans quoi il lui serait émotionnellement impossible de remplir sa mission. Cela ne veut cependant pas dire qu'il soit détaché d'une quelconque implication personnelle avant la bataille, ni même de compassion à l'issue de la bataille. Cela ne doit pas le rendre inhumain…[69]

Il est possible que je sois trop pointilleux en essayant de faire la distinction entre la non-humanisation de Brough et une interruption de l'impulsion empathique. Cependant, il semble pertinent de décrire cette étape nécessaire non pas comme une véritable attribution d'un statut non humain à l'ennemi, mais plutôt comme une tentative de gestion de ses propres facultés mentales. Au fil du temps, une disposition naturelle se développera en fonction de l'un ou de l'autre. Il semble alors préférable de la limiter aux différentes réactions possibles envers les autres d'un point de vue affectif plutôt que de prendre l'habitude de réifier autrui. Ménager une disposition

---

69. Nigel Biggar, *In Defense of War* (Oxford: Oxford University Press, 2013), 127.

ayant un impact limité permettra plus facilement à un soldat de respecter les ennemis tombés au front de la manière dont Brough le recommande, puisque leur humanité n'est alors jamais niée. La non-humanisation se prête trop facilement aux dangers d'un état d'esprit bureaucratique ou d'une perspective du *jus in bello* qui serait trop prompte au catalogage, mettant ainsi en péril la bonne intention.

Ainsi, au lieu de déshumaniser les ennemis en les catégorisant comme sous-humains ou non-humains, je suggère une gestion de l'empathie qui soit comparable à celle des sens. Tout comme il est possible que l'ouïe s'aiguise en détectant certains sons plutôt que d'autres, il est également possible d'activer son empathie de manière sélective. Cette harmonisation empathique se produit déjà dans divers contextes, dont des moments teintés d'immoralité durant lesquels on peut être trop partial. Cette partialité est particulière-ment commune dans la guerre, car l'empathie à l'endroit de camarades de combat peut diluer celle dont il faudrait faire preuve envers l'ennemi ou les non-combattants. Le cas des meurtres justifiés en temps de guerre compte néanmoins comme un moment moralement indiqué pour l'empathie.

En marge de cette concession faite au meurtre justifié, l'empathie ne doit pas être supprimée dans la guerre. En effet, elle ne saurait l'être dans une finalité quelconque, étant donné la nature instinctive de l'empathie de base, compte tenu des moments empathiques inévitables se produisant même dans la guerre et au vu de l'introspection nécessaire aux soldats à l'issue du combat. Les soldats sont humains, et donc, préprogrammés pour l'empathie, ce qui fait de la création d'un automate humain un objectif impossible, même si on pouvait le doter d'une formation militaire approfondie. Il s'agit aussi d'un objectif immoral, puisqu'un automate ne peut montrer de disposition à une paix juste et durable ; devant être équipé d'un simple programme d'activités, l'automate ne peut pas avoir la capacité de jugement nécessaire pour exercer correctement la force létale dans tout l'éventail de circonstances auxquelles un soldat pourrait être confronté. Troisièmement, il s'agit d'un objectif déraisonnable d'un point de vue tactique : un automate ne peut pas s'adapter à des circonstances véritablement nouvelles puisqu'il ne peut être équipé que d'un catalogue d'actions possibles, aussi élaboré soit-il.

Des alternatives à la déshumanisation

Compte tenu de la nature inévitable de l'empathie, de l'humanisation d'autrui qu'elle suscite, et du besoin moral vital de conserver à l'ennemi son humanité dans la guerre, il est important d'identifier des alterna-tives à la perspective moderne qui ne laisse aucune place à l'humanité de l'ennemi. Cette vision moderne suggère que la valeur d'un soldat dépend de l'avilissement condescendant ou dédaigneux qu'il impose à l'ennemi, et que cet avilissement est une preuve directe de sa valeur en tant que soldat. Considérons, au contraire, l'attitude des Grecs anciens telle que la dépeint Homère, ou, plus révélatrice encore, l'attitude des premiers chrétiens, qui permet de comprendre un ennemi « honorable en tant que lui-même » même lorsqu'on le combat jusqu'à la mort.[70]

Dans son étude approfondie de *l'Iliade* d'Homère, Jonathan Shay ne trouve aucune tentative de Grecs ou de Troyens visant à déshumaniser le camp adverse au cours de la bataille pour la prise de Troie.[71] Aucune des deux parties n'emploie de termes péjoratifs à l'encontre de l'adversaire, contrairement à la pratique courante dans les guerres modernes. De façon plus générale, les Grecs comme les Troyens n'expriment pas non plus de manque de respect. Au contraire, ils citent à plusieurs reprises leur admiration pour les prouesses de leur adversaire au combat. A l'issue d'un duel prolongé qui s'est soldé par un nul, le guerrier troyen Ajax déclare :

> Nous nous rencontrerons à nouveau une autre fois – et nous nous battrons jusqu'à ce que le pouvoir invisible décide entre les nôtres, accordant victoire à l'une ou l'autre. Ensuite, ils se dira, parmi [les Grecs] et les Troyens: « Ces deux se sont battus et n'ont fait aucun quartier dans le combat, mais ils se sont séparés en amis.[72]

Shay note également que « le contraste avec la lutte contre les « Viêt-Cong » au Vietnam ne pourrait être plus sévère.[73]

La seule entorse faite à cette attitude respectueuse est le traitement épouvantable infligé au cadavre d'Hector après qu'Achille l'a vaincu au combat. Achille mutile le corps avant de l'exposer à la honte publique. Comme le souligne Shay, ce comportement a cependant été sévèrement condamné aussi bien par les Grecs que par les Troyens, car il allait à l'encontre de normes profondément ancrées dans les deux cultures.[74] Qui plus est, Homère dépeint Achille comme un guerrier particulièrement respectueux et généreux envers ses adversaires, avant qu'un profond changement de caractère visiblement entraîné par la trahison de son commandant ne vienne altérer son jugement.

---

70. Phrase de Shay plus haut dans le texte.
71. Shay 1994, 103-120.
72. Ibid., 108-109.
73. Ibid.
74. Ibid., 29.

Certes, les Grecs et les Troyens partageaient une communauté de culture ce qui encourageait ce sentiment de respect mutuel. Il était facile pour les deux parties de se considérer comme égales en statut et en valeur humaine. Shay note que « plus tard, les Grecs avilissaient leurs ennemis étrangers « barbares » autant que les Américains modernes [ont pu le faire pendant la Seconde Guerre mondiale et durant la guerre du Vietnam]. »[75] Néanmoins, l'exemple grec et troyen demeure une exception notable à une déshuman-isation présumée nécessaire pour l'accomplissement des devoirs militaires. Malgré tout, le respect mutuel qui unissaient les Grecs et les Troyens ne diminuait en rien leur ténacité au combat.[76]

Selon Shay, le contraste criant entre l'attitude de la Grèce antique envers ses ennemis et celle de ses homologues modernes s'explique par une tendance à la déshumanisation des adversaires inhérente aux religions bibliques.[77] Selon lui, les traditions juives, chrétiennes et islamiques mettent l'accent sur la déshumanisation des ennemis en tant qu'expression de piété. « Alors qu'ils déshumanisent l'ennemi, les soldats américains actuels et leurs diri-geants affirment leur loyauté envers Dieu, exprimant ainsi une tradition culturelle fortement ancrée par les Écritures bibliques. »[78] Shay fait égale-ment l'examen de l'histoire de David et Goliath, mettant en évidence le discours qui compare Goliath à un animal et le présente « comme une monstruosité morale doublée d'un monstre physique dont il est inconcev-able de souffrir la présence en tant que contrepartie dans le compromis politique...»[79] Shay conclut:

> La vision du monde judéo-chrétienne (et islamique) a triomphé si parfaitement sur la vision du monde homérique que déshon-orer l'ennemi semble maintenant naturel, vertueux, patriotique, pieux. Pourtant, dans *l'Iliade,* seul Achille manque de respect à l'ennemi. Dans le monde d'Homère, il ne s'agit pas d'un état naturel, mais d'un état inhumain dans lequel Achille est tragique-

---

75. Shay 1994, 111, note 6. Shay cite les recherches d'Edith Hall dans *Inventing the Barbar-ian* (New York: Oxford University Press, 1991).

76. Ce respect n'adoucissait pas non plus le traitement réservé par le vainqueur aux combattants et aux non-combattants capturés au combat. Les deux partis comprenaient qu'en tombant au combat, ils seraient massacrés, leurs villes pillées et leurs familles réduites en esclavage. Aussi terribles que ces actions puissent paraître, elles ne procédaient pas d'une perception des vaincus comme étant des sous-hommes. Voir Shay 1994, 103.

77. Shay 1994, 103, 111–120.

78. Ibid., 111.

79. Ibid., 103, 112.

ment tombé. Les guerriers d'Homère n'ont jamais été affaiblis
par le respect qu'ils accordaient à l'ennemi.[80]

Il est impossible de nier la déshumanisation entreprise au nom de Dieu,
ni la ferveur religieuse qui l'alimente encore trop souvent. Pourtant,
l'affirmation de Shay semble à la fois disproportionnée et incomplète. Dans
son analyse des commentaires faits par David à l'adresse de Goliath, mais
aussi à son propos, il n'est pas aussi clair que le prétend Shay que David ait
voulu rabaisser Goliath au statut inférieur d'un animal ou d'un monstre.
David compare le défi que représente son combat contre lui à des défis
antérieurs, tels son combat contre un lion ou un ours, mais cette comparaison n'est pas nécessairement humiliante, car elle peut également être
appréciée comme une reconnaissance élogieuse de la férocité au combat de
Goliath. David tire clairement son courage d'une foi en la faveur de Dieu à
son égard, et cette présomption peut s'apparenter à une vision arrogante et
méprisante d'autrui, mais il n'est à aucun moment évident que David fasse
preuve d'arrogance ou de mépris. Son attitude pourrait s'expliquer par une
foi réelle et un désir d'attribuer à Dieu le mérite de la victoire qu'il anticipe.

Quoi qu'il en soit, le silence de Shay quant au plaidoyer issu des traditions juives, chrétiennes et islamiques en faveur du traitement humain des
ennemis est plus qu'étonnant. Je concentrerai mon attention sur la tradition
chrétienne, à la fois parce que ses premiers membres furent les fondateurs
de la tradition de la guerre juste et parce que la mission des chrétiens concernant leurs ennemis est si rigoureuse : selon la célèbre citation de Jésus,
on doit aimer ses ennemis comme soi-même.[81]

D'aucuns trouveront cette injonction indéfendable, car c'est une contradiction pour un soldat de prétendre aimer l'ennemi qu'il doit tuer. Peut-être
les intentions du soldat sont-elles motivées par une réelle affection pour
une victime en tuant son agresseur, mais il semble absurde de prétendre
qu'il puisse aussi agir avec la même affection envers l'agresseur en question.
Au lieu de cela, la tendance moderne à la déshumanisation de l'agresseur
s'impose comme une réaction plus réaliste. Toutefois, Saint Augustin
d'Hippone défend l'amour de l'agresseur, d'une part parce qu'il identifie
l'amour comme une disposition sensible du cœur du soldat, d'autre part en
suggérant que la contrainte de l'agresseur par la force lui profite autant qu'à
la victime : « l'individu que l'on prive d'une liberté qui aide à soutenir les

---

80. Shay 1994, 115.
81. Matthieu 5:43-45; Luc 6:27-28, 35.

vices est frappé *miséricordieusement…*» [82] Restreindre un agresseur qui accepte de se réformer est une chose, mais Saint Augustin maintient cet avantage même si l'agresseur est tué puisque dans la vision chrétienne du monde, chaque personne doit répondre des torts qu'il a commis sur cette terre, et la mort de cet agresseur l'empêche de causer des torts supplémentaires.

Saint Augustin propose aussi une autre réponse qui ne fait pas appel à une vie après la mort, ni n'exige de force, à moins de tuer. Dans une lettre adressée à un commandant militaire qui exprimait des doutes quant à sa capacité à être à la fois chrétien et soldat, Augustin écrit :

> Restez donc ami de la paix, même en combattant, afin que la victoire vous serve à ramener l'ennemi aux avantages de la paix. « Bienheureux les pacifiques, dit le Seigneur, parce qu'ils seront appelés enfants de Dieu (3). » (Matthieu 5:9)….Que ce soit donc la nécessité et non pas la volonté qui ôte la vie à l'ennemi dans les combats. De même qu'on répond par la violence à la rébel-lion et à la résistance, ainsi on doit la miséricorde aux vaincus et aux captifs, surtout quand les intérêts de la paix ne sauraient en être compromis. [83]

Deux fragments de ce passage sont particulièrement pertinents quant à une possible défense de l'humanité des ennemis dans la guerre. Augustin conseille à ce commandant d'être un ami de la paix, ce qui pourrait signifier soit la coexistence réconciliatrice d'une paix positive, soit l'élimination de la paix négative. Cette dernière est rapidement exclue, cependant, comme Augustin encourage ce soldat à « ramener l'ennemi aux avantages de la paix » et plus tard, à accorder la miséricorde « aux vaincus ». La paix qu'Augustin veut pour ce soldat implique la participation de ses ennemis, et non leur assujettissement ou leur élimination ; en cela, cette paix respecte leur humanité.

Deuxièmement, Augustin insuffle à ce soldat que « ce soit donc la nécessite et non pas la volonté qui ôte la vie à l'ennemi. » Il recommande au soldat de tuer avec regret et non pas de tout cœur, presque d'une manière telle que l'ennemi doive lui forcer la main. Nigel Biggar propose une version contemporaine de cette idée :

> Néanmoins, il peut être permis le choix d'agir de manière à causer la mort d'un être humain, à condition que ce qui est prévu

---

82. Saint Augustin d'Hippone, Lettre 138 (les italiques sont ajoutés par mes soins) ; traduc-tion par http://jesusmarie.free.fr/.
83. Ibid., Lettre 189.

soit autre chose que sa mort (p. ex. la défense des innocents), que la possibilité (ou même la certitude) de sa mort soit acceptée avec une réticence appropriée et manifeste, et que cette acceptation soit nécessaire, non subversive et proportionnée. Moralement parlant, causer délibérément la mort de cette façon n'est pas la même chose que la causer par simple intention de tuer. [84]

À première vue, la suggestion de Biggar selon laquelle un soldat n'a pas l'intention de tuer semble aussi absurde que celle de prétendre aimer ses ennemis alors même qu'on les tue. Toutefois, si, par l'emploi du terme « intention » Biggar fait référence à un but global, alors il plaide simplement pour que les soldats emploient la bonne intention vers une paix juste et durable, au lieu de donner libre cours à leur aspiration prédominante qui se traduit par l'intention de tuer.

Ce résumé des perspectives grecque et chrétienne n'est destiné qu'à montrer l'intérêt de conserver leur humanité à ses ennemis au beau milieu du combat. Ces perspectives méritent un traitement plus complet, et il y a sans doute d'autres exemples démontrant un respect pour l'humanité de l'ennemi [85], mais à ce stade de mon travail, je me contenterai d'établir la plausibilité d'alternatives à la déshumanisation dans le but de rendre possible la compatibilité de l'empathie avec la mission du soldat.

Remettre le meurtre à sa place

Les soldats dotés d'empathie sont plus aptes à concevoir l'acte de tuer comme une tâche nécessaire et regrettable au lieu de le considérer comme leur but primordial. L'empathie aide les soldats à résister à la déshumanisation d'autrui, en particulier des ennemis. En d'autres termes, l'empathie impose l'humanité de l'ennemi comme une évidence factuelle, en révélant des

---

84. Biggar 2013, 10
85. On a soumis à mon attention une autre suggestion prometteuse, bien qu'elle exige une étude plus approfondie, concernant l'attitude du chasseur envers sa proie selon l'éthique de la chasse de certaines communautés amérindiennes. Dans la pratique des Ojibwe, par exemple, « un chasseur fait un discours de gratitude au monde animal/spirituel pour exprimer sa gratitude par avance ou après une récolte. » Egalement : « La manipulation de la carcasse du cerf et l'élimination des portions inutilisées devraient être faites de façon à conserver sa dignité à l'esprit de l'animal. » Voir Nicholas James Reo, Kyle Powys Whyte, « Hunting and Morality as Elements of Traditional Ecological Knowledge », *Human Ecology,* vol. 40:1 (février 2012), 15-27. Bien que j'hésite à mettre en relation les soldats ennemis avec des proies, cette attitude de respect de la part du chasseur semble être liée aux efforts entrepris pour la conservation de son humanité. Il serait utile d'approfondir des recherches afin de vérifier que les Ojibwe encouragent véritablement cette attitude parmi leurs guerriers au combat et pas seulement pendant la chasse. Mes remerciements vont à Monte Hoover pour cette référence.

éléments constitutifs de son expérience humaine, mais aussi de ses valeurs, désirs et intentions. Certes, ces éléments sont utiles à la prise de décisions tactiques dans la lutte contre l'ennemi, mais sont bien plus indispensables encore lorsqu'ils permettent de meilleurs jugements concernant une paix partagée et la bonne intention orientée vers cette paix.

Il faudrait toujours privilégier la paix dans ses objectifs ultimes, ce à quoi on devrait aussi inciter les soldats. En effet, leur bonne conduite au combat a une influence directe sur toute perspective de paix. Bien que les actions de tuer, blesser, causer l'invalidité, menacer et détenir d'autres personnes par la force soient inhérentes au combat, elles doivent être menées en fonction de l'objectif global qu'elles servent. En outre, alors que les pulsions empathiques devraient être atténuées chez les soldats dans le but de mener judicieusement ces actions de combat, il ne peut y avoir qu'une interruption temporaire de leur faculté empathique, et non pas un déni de l'humanité de l'ennemi.

III. L'empathie dans la guerre

La partie précédente de ce travail délimite les contours du soutien que l'empathie apporte à la bonne intention parmi les soldats, et décrit comment ces derniers peuvent conserver une compréhension empathique de l'ennemi qui soit en conjonction avec leur tâche justifiée de tuer. La partie qui suivra a pour but de montrer la pertinence spécifique de l'empathie pour les responsabilités du « mener la guerre », selon l'expression choisie par James Dubik. L'empathie est tout aussi pertinente pour les principes traditionnels de la guerre tels que la discrimination et la proportionnalité, mais, par souci de concision, mon propos sera centré sur la critique novatrice faite par Dubik de la tradition de la guerre juste.

Dubik opère une distinction précise entre *le mener* la guerre et *le faire* la guerre afin de mieux décrire les activités liées au combat.[86] L'expression *faire la guerre* fait référence au large éventail des activités qui se déroulent sur le champ de bataille lui-même, en particulier le maniement de la force létale dirigée contre l'ennemi à travers l'emploi des armes. En revanche, à travers l'expression *mener la guerre*, Dubik fait référence aux activités qui anticipent, dirigent, coordonnent et soutiennent les combats sur le champ de bataille – soit l'intendance complète d'une guerre, sans se limiter aux actions spécifiques sur le lieu de bataille au cœur du champ de bataille.[87]

---

86. James M. Dubik, *Just War Reconsidered – Strategy, Ethics, and Theory* (Lexington: University Press of Kentucky, 2016), 3-4.
87. Ibid., 15.

L'empathie a un rôle important à jouer dans les actions destinées à mener la guerre. Dans les paragraphes qui suivent, je me livrerai à un examen des contributions de l'empathie à la planification stratégique et à l'évaluation des progrès de la guerre. Comme le fait remarquer Dubik :

> Bien que l'autorité décisionnelle ultime repose sur un très petit groupe de personnes – parfois une seule – les décisions d'ampleur sont précédées d'une analyse détaillée de solutions de remplacement, d'études de faisabilité et de monceaux de papiers où sont exposées des logiques argumentées issues de nombreux comités et groupes d'étude, des organisations qui s'y rattachent, ainsi que d'organisations du personnel. La qualité des décisions finales reflète souvent la qualité de ce travail préparatoire. [88]

Je prétends que l'empathie améliore ce travail en amont et les décisions qui en découlent. En tant que membre de nombreux comités, groupes d'étude et groupes de personnel, je me rends à l'évidence que ces rôles, et les bureaux sans fenêtre où ils s'exercent souvent, peuvent étouffer une considération empathique d'autrui (et ce, à certains égards, de manière plus définitive que les aléas du combat). Pourtant, les conséquences qui sont en jeu exigent les perspectives les plus justes afin de comprendre la vision du monde et les motivations des acteurs humains dans la guerre ; elles demandent une réflexion critique et créative pour faire l'examen rigoureux de toutes les présuppositions, et évaluer la progression de la guerre honnêtement et de manière significative. En outre, en faisant bien ce travail, on conserve sa légitimité à la guerre à plus d'un égard. La légitimité, souligne Dubik, est une « fonction de la guerre juste (question liée au *jus ad bellum*) et de sa progression vers un probable succès (question liée au *jus in bello*). [Elle] est directement liée à la compétence des dirigeants politiques et des hauts gradés militaires dans l'exécution des responsabilités qui leur incombent pour mener la guerre. » [89] À mesure que l'empathie améliore le processus de planification et d'évaluation de la guerre, elle contribue également à engager de véritables progrès dans la guerre, contribuant ainsi à sa légitimité.

De la planification stratégique

Dans son analyse des obstacles auxquels les soldats sont confrontés en temps de guerre, Dubik opère une distinction entre les problèmes techniques

---

88. Ibid., 18.
89. Dubik 2016, 155.

et les problèmes d'adaptation. [90] Les soldats peuvent remédier aux problèmes techniques selon l'état de leurs connaissances et d'après leur expérience acquise ; ces problèmes « peuvent être résolus grâce à une expertise confirmée et par le recours aux structures, procédures et modes de fonctionnement de l'armée ».[91] Un problème technique peut être complexe, mais ses solutions sont facilement identifiables. En revanche, les problèmes d'adaptation, en ce qu'ils échappent aux compétences de l'armée, s'avèrent souvent difficiles à comprendre, et encore plus à résoudre. Etant donné que le contexte d'un problème d'adaptation est « en constante évolution, la solution la mieux adaptée change aussi constamment ». [92] Dubik observe que les défis tactiques de la guerre sont, en règle générale, de nature technique, alors que les défis stratégiques sont plutôt adaptatifs. Ainsi, avoir à mener la guerre implique principalement des problèmes d'adaptation.

La première étape, et certainement la plus importante, dans la gestion des problèmes d'adaptation est d'en comprendre les détails. L'un des défis les plus fondamentaux de cette étape est de reconnaître les lacunes de ses propres cadres conceptuels. Lorsqu'un problème d'adaptation implique des acteurs humains, en particulier des ennemis, une compréhension empathique de ces humains permet de surmonter les erreurs liées aux conceptions préexistantes à leur sujet. En d'autres termes, l'empathie permet de surmonter les idées reçues ainsi que les préjugés culturels, idéologiques, raciaux ou sociaux. Par exemple, une approche empathique envers les Japonais durant la seconde guerre mondiale leur aurait conféré un caractère humain rendant plus difficile de sous-estimer leurs capacités. Au lieu de cela, des stéréotypes racistes avaient pris un ascendant réel sur les planificateurs alliés au début de la guerre, donnant cours à une dévalorisation de l'ennemi : les Japonais étaient « trop myopes et sujets au vertige pour pouvoir piloter un avion de combat, et avaient trop peur de se battre dans la jungle qu'ils croyaient habitée par des fantômes et des démons. » [93] Il est évident que sous-estimer l'ennemi entraîne des pertes humaines bien inutiles.

Face à une difficulté d'ordre adaptatif, une tentation primordiale consistant à la catégoriser à tort comme un problème technique s'impose parfois. Dans la culture militaire en particulier, comme elle est très orientée vers l'action, c'est une solution alléchante que de traiter un problème peu familier et gênant par l'emploi d'une solution familière et pratique. À titre d'exemple

---

90. Ibid., 141-143.
91. Ibid., 141-142.
92. Ibid., 142.
93. Shay 1994, 120.

de ce type d'erreur, on considèrera l'échec d'une méthode de planification d'opérations militaires connue sous le nom d'« Opérations basées sur les effets » (*Effect-Based Operations*). [94]

Il s'agit d'une conception particulière de la planification d'opérations militaires prenant ses sources dans l'US Air Force, mais également employée sous une forme ou une autre par d'autres armées. [95] Elle tire son nom de ses objectifs, principalement centrés sur des effets néfastes à atteindre, plutôt que les considérations traditionnelles liées à la quantité de ressources nécessaires contre les forces ennemies (en termes d'unités, de munitions ou de systèmes d'armes). Les planificateurs de la force aérienne ont mis au point l'EBO afin de mobiliser plus efficacement les ressources nécessaires contre des cibles clé des forces ennemies. Par exemple, un pilote peut cibler un seul radar ennemi attaché à la transmission de données cruciales à plusieurs systèmes d'armes de défense aérienne, plutôt que de cibler individuellement chacun de ces systèmes. Alliée à une économie de moyens, cette approche paralyse l'ennemi par des attaques sélectives et simultanées. La première application militaire majeure de l'EBO date de la campagne aérienne de 1990 dont l'objectif réussi s'inscrit dans le premier volet de l'action destiné à chasser du Koweït les forces militaires de Saddam Hussein. Cette méthode de planification a également donné lieu à une campagne aérienne inscrite dans la doctrine « choc et effroi » au début de l'invasion de l'Irak en 2003.

Les modes opératoires de l'EBO ont permis aux planificateurs militaires de rendre compte de tous les facteurs pertinents participant des capacités d'une force ennemie. S'agissant de l'analyse d'un système relativement fermé, comme les armes de défense aérienne, l'EBO s'est avéré utile pour mettre en évidence certaines vulnérabilités de l'ennemi et ainsi orienter un emploi judicieux de la force militaire. Toutefois, les succès tactiques obtenus grâce à la planification par EBO ont encouragé l'extension de ce mode de planification militaire à des missions stratégiques plus importantes. Les planificateurs ont ainsi voulu l'employer pour saisir des facteurs politiques, militaires, économiques et sociaux grâce à une grille d'information ambitieuse mais simpliste ; ils en sont venus à traiter « quelque chose d'aussi complexe que l'activité humaine [comme] un domaine essentiellement passif et sans vie ».[96]

---

94. U.S. Armed Forces, Joint Publication 3-0, *Operations* (Washington, DC : Joint Staff, septembre 2006) ; revue et corrigée en août 2011, puis en janvier 2017.
95. Gary Cheek, "Effects-Based Operations: the End of Dominant Maneuver?" *Transformation Concepts for National Security in the 21st Century,* ed. Williamson Murray (2002), 73-100.
96. Milan Vego, « Systems versus Classical Approach to Warfare », *Joint Force Quarterly* 52 (1st Quarter 2009), 42.

Par exemple, on choisit désormais plus facilement les chefs tribaux en tant que cibles clé à « atteindre » avec les ressources disponibles, qu'on ne cible les radars de défense aérienne. Une mentalité concomitante à l'emploi de l'EBO a su attirer l'attention loin des considérations traditionnelles--liées à une supériorité de puissance de combat ou de maintien d'une force de réserve en cas de surprises--et a su promettre à la place, avec un niveau alléchant de certitude et d'efficacité, l'assujettissement des forces ennemies suivant leur démantèlement. Dès 2008, des critiques de cette forme de planification ont commencé à émerger :

> Des concepts décrits en termes de guerre centrée sur un réseau d'opérations, actic ns rapides et décisives, choc et effroi, ainsi que diverses permutations d'opérations basées sur les effets produits, ont adopté ce qui apparaissait de plus en plus comme un argument fondé sur la croyance que la guerre future serait avant tout menée dans le domaine de la certitude et pourrait donc être gagnée rapidement et efficacement, à faible coût, par des forces militaires limitées en nombre.[97]

Plus tard la même année, un haut commandant militaire chargé de la doctrine de l'Opération basée sur les effets a publié un mémorandum assez désobligeant qui interdisait aux forces américaines d'utiliser l'EBO pour la planification militaire.[98] Le secrétaire à la défense faisait remarquer dans ce document que la méthode de l'EBO « essaie mécaniquement de fournir certitude et prévisibilité dans un environnement incertain », qu'elle est « trop normative et trop perfectionnée » et qu'elle « ignore les dimensions humaines de la guerre (p. ex., passion, imagination, volonté et imprévisibilité). »[99] En revanche, il était d'accord sur le fait que « certains éléments de [l'EBO] se sont révélés utiles afin de s'intéresser aux « systèmes fermés », comme le ciblage des endroits où les effets peuvent être mesurés selon les méthodes d'analyse et de ciblage [de l'US Air Force]. Cependant, ces concepts ont été mal employés dans certaines opérations, car ils ont été détournés de l'intention initiale de la méthode, ce qui a d'ailleurs entraîné dispersion et désordre. »[100]

---

97. H.R. McMaster, « On War: Lessons to be Learned », *Survival* 50:1 (March 2008), 21.
98. Le général James Mattis (secrétaire américain à la Défense), « USJFCOM Commander's Guidance on Effects- Based Operations », Joint Force *Quarterly* 51 (4th Quarter 2008), 105-108.
99. Ibid., 106-107.
100. Ibid.

Le nom de cette méthode de planification, *Opérations basées sur les effets,* implique une plus grande sagesse que ne le laisse paraître cette critique. Certainement, le fait de concentrer l'attention sur les effets souhaités peut rendre le choix des moyens pour y arriver à la fois plus efficace et plus respectable sur le plan éthique (afin de minimiser les dommages collatéraux, par exemple). Toutefois, l'application des principes de l'EBO à de plus larges préoccupations stratégiques repose sur une hypothèse d'une arrogante fierté, car elle croit la force militaire capable de faire advenir certains effets sans avoir besoin ni de s'adapter au comportement imprévisible de l'ennemi ou à d'autres instances, ni de se rallier la coopération des alliés et des groupes-clés de non-combattants. Cette erreur était, d'un point de vue métaphorique, une tentative de *fabriquer* des effets qui ne pouvaient qu'être *naturels*– en effet, les unités militaires n'auraient pu contrôler tous les facteurs (et en particulier, des humains peu coopératifs) mais ont vaniteusement supposé le contraire. Il s'agit d'une erreur épistémologique, en ce que les soldats ont échoué à évaluer les limites de ce dont ils avaient un contrôle réel. L'erreur consistait en une tentative de transformer une méthode de planification tactique, convenant aux systèmes fermés de composants matériels, en un concept de planification stratégique, convenant à des systèmes ouverts et imprévisibles, car incluant une composante humaine. Une plus grande appréciation de l'empathie, et des notions de compréhension et de respect qu'elle implique, aurait pu empêcher la validation de l'hypothèse selon laquelle les effets souhaités pouvaient être fabriqués.

Outre cette erreur épistémologique concernant le traitement d'un problème adaptatif comme un problème technique, cette méthode de planification stratégique basée sur les effets a entraîné une erreur morale de traitement des humains en tant qu'objets adaptables à des généralisations faisant figure de lois. Cette erreur morale est une forme de déshumanisation qui réifie les acteurs humains. Selon cette méthode, les planificateurs militaires font un mauvais usage de connaissances culturelles en les traitant comme des lois de comportement aussi inaltérables que les lois de la physique. Ainsi, les planificateurs envisagent l'ennemi ou les humains au sens large d'une manière mécanique et tentent d'appliquer des hypothèses simplistes à des populations entières. Il s'agit souvent d'une déshumanisation bureaucratique, et pas nécessairement d'une sous-humanisation viscérale comme celle que l'on peut connaître dans le stress au combat, en dépit du fait qu'elle puisse aussi en émaner. Quoi qu'il en soit, elle produit des effets tout aussi troublants autant d'un point de vue moral que d'un point de vue pratique. Ce genre de déshumanisation conduit à traiter la guerre comme étant du domaine des sciences physiques et envisage les acteurs humains comme de simples objets manipulables. Ainsi, la dénomination d'« Opérations basées sur les effets » est trompeuse parce que les effets prévus ont été choisis péremptoirement à partir de ce qu'on pourrait qualifier, pour le moins, d'un moment de déshumanisation bureaucratique. L'empathie est un antidote, à cette prédisposition déshumanisante à la guerre en tant que science physique, ainsi qu'à la connaissance culturelle perçue comme un ensemble de généralisations des comportements de l'autre qu'on élève erronément au statut de lois inaliénables.

Des principes d'évaluation

L'empathie améliore l'évaluation des progrès effectués vers des objectifs militaires donnés en privilégiant l'évaluation des résultats obtenus au lieu de la seule évaluation des stratégies adoptées. Face au désordre des contre-insurrections en Irak et en Afghanistan, le personnel militaire américain a été constamment tenté d'évaluer ces progrès en se fondant exclusivement sur les stratégies adoptées. Bien que celles-ci soient nécessairement plus faciles à maîtriser, elles ne conviennent évidemment pas à une évaluation de l'état d'avancement des opérations. Néanmoins, un chef du département d'État d'une équipe de reconstruction régionale en Irak fait la remarque suivante :

> Nous avons mesuré l'impact de nos projets par les effets qu'ils ont eu sur nous, et non pas par leurs effets sur les Irakiens. *Résultats* était le mot manquant dans le vocabulaire convenant à la reconstruction de l'Irak. Tout n'a été mesuré qu'en partant de ce que nous avions investi - argent, heures de travail, personnel engagé…rédaction de communiqués de presse. [101]

La nature de l'empathie en tant que mode de pensée réceptif à l'expérience d'autrui guide les soldats, partis d'une perspective centrée sur les ressources employées, vers une perspective ancrée dans des résultats concrets--et qui tient compte du point de vue de la population quant aux efforts militaires engagés. Bien que le jugement des populations locales ne doive pas être le seul facteur dans l'évaluation des progrès effectués, il doit être partie prenante, en particulier compte tenu des initiatives de reconstruction coopératives inhérentes aux contre-insurrections (ou entreprises à la suite de conflits conventionnels).

---

101. Peter Van Buren, *We Meant Well: How I Helped Lose the Battle for the Hearts and Minds of the Iraqi People* (New York: Metropolitan Books, 2011), 144.

Une autre raison pour laquelle les ressources engagées peuvent dominer les évaluations est la facilité qu'il y a à les quantifier. Etant donné la pression toujours omniprésente liée à la gestion du temps, les planificateurs militaires peuvent aisément succomber à cette facilité de la quantification objective. Toutefois, l'empathie maîtrise cette tendance en mettant l'accent sur une évaluation plus globale des opérations militaires, notamment des opinions des alliés, des parties neutres et des non-combattants. En revanche, si elle n'en demeure pas moins importante, la compréhension empathique ne peut pas être la seule considération à prendre en compte dans l'évaluation des progrès militaires effectués.

Parmi les planificateurs et les dirigeants, ceux qui sont en proie à une mentalité bureaucratique et trop axée sur une perception quantitative des ressources ne parviennent pas à évaluer l'effort de guerre avec précision. Il faut garder en mémoire l'exemple de la guerre du Vietnam, durant laquelle cet état d'esprit était couplé à une intention meurtrière visant à produire des mesures quantitatives, telles que le nombre de pertes humaines ennemies, afin de fournir une mesure des progrès du conflit. Un historien militaire a fait remarquer que, lorsqu'on est pris dans cet état d'esprit, « si l'on ne peut pas tenir une comptabilité de ce qui est important, ce qu'on peut comptabiliser devient alors important. »[102] Caractérisée par l'humanisation de l'ennemi et d'autrui ainsi que par un élan vers la bonne intention, l'empathie s'attache à compenser cette erreur en remettant au centre des débats une paix juste et durable entre les belligérants.

Comme on l'a montré dans des exemples de conflits mentionnés précédemment, une empathie sélective peut fausser l'évaluation des progrès effectués au lieu d'y contribuer. Si les dirigeants se préoccupent uniquement de la compréhension empathique des soldats, au détriment des autres, le seul critère d'évaluation des progrès effectués pourrait tout aussi bien être le retour au bercail de chaque soldat, indépendamment des progrès accomplis dans la mission. Cette empathie sélective peut alors devenir trop réticente à la prise de risques nécessaire aux opérations militaires.

IV. Conclusion

Lorsque le but d'être un soldat, avec tout ce que cela comporte, est orienté vers l'édification d'une paix juste et durable, le rôle de l'empathie devient alors aussi clair que crucial. L'empathie incite les soldats à maintenir cette

---

102. James Willbanks (documentaire Burns, épisode 4).

paix au cœur de leur intention, plutôt que de chercher une paix négative impliquant l'assujettissement ou l'éradication de l'adversaire. L'empathie permet aux soldats de mettre à l'écart la « tradition universelle guerrière » consistant à déshumaniser les combattants ennemis et les civils.[103] Ainsi, ils sont capables de faire preuve d'une retenue appropriée dans leur jugement de même que pour ce qui concerne les actions énergiques véritablement nécessaires à la guerre De cette manière, les soldats maintiennent fidèlement les principes traditionnels de la guerre comme la discrimination et la proportionnalité. Cette même compréhension empathique d'autrui, et la bonne intention qui y est intimement liée, améliorent également la manière dont les soldats s'acquittent de leurs responsabilités, telles qu'elles s'appliquent dans la planification de campagnes militaires respectueuses de certaines limites morales et pratiques, et concernant l'évaluation honnête et globale des progrès effectués.

Références

Saint Thomas d'Aquin. *Summa theologiae.* Translated by Fathers of the English Dominican Province. Second and Revised Edition, 1920. Online Edition Copyright © 2008 by Kevin Knight. <http://www.newadvent.org/summa/>.

Saint Augustin d'Hippone. *The City of God.* Trans. R. Ryson. Cambridge: Cambridge University Press, 1998.

——. *Contra Faustum* XXII, Translated by Richard Stothert. From *Nicene and Post-Nicene Fathers*, First Series, Vol. 4. Edited by Philip Schaff. Buffalo, NY: Christian Literature Publishing Co., 1887. Revised and edited for New Advent by Kevin Knight. <http://www.newadvent.org/fathers/140622.htm>.

——. Letter 138. Translated by J.G. Cunningham. From *Nicene and Post-Nicene Fathers*, First Series, Vol. 1. Edited by Philip Schaff. Buffalo, NY: Christian Literature Publishing Co., 1887. Revised and edited for New Advent by Kevin Knight. <http://www.newadvent.org/fathers/1102138.htm>.

——. Letter 189. Translated by J.G. Cunningham. From *Nicene and Post-Nicene Fathers*, First Series, Vol. 1. Edited by Philip Schaff. Buffalo, NY: Christian Literature Publishing Co., 1887. Revised and edited for New Advent by Kevin Knight. <http://www.newadvent.org/fathers/1102189.htm>.

Batson, C. D. (2009). "These Things Called Empathy." *The Social Neuroscience of Empathy.* Ed. Jean Decety and William Ickes. Cambridge, MA: MIT Press.

——, (1991). *The Altruism Question: Toward a Social-psychological Answer.* Hillsdale, NJ: Erlbaum.

Bell, Daniel (2009). *Just War as Christian Discipleship: Recentering the Tradition in the Church rather than the State.* Grand Rapids, MI: Brazos Press.

Biggar, Nigel (2013). *In Defence of War.* Oxford: Oxford University Press.

---

103. Brough 2007, 151.

Bloom, Paul (2016). *Against Empathy*. New York: HarperCollins.

Bolgiano, David, and John Taylor (2017). "Can't Kill Enough to Win? Think Again." *Proceedings Magazine*, Vol. 143/12/1,378. U.S. Naval Institute, December 2017. <https:// www.usni.org/magazines/proceedings/2017-12/cant-kill-enough-win-think- again>.

Brough, Michael (2007). "Dehumanization of the Enemy and the Moral Equality of Soldiers," in *Rethinking the Just War Tradition*. Eds. Michael Brough, John Lango, Harry van der Linden. Albany, NY: State University of New York Press, 149-167.

Burkhardt, Todd (2017). *Just War and Human Rights: Fighting with Right Intention*. Albany, NY: SUNY Press.

Burns, Ken and Lynne Novick (2017). "The Vietnam War." Documentary. Florentine Films and WETA.

CNN Politics. "Troops alone will not yield victory in Afghanistan." CNN.com (10 September 2008). <http://www.cnn.com/2008/POLITICS/09/10/mullen. afghanistan>.

Capizzi, Joseph (2015). *Politics, Justice, and War: Christian Governance and the Ethics of Warfare*. Oxford: Oxford University Press.

Cavanaugh, Matt (2015). "The Military's Purpose is not to Kill People and Break Things." *War on the Rocks*. 26 August 2015. <https://warontherocks.com/2015/08/the-militarys- purpose-is-not-to-kill-people-and-break-things/>.

Cheek, Gary (2002). "Effects-Based Operations: the End of Dominant Maneuver?" *Transformation Concepts for National Security in the 21st Century*. Ed. Williamson Murray. Strategic Studies Institute, U.S. Army War College, 73-100. <https://ssi. armywarcollege.edu/pubs/display.cfm?pubID=252>.

Coates, A.J. (2016). *The Ethics of War*. 2nd ed. Manchester, UK: Manchester University Press.

Coplan, Amy (2011). "Understanding Empathy: Its Features and Effects." *Empathy: Philosophical and Psychological Perspectives*. Eds. Amy Coplan and Peter Goldie. New York: Oxford University Press.

Coplan, Amy and Peter Goldie (2011). "Introduction." *Empathy: Philosophical and Psychological Perspectives*. Eds. Amy Coplan and Peter Goldie. New York: Oxford University Press, ix-xlvii.

Darwall, Stephen (1998). "Empathy, Sympathy, and Care." *Philosophical Studies* 89: 261-282.

Dubik, James (2016). *Just War Reconsidered — Strategy, Ethics, and Theory*. Lexington: University Press of Kentucky.

Frowe, Helen (2011). *The Ethics of War and Peace*. London: Routledge.

Gallagher, Shaun (2012). "Empathy, Simulation, and Narrative." *Science in Context*, vol. 25, no. 3, 355-381.

Gourley, Jim (2015). "The military's purpose isn't to break things and kill people, but it should be." *Foreign Policy*. 24 September 2015. <http://foreignpolicy. com/2015/09/24/the- militarys-purpose-isnt-to-break-things-and-kill-people-but-it-should-be/>

Hoffman, Bruce (2006). *Inside Terrorism*. Revised and expanded edition. New York: Columbia University Press.

Klay, Phil (2017). "What We're Fighting For." *New York Times*. 10 February 2017.

Linn, Brian (2009). *The Echo of Battle: The Army's Way of War*. Cambridge, MA: Harvard University Press.

MacIntyre, Alasdair (2016). *Ethics in the Conflicts of Modernity: An Essay on Desire, Practical Reasoning, and Narrative*. New York: Cambridge University Press.

——, (2007). *After Virtue: A Study in Moral Theory*. 3rd ed. Notre Dame: University of Notre Dame Press.

Matravers, Derek (2017). *Empathy*. Malden, MA: Polity Press.

Mattis, James (2008). "USJFCOM Commander's Guidance on Effects-Based Operations," *Joint Force Quarterly*. Vol. 51 (4th Quarter 2008), 105-108.

McMahan, Jeff (2005). "Just Cause for War." *Ethics and International Affairs* 9:3 (December 2005), 1-21.

McMaster, H.R. (2008). "On War: Lessons to be Learned." *Survival* 50:1 (March 2008), 19-30.

Morris, Errol (2003). "The Fog of War: Eleven Lessons from the Life of Robert S. McNamara." Documentary. Sony Pictures Classics.

Orend, Brian (2006). *The Morality of War*. Toronto: Broadview Press.

Orend, Brian (2001). "A Just War Critique of Realism and Pacifism." *Journal of Philosophical Research*, Vol. XXVI, 435-477.

Pickstock, Catherine (1998). *After Writing*. Malden, MA: Blackwell Publishers.

Prinz, Jesse (2011). "Is Empathy Necessary for Morality?" *Empathy: Philosophical and Psychological Perspectives*. Ed. Amy Coplan and Peter Goldie. New York: Oxford University Press, 211-229.

Reo, Nicholas James, and Kyle Powys Whyte (2012). "Hunting and Morality as Elements of Traditional Ecological Knowledge." *Human Ecology*. Vol. 40:1 (February 2012), 15-27.

Rodin, David (2004). "Terrorism without Intention," *Ethics* 114 (July 2004), 752-771.

Ross, Janell (2015). "Mike Huckabee says the military's job is to 'kill people and break things.' Well, not quite." *The Washington Post* (7 August 2015).

Schofield, John M (1881). "Notes on 'The Legitimate in War.'" *Journal of the Military Service Institution*. Vol. 2, 1-10.

Shay, Jonathan (1994). *Achilles in Vietnam: Combat Trauma and the Undoing of Character*. New York: Scribner.

Smith, Joel (2015). "What is Empathy For?" *Synthese*, vol.194, 709-722.

Stueber, Karsten (2006). *Rediscovering Empathy: Agency, Folk Psychology, and the Human Sciences*. Cambridge, MA: MIT Press.

Tacitus, Publius Cornelius. *The Works of Tacitus: The Oxford Translation, Revised with Notes*, Vol. 2. London: Bell and Daldy, 1872.

United Nations. "Declaration on Measures to Eliminate International Terrorism." Annex to UN General Assembly Resolution 49/60, "Measures to Eliminate International Terrorism." (9 December 1994). <https://www.un.org/documents/ga/res/49/a49r060.htm>.

U.S. Armed Forces. Joint Publication 3-0, *Operations* (Washington, DC: Joint Staff, September 2006); superseded in August 2011, then again in January 2017.

Van Buren, Peter (2011). *We Meant Well: How I Helped Lose the Battle for the Hearts and Minds of the Iraqi People.* New York: Metropolitan Books.

Vego, Milan (2009). "Systems versus Classical Approach to Warfare." *Joint Force Quarterly.* Vol. 52 (1st Quarter 2009), 40-48.

Walzer, Michael (1977). *Just and Unjust Wars: A Moral Argument with Historical Illustrations.* Philadelphia: Basic Books.

Weinstein, Adam (2017). "No, We Can't Kill Our Way To Victory Despite What 2 Misguided Lieutenant Colonels Might Think." *Task and Purpose* (8 December 2017). <https://taskandpurpose.com/no-cant-kill-way-victory-despite-2-misguided-lieutenant- colonels-might-think/>.

Wood, David (2016). *What Have We Done: The Moral Injury of Our Longest Wars.* New York: Little, Brown and Company, Kindle edition.

Zahavi, Dan (2014). *Self and Other: Exploring Subjectivity, Empathy, and Shame.* New York: Oxford University Press.

Just War Traditions and Revisions
Thesis Summary

Joseph O. Chapa

I have a moral right not to be killed. You have a moral duty not to kill me.[1] But my right is not "unalienable," *pace* Jefferson. There are actions I can commit that would cause me to lose my right and therefore absolve you of your duty. This language of rights has had a profound influence on just war theory. Medieval and early modern just war theorists were concerned about whether an agent acted rightly or wrongly; in good faith or bad; righteously or sinfully; but they lacked the language of rights violations and infringements. Walzer's seminal 1977 work, *Just and Unjust Wars*, is often credited with reinvigorating just war thought within the academy. One of Walzer's contributions in that work was, as Brian Orend puts it, "the cementing of human rights theory within the core propositions of just war theory."[2] On Walzer's view, whether one acts rightly or wrongly in war can decisively depend upon whether one violates a person's rights. Thus, the reason that one may kill combatants but may not kill noncombatants is cast, in Walzer's account, in the language of rights. Combatants are liable to be killed as a class because "as a class [they] are set apart from the world of peaceful activity."[3] Though Walzer's account is thorough and influential, in many respects, his treatment of liability and immunity to harm, though invoking the language of rights, is left open to questions about the substance of those rights. Walzer's account is open, for example, to the charge that arose in earnest in the 1990s. If combatants—even combatants who fight for a just cause—are liable to be killed, then correlatively, they have no right not to be killed; but what, many contemporary theorists have asked, has the combatant on the just side

---

1. The views expressed throughout this thesis are my own and do not necessarily reflect those of the US Air Force, the Department of Defense, or the US government.
2. (Walzer 1977; For commentary on Walzer's importance, see e.g. McMahan 2012; Orend 2013: 24–25; Sussman 2014: 14; Lazar 2017; Jenkins, Robillard, and Strawser 2018: 1–3) Throughout the thesis, I refer to the 5th edition of *Just and Unjust Wars*. The one exception is where I explicitly refer to Walzer's preface to the 4th edition in "Just War Traditions and Revisions."
3. (Walzer 2015: 144–45)

done to forfeit his right not to be killed? The just war literature that has developed in response to Walzer has been largely dominated by a focus on this question. As Ryan Jenkins, Michael Robillard, and B. J. Strawser have aptly described it, "a schism is under way in the military ethics community, and the concept of liability is the wedge."[4]

The disagreement between those who broadly accept Walzer's account and those who broadly reject it is often referred to as a disagreement between "traditionalists" and "revisionists." I shall refrain from using these terms. This is first because they are misleading even at a superficial level and second because even once one is armed with a more nuanced understanding, these terms are contentious. Throughout the thesis, I will refer to what is sometimes called "revisionist" just war theory as the "reductivist-individualist" account, or sometimes just as the "reductivist" view for short. Likewise, I will refer to what is sometimes called the "traditionalist" view as the "exceptionalist-collectivist" account, or sometimes just "exceptionalist" for short.

In this chapter, I argue against the exceptionalist-collectivist account and for the reductivist-individualist account. In the first half of the chapter, I appeal largely to two hypothetical cases set in a real world context to show that the exceptionalist account appears to offer conflicting conclusions. In the first case, a US infantry patrol in the Vietnam War is tasked with attacking enemy combatants. Once all the targets are killed, the patrol investigates and learns that those killed were, in fact, noncombatants. On my understanding, the exceptionalist account will conclude that the attack was objectively wrongful—the noncombatants' rights not to be killed were violated. This conclusion holds even though the patrol members had an evidence-relative justification for killing them. I argue that this same structure ought to apply to the *jus ad bellum* case of an unjust war. A policymaker commits forces to attack an enemy for a cause that is objectively unjust. If so, the combatants cause objectively unjust harm to their targets—they lack a fact-relative justification. And, if the US patrol case is to be our guide, the victims of that objectively unjust attack are permitted defensively to harm their attackers and their attackers are liable to defensive harm. And yet, the exceptionalist must reject this analogy and insist that when a policymaker commits forces to an unjust cause, even if the war is unjustified, the combatants who are killed are liable to be killed by virtue of their being military members at war.

---

4. (Jenkins, Robillard, and Strawser 2018: 1)

In the second half of the paper, I defend the individualist position. One important critique of the reductivist-individualist account is that the set of people who are liable to be defensively harmed is not coextensive with the set of combatants. Therefore, a significant number of combatants on the unjust side are not liable to be harmed while a significant set of civilians on the unjust side are liable to be harmed. I defend the individualist position against this critique with a novel account of signaling as threatening in war. Even on the individualist account, I argue, when a soldier dons a uniform and fills a post, she signals to the enemy that she is participating in hostilities. And by participating in hostilities, she contributes to the threat her side poses to the other side—even if she never fires a shot. I appeal to military deception as an archetype of signaling as threatening and argue that mere participation in the warfighting arm of the military organization contributes to the threat. Therefore, combatants on the unjust side become liable to defensive harm even if they are not directly involved in employing weapons. Ultimately, I argue that on a reductivist-individualist account, the set of liable persons and the set of military persons on the unjust side overlap to a greater degree than might first appear. This paper can be seen primarily as a defense of the reductivist-individualist account of just war theory.

References

Jenkins, Ryan, Michael Robillard, and Bradley Jay Strawser. 2018. Editors' Introduction. In *Who Should Die? The Ethics of Killing in War*, ed. R. Jenkins, M. Robillard and B. J. Strawser, 1–12. Oxford: Oxford University Press.

Lazar, Seth. 2017. "War." The Stanford Encyclopedia of Philosophy.

McMahan, Jeff. 2012. "Rethinking the 'Just War' Part I." *The New York Times*, 11 November.

Orend, Brian. 2013. *The Morality of War*. 2nd ed. Peterborough, Ont.: Broadview Press.

Sussman, Naomi. 2014. "Introduction: The Substantive Unity of Michael Walzer's Pluralism." In *Reading Walzer*, ed. Y. Benbaji and N. Sussman, 1–18. New York: Routledge.

Walzer, Michael. 1977. Just and Unjust Wars : A Moral Argument with Historical Illustrations. 1st ed. New York: Basic Books.

———. 2015. Just and Unjust Wars : A Moral Argument with Historical Illustrations. 5th ed. New York: Basic Books.

Tradiciones y revisiones de la guerra justa
Resumen de tesis

Joseph O. Chapa
Traducción al español de Haydeé Espino

Tengo el derecho moral a que no me maten. Tú tienes el deber moral de no matarme.[1] Sin embargo, pese al planteamiento de Jefferson, mi derecho no es "inalienable". Algunos de mis actos podrían conducir a la pérdida de este derecho y por consiguiente eximirte de tu deber. Este lenguaje de derechos ha tenido una enorme influencia en la teoría de la guerra justa. A los teoristas medievales y de principios de la era moderna les inquietaba el hecho de que un agente actuara de manera correcta o incorrecta; de buena o de mala fe; justa o pecaminosamente; sin embargo, carecían del lenguaje relacionado con las faltas y la violación de derechos. Es a la obra fundacional de Walzer, *Guerras justas e injustas*, de 1977, a la que a menudo se atribuye el mérito de revitalizar el pensamiento de la guerra justa dentro de la academia. Una de las contribuciones de Walzer en dicha obra era, en palabras de Brian Orend: "La consolidación de la teoría de los derechos humanos dentro de las propuestas medulares de la teoría de la guerra justa.".[2] Según Walzer, la actuación correcta o incorrecta de un individuo en la guerra puede depender decisivamente de si se violan los derechos de otra persona. Por ello, la razón por la que se puede matar a los combatientes, pero no a los no combatientes toma forma, según Walzer, en el lenguaje de los derechos. Los combatientes son responsables de ser asesinados como una colectividad porque "como una colectividad se encuentran apartados del mundo de la actividad pacífica".[3] Aunque el razonamiento de Walzer es, de muchas maneras, elaborado e influyente, su tratamiento de la responsabilidad

---

1. Las opiniones expresadas a lo largo de la presente tesis son solo mías y no reflejan necesariamente las de la Fuerza Aérea de los Estados Unidos., las del Departamento de Defensa, o las del Gobierno de los Estados Unidos.
2. (Walzer 1977; Para un comentario sobre la importancia de Walzer's, véase e.g. McMahan 2012; Orend 2013: 24-25; Sussman 2014: 14; Lazar 2017; Jenkins, Robillard, y Strawser 2018: 1-3) A lo largo de la presente tesis, hago referencia a la quinta edición de *Just and Unjust Wars*. La única excepción es donde explícitamente me refiero al prefacio de Walzer de la cuarta edición de "Just War Traditions and Revisions."
3. (Walzer 2015: 144-45)

y la inmunidad, si bien invoca el lenguaje de los derechos, queda abierto a cuestionamientos sobre la esencia de aquellos. El razonamiento de Walzer queda abierto, por ejemplo, a la acusación que adquirió gran trascendencia durante la década de los noventas. Si los combatientes —incluso aquellos que luchan por una causa justa— son responsables de ser asesinados, entonces, correlativamente, no tienen el derecho a no ser asesinados. Sin embargo, lo que varios teóricos contemporáneos se han planteado es: ¿Ha renunciado el combatiente del lado justo a su derecho a no ser asesinado? La literatura de la guerra justa desarrollada en respuesta al razonamiento de Walzer se ha visto ampliamente dominada por esta interrogante como foco central. Tal y como Ryan Jenkins, Michael Robillard y B. J. Strawser lo describen acertadamente: "Un cisma se cierne sobre la comunidad ética militar y el concepto de responsabilidad es su cuña."[4]

Al desacuerdo entre quienes aceptan ampliamente el razonamiento de Walzer y aquellos que abiertamente lo rechazan se le conoce como el desacuerdo entre "los tradicionalistas" y "los revisionistas". Yo me abstendré de utilizar dichos términos. Esto se debe, en primer lugar, a que resultan engañosos incluso en un nivel superficial y, en segundo, a que incluso una vez que uno se reviste de un entendimiento más profundo, dichos términos resultan controvertidos. A lo largo de la tesis, me referiré a lo que a veces se le denomina teoría "revisionista" de la guerra justa como la corriente "reduccionista-individualista", y otras, para abreviar, simplemente como el "reduccionismo". Me referiré asimismo a lo que a veces se le denomina la visión "tradicionalista" como la corriente "excepcionalista-colectivista" o simplemente como "excepcionalista", para abreviar.

En este capítulo, argumento en contra de la corriente excepcionalista-colectivista y a favor de la reduccionista-individualista. En la primera mitad del capítulo hago alusión en gran medida a dos casos hipotéticos situados en el contexto del mundo real con el fin de demostrar que la corriente excepcionalista parece aportar conclusiones contradictorias. En el primer caso, a una patrulla de infantería estadounidense de la guerra de Vietnam se le asigna atacar a los combatientes enemigos. Luego de matar a todos sus objetivos, la patrulla investiga y descubre que a quienes se dio muerte eran, de hecho, no combatientes. A mi ver, la corriente excepcionalista concluirá que el ataque fue objetivamente ilícito —el derecho de los no combatientes a no ser asesinados no fue violado. Esta conclusión es válida aun cuando

---

4. (Jenkins, Robillard y Strawser 2018: 1)

los miembros de la patrulla tenían una justificación evidente-relativa para matarlos. Sostengo que esta misma estructura debe aplicarse en caso de *jus ad bellum* de una guerra injusta. Un hacedor de políticas compromete a las fuerzas armadas para que ataquen al enemigo por una causa objetivamente injusta. En ese caso, los combatientes infligen un daño objetivamente injusto a sus objetivos —carecen de una justificación epistémico-relativa —. Y si el caso de la patrulla estadounidense fungiera como nuestra guía, las víctimas de dicho ataque objetivamente injusto pueden a manera de defensa infligir daño a sus atacantes, y sus atacantes serán responsables del daño por defensa. Aun así, el excepcionalista debe rechazar esta analogía e insistir en que cuando algún hacedor de políticas compromete a las fuerzas a una causa injusta, incluso si la guerra fuera injustificada, los combatientes caídos son responsables de ser asesinados por tratarse de elementos militares en guerra.

En la segunda mitad del presente trabajo defiendo la postura individualista. Una crítica importante de la corriente reduccionista-individualista es que el grupo de personas que son responsables de su daño a manera de defensa no se coextiende con el grupo de los combatientes. Por lo tanto, un número importante de combatientes del lado injusto no será responsable de su propio daño, mientras que un grupo significativo de civiles del lado injusto lo será. Defiendo la postura individualista contra dicha crítica con un novedoso razonamiento sobre las señales como amenazas en la guerra. Incluso desde la corriente individualista, sostengo que cuando un soldado porta el uniforme y ocupa su puesto, le envía al enemigo señales de que participa en actividades hostiles. Y al participar en dichas actividades hostiles coadyuva a la amenaza que su lado representa sobre el otro —aunque no dispare ni una sola bala—. Apelo al engaño militar como un arquetipo de señas amenazantes y argumento que la mera participación en el brazo armado de la guerra de una organización militar coadyuva a la amenaza. Por lo tanto, los combatientes del lado injusto se vuelven responsables del daño por defensa aun cuando no se involucren directamente en el manejo de armas. Finalmente, sostengo que desde una corriente reduccionista-individualista el grupo de personas responsable y aquel que pertenece a las fuerzas militares en el lado injusto se superponen en mayor grado de lo que aparentan a primera vista. El presente trabajo puede considerarse primordialmente como una defensa de la corriente reduccionista-individualista de la teoría de la guerra justa.

Referencias

Jenkins, Ryan, Michael Robillard, and Bradley Jay Strawser. 2018. Editors' Introduction. In *Who Should Die? The Ethics of Killing in War*, ed. R. Jenkins, M. Robillard and B. J. Strawser, 1–12. Oxford: Oxford University Press.

Lazar, Seth. 2017. "War." The Stanford Encyclopedia of Philosophy.

McMahan, Jeff. 2012. "Rethinking the 'Just War' Part I." *The New York Times*, 11 November.

Orend, Brian. 2013. *The Morality of War*. 2nd ed. Peterborough, Ont.: Broadview Press.

Sussman, Naomi. 2014. "Introduction: The Substantive Unity of Michael Walzer's Pluralism." In *Reading Walzer*, ed. Y. Benbaji and N. Sussman, 1–18. New York: Routledge.

Walzer, Michael. 1977. Just and Unjust Wars : A Moral Argument with Historical Illustrations. 1st ed. New York: Basic Books.

———. 2015. Just and Unjust Wars : A Moral Argument with Historical Illustrations. 5th ed. New York: Basic Books.

Des traditions de la guerre juste et de ses réformes
Résumé de l'article

Joseph O. Chapa

Chaque être humain a le droit moral de ne pas être tué. Tout comme chacun a le devoir moral de ne pas tuer.[1] Toutefois ce droit n'est pas « inaliénable », contrairement à l'opinion de Jefferson. On peut commettre certaines actions qui entraînent la perte de ce droit et donc absoudre quiconque de son devoir moral de ne pas tuer. Cette rhétorique des droits accordés aux uns et aux autres a eu une profonde influence sur la théorie de la guerre juste. Dès l'époque médiévale les théoriciens de la guerre juste cherchaient déjà à déterminer si un agent agissait à tort ou à raison, de bonne ou de mauvaise foi, d'une manière juste ou moralement injuste, mais ne disposaient pas à cet effet d'une rhétorique de l'infraction et de la violation des droits. Écrit en 1977, le travail précurseur de Walzer intitulé *Just and Unjust Wars* (Guerres justes et injustes, Trad. de l'anglais (États-Unis) par Simone Chambon et Anne Wicke, Gallimard 2006) est généralement reconnu pour avoir donné un nouvel élan de pensée à la tradition de la guerre juste au sein de l'académie. Comme le confirme Brian Orend, Walzer a notoirement contribué au « cimentage de la théorie des droits de l'homme au cœur des propositions fondamentales de la théorie de la guerre juste ».[2] Selon l'optique de Walzer, le fait d'agir à tort ou à raison dans la guerre peut dépendre décisivement de violations des droits de la personne. Ainsi, pour la première fois, Walzer énonce en termes de droit la raison pour laquelle on peut tuer des combattants, mais pas des non-combattants. Les combattants sont susceptibles d'être tués parce que « la catégorie à laquelle ils appartiennent reste à l'écart du monde de

---

1. Les points de vue exprimés dans cette thèse n'engagent que moi et ne reflètent pas nécessairement ceux de l'US Air Force, du Département de la Défense ou du gouvernement américain.

2. (Walzer 1977. Pour un commentaire sur l'importance de Walzer importance, voir par exemple McMahan 2012, Orend 2013: 24-25, Sussman 2014: 14, Lazar 2017, Jenkins, Robillard, et Strawser 2018: 1-3) En majeure partie, ce travail fait référence à la 5e édition de *Just and Unjust Wars,* à l'exception d'une seule occurrence où l'on réfère à la préface de la 4e édition de cet ouvrage dans "Just War Traditions and Revisions."

l'activité non guerrière. »[3] Bien que l'analyse de Walzer soit aussi approfondie qu'influente, à bien des égards, son traitement de la responsabilité légale et de l'immunité contre un préjudice possible invoque la rhétorique du droit tout en laissant une appréciation totalement ouverte de la nature des droits invoqués. De fait, l'appréciation de Walzer est soumise à une accusation sérieuse portée dans les années 1990. À savoir que si les combattants, même ceux qui se battent pour une cause juste, sont susceptibles d'être tués, on peut alors considérer que, corrélativement, ils sont destitués du droit de ne pas l'être. À cela, de nombreux théoriciens contemporains répondent par la question suivante : que le combattant rangé du côté de la cause juste a-t-il fait pour devoir renoncer à son droit de ne pas être tué ? Autant dire que le pan de littérature de la guerre juste qui a fait son émergence en réponse à Walzer fut largement dominé par cette question. Comme l'ont bien décrit Ryan Jenkins, Michael Robillard et B. J. Strawser : « un schisme est en cours dans le milieu de l'éthique militaire, et le concept de responsabilité morale en est la pierre angulaire ».[4]

Ce désaccord entre ceux qui adhèrent au discours de Walzer et ses détracteurs est souvent qualifié de conflit entre « traditionalistes » et « révisionnistes ». Toutefois, je m'abstiendrai d'employer ces termes, premièrement, parce qu'ils sont trompeurs, même superficiellement, et deuxièmement, parce qu'ils sont litigieux, même dans une compréhension plus nuancée de leur sens. Tout au long de cette thèse, je fais appel à une perspective que l'on taxe parfois de théorie « révisionniste » de la guerre juste en tant que discours « réductiviste-individualiste » (on dit aussi perception « réductiviste » pour faire court). De même, je me référerai au point de vue dit « traditionnaliste » en tant que discours « exceptionnaliste-collectiviste » (qu'on appelle aussi en un mot « exceptionnel »).

Dans ce chapitre, je m'oppose au discours exceptionnaliste-collectiviste et défends le discours réductiviste-individualiste. En premier lieu, j'en appelle en grande partie à deux cas hypothétiques rapportés à un contexte réel afin de montrer que le discours exceptionnel entraîne des conclusions contradictoires. Considérons le premier cas de figure : pendant la guerre du Vietnam, une patrouille d'infanterie américaine est chargée d'attaquer des combattants ennemis. Une fois que toutes les cibles ont été anéanties, une enquête de la patrouille révèle que les morts étaient, en fait, des non-combattants. D'après

---

3. (Walzer 2015: 144-45)
4. (Jenkins, Robillard, and Strawser 2018: 1)

ce que je crois comprendre, le discours exceptionnel en conclura que l'attaque dirigée contre ces non-combattants était objectivement injustifiée, en raison d'une violation de leur droit de ne pas être tués. Cette conclusion est également valable si les membres de la patrouille détenaient des éléments de preuve à l'appui d'une justification au meurtre ces non-combattants. Je soutiens que ce même mode de pensée devrait s'appliquer au cas du *jus ad bellum,* le droit à la guerre, dans une guerre injuste. Un responsable politique engage des ressources militaires pour attaquer un ennemi en vertu d'une cause objectivement injuste. Si c'est en effet le cas, les combattants causent un préjudice délibérément injuste à leurs cibles, en ce qu'ils n'ont pas de justification qui soit fondée sur des faits pour faire la guerre. De même, si l'on doit prendre ce cas en exemple, les victimes de cette attaque sont alors autorisées à nuire à leurs attaquants de manière défensive de même que leurs attaquants sont alors susceptibles de subir des dommages défensifs. Cependant, la perspective exceptionnaliste doit rejeter cette analogie en insistant sur le fait que lorsqu'un responsable politique engage des ressources en hommes et en matériel pour une cause injuste, et donc, même si la guerre est injustifiée, les combattants qui sont tués sont susceptibles de l'être en raison de leur seule présence dans la guerre en tant que tels.

Dans la seconde partie de cette thèse, je défends le point de vue individualiste. Une critique majeure de la perception réductiviste-individualiste consiste à dire que l'ensemble des personnes susceptibles d'être blessées défensivement ne coïncide pas avec l'ensemble des combattants. Par conséquent, un nombre important de combattants se trouvant du côté injuste de la guerre n'est pas susceptible d'être touché alors qu'un nombre important de civils courent ce risque. Je défends la perspective individualiste contre cette critique par le truchement d'un discours novateur portant sur l'identification en tant que menace dans la guerre. Je soutiens que, même selon la perspective individualiste, quand un soldat enfile un uniforme et occupe un poste donné, il envoie un signal d'identification à l'ennemi confirmant sa participation aux hostilités. C'est-à-dire qu'en y prenant part, il ajoute à la menace que son camp représente pour le camp adverse, même en n'ayant jamais tiré un seul coup de feu. Ainsi, j'envisage la déception comme un archétype de l'identification en tant que signe de menace et je soutiens que la simple participation à une branche de l'organisation militaire engagée dans le combat contribue à cette menace. Par conséquent, les combattants se trouvant du côté injuste de la guerre deviennent passibles de préjudices défensifs même s'ils ne sont pas directement impliqués dans l'utilisation d'armes. En forme de conclusion, je soutiens que, d'un point de vue réductiviste-individualiste, les responsables et les militaires se trouvant du côté injuste de la guerre sont deux groupes convergeant à un même but dans une bien plus grande mesure qu'il ne pourrait y paraître. Cet article peut être considéré principalement comme une défense de la perspective réductiviste-individualiste de la théorie de la guerre juste.

Références

Jenkins, Ryan, Michael Robillard, and Bradley Jay Strawser. 2018. Editors' Introduction. In *Who Should Die? The Ethics of Killing in War,* ed. R. Jenkins, M. Robillard and B. J. Strawser, 1–12. Oxford: Oxford University Press.

Lazar, Seth. 2017. "War." The Stanford Encyclopedia of Philosophy.

McMahan, Jeff. 2012. "Rethinking the 'Just War' Part I." *The New York Times,* 11 November.

Orend, Brian. 2013. *The Morality of War.* 2nd ed. Peterborough, Ont.: Broadview Press.

Sussman, Naomi. 2014. "Introduction: The Substantive Unity of Michael Walzer's Pluralism." In *Reading Walzer,* ed. Y. Benbaji and N. Sussman, 1–18. New York: Routledge.

Walzer, Michael. 1977. Just and Unjust Wars : A Moral Argument with Historical Illustrations. 1st ed. New York: Basic Books.

———. 2015. Just and Unjust Wars : A Moral Argument with Historical Illustrations. 5th ed. New York: Basic Books.

Contributors and Translators

Hunter Cantrell earned his MA in Philosophy at Georgia State University. He is an Instructor at the United States Military Academy, West Point, and captain in the United States Army.

Joseph Chapa earned his DPhil (PhD) at the University of Oxford. He is a lieutenant colonel in the United States Air Force and works on the Air Staff focusing on issues relating to the ethics of artificial intelligence.

Kevin Cutright earned his PhD in Philosophy at Saint Louis University. He is an Academy Professor at the United States Military Academy, West Point, and is a lieutenant colonel in the United States Army.

French Translations
Fabienne Pizot-Haymore, translator
Nathalie Letourneau, proofreader

Spanish Translators
Haydeé Espino
Victoria A. García